LOCAL BAPTISTS, LOCAL POLITICS

LOCAL BAPTISTS, LOCAL POLITICS

Churches and Communities in the Middle and Uplands South

Clifford A. Grammich Jr.

America's Baptists
Keith Harper, Series Editor

The University of Tennessee Press / Knoxville

Copyright © 1999 by The University of Tennessee Press / Knoxville.
All Rights Reserved. Manufactured in the United States of America.
First Edition.
Cloth: 1st printing, 1999.
Paper: 1st printing, 2022.

Library of Congress Cataloging-in-Publication Data

Grammich, Clifford A. (Clifford Anthony), 1963–
Local Baptists, local politics : churches and communities in
the middle and uplands south / Clifford A. Grammich, Jr. — 1st ed.
p. cm.
Includes bibliographical references and index.
ISBN 978-1-62190-751-0
1. Baptists—Southern States. 2. Christianity and
politics—Baptists. 3. Christianity and politics—Southern States.
I. Title.
BX6241.G73 1999
286'.0975—dc21
98-40212

For Kathy

Give her of the fruit of her hands,
and let her own works praise her in the gates.

—Proverbs 31:31

and for Jimmy, Mary Kate, and Anthony

I have no greater joy than to hear
that my children walk in truth.
—3 John 1:4

CONTENTS

Foreword / XIII

Introduction to the Paperback Edition / XV

Acknowledgments / XLIII

Politics and the Bible: An Introduction / 1

1. National Themes in Local Settings / 27

2. Histories and Their Implications: Some Characteristics of Sectarian Baptists / 56

3. The Strengths of Adaptation for Labor: Organized Labor and Traditional Protestantism / 113

4. The Limits of Adaptation for Reform: The Problem of Local Versus Public Goods / 137

5. A Theme and Its Variations: Sectarianism and Politics Revisited / 187

Appendix: Sources and Methodology / 205

Notes / 207

Bibliography / 233

Index / 239

MAPS

0.1 Seventeen Core Counties with Historic Concentrations
of Old Regular and United Baptists / XXVII

1. Central Baptist Distribution by County, 1990 / 61

2. Duck River and Kindred Baptist Distribution by County, 1990 / 67

3. Duck River and Kindred Baptist Core Counties / 68

4. "Old" Missionary Baptist Distribution by County, 1990 / 73

5. "Old" Missionary Baptist Analysis Areas, 1990 / 74

6. Old Regular Baptist Distribution by County, 1990 / 80

7. Old Regular Baptist Core Counties / 81

8. Eastern District Primitive Baptist Association
Distribution by County, 1990 / 86

9. United Baptist Distribution by County, 1990 / 89

10. United Baptist Analysis Areas / 91

11. Magoffin, Jefferson, and Fayette Counties, Kentucky / 141

TABLES

0.1 Churches and Members of Select Old Regular Baptist Associations, 1990–2020 / xxii

0.2 Members of Sardis and Indian Bottom Old Regular Baptist Associations in Select Counties, 1990–2020 / xxv

0.3 Demographic Characteristics in the Seventeen Core Counties, 2000 and 2019–2020 / xxix

0.4 Socioeconomic Characteristics in the Seventeen Core Counties, 2019 / xxx

0.5 Percentage Democratic Vote for President in the Seventeen Core Counties, 1996–2020, Compared with National Vote / xxxi

1. Central Baptist Area Characteristics / 64

2. Duck River and Kindred Baptist Core Area Characteristics / 70

3. "Old" Missionary Baptist Area Characteristics / 75

4. Old Regular Baptist Core Area Characteristics / 82

5. Eastern District Primitive Baptist Core Area Characteristics / 87

6. United Baptist Area Characteristics / 92

7. Magoffin County Population Characteristics / 143

8. Magoffin County Families and Poverty / 144

FOREWORD

When Clifford A. Grammich published *Local Baptists, Local Politics* in 1999, he caught the eye of several distinguished scholars. Charles A. Lippy described the work as "meticulously researched" that demonstrated how diverse Baptists could be. Samuel S. Hill praised Grammich for his fairness and for resisting the temptation to be reductionistic. High praise, indeed!

Grammich focused on six Baptist groups concentrated in the Middle and Upper South. According to his analysis, these Baptists defy all stereotypes that dismiss them as focused strictly on saving souls and "other worldliness." In reality, their biblical literalism along with cultural mores and folkways shape their politics, even though they do not necessarily share a common political ideology. That is, Baptists tend to vote according to personal, even pragmatic concerns.

This paperback edition of *Local Baptists, Local Politics* focuses on politics in the early twenty-first century. In the detailed new preface, Grammich builds on his earlier analysis. Do Baptists still vote according to personal, pragmatic concerns? Did the "Trump Phenomenon" influence religiously minded voters? Has Grammich's original analysis stood the test of time? We invite you to read on.

The University of Tennessee Press is pleased to offer this edition of *Local Baptists, Local Politics*. We hope that it encourages more inquiry into the nexus between politics and religion. And we especially recommend it to anyone who still feels that somehow "politics and religion don't mix."

Keith Harper
Southeastern Baptist Theological Seminary

INTRODUCTION TO THE PAPERBACK EDITION

The lessons of the first edition of this work, published in 1999, were twofold. First, it demonstrated that those emphasizing literal belief in a sacred text can adapt their religion to local circumstances and needs. To be sure, the groups I studied for this work share many common characteristics and core values, particularly related to cultural conservatism. Beyond claiming a literal belief in the Bible, their members are white, often of modest means, and, as the title notes, concentrated in rural areas of the middle and uplands South. But because these churches believe theological authority is local, they may differ on some politics. In particular, their members may position themselves where one might not expect cultural conservatives within contemporary U.S. politics. Second, the social circumstances of these groups' adherents can limit the support religion may offer them. Individuals in isolated rural areas can find a religion based on local authority to be appealing in many ways. But a religion based on local authority may offer only limited support in modern society.

My original work drew these lessons by placing these groups in context and exploring some of their communities in depth. It began with how one might draw political lessons from a sacred text, then noted how broader cultural and economic issues affected the local settings of these groups, including the histories of these groups. It documented how these groups offered more support in a labor struggle than organized labor's erstwhile allies in more formal churches, while noting the limits these groups confronted in addressing a complex environmental issue.

These lessons stand, and they may be worth exploring in other settings where local theological authority flourishes. While I am grateful for the opportunity to again present this work as part of the America's Baptists series, I have not changed any of the original material. Both current personal circumstances and the circumstances of these groups prohibit the intensive research I was able to undertake originally.

At the same time, after over twenty years since the original publication of the book, the reader deserves some updated discussion on the current context of these groups. To that end, in this preface I place the original research in an updated context in four ways: 1) I review relevant recent history of religion and politics in the United States; 2) I discuss current context for some of these groups, including changes in numbers relevant to other religious bodies; 3) I explore some aspects of the current local, state, and national settings in which these groups now find themselves; 4) I revisit the lessons one might draw from this research.

RECENT RELEVANT RESEARCH ON U.S. RELIGION AND POLITICS

Several works in the past quarter century have explored similar religious groups both in the middle and uplands South and elsewhere. Many have done so in the context of history and economic change. Much work continues to discuss how Christian churches emphasizing Biblical authority and inerrancy grew with political conservatism. Yet even within this work there has been discussion of different paths, where one might also place the Baptists of this work.

Echoes of these groups are evident among other religious groups in the South. For many adherents of these and similarly situated groups, Bethany Moreton claims, subsistence, more than career advancement in an industrial economy, has been a primary goal.[1] Religion can offer a sanctuary for developing and protecting personal virtue and familial roles.

These groups, like others, may find that the rudimentary structure of their churches offers limited advantage during profound social change. One recent history shows how "plain-folk" religion came to dominate the politics of a region far removed from its homeland and, beyond that, the nation.[2] Yet the rise of plain-folk religion was not the same for all its adherents. While much of plain-folk religion transplanted to Southern California grew to define conservatism there and across the nation, some elements did not. Many pastors of the religion, who often had other jobs in addition to their pastoral duties, lacked training and would not follow elaborate doctrinal codes. Politically, these adherents were "small-d Democrats," but they remained open to other possibilities, which they would soon explore.[3] An early populist movement in Southern California, fueled in large part by adherents of plain-folk religion, found itself in political crossfire between those seeking to co-opt the movement for their own purposes and those seeking to develop a more cosmopolitan, progressive politics. As Darren Dorchuk explains, being "[a]ccosted by the Left [and] bombarded by the Right" led many adherents to abandon politics or to begin moving their politics in a more conservative direction.[4] For some, the rudimentary religious structures proved inadequate to bridge the gap between their populism and broader liberalism. This is a theme evident in the original text of this book, as well as some developments I review. Many, then and now, did adapt to more conservative politics through their church structures. But such adapters are beyond the world of the Baptists of my work and adherents of similar churches.

    A more contemporary analysis, and one based closer to the areas I researched, also finds adaptability of this religion, but one that, politically and buffeted by recent cultural issues, may be described as "Republican by default."[5] Such churches, Joe Bageant claims, "are theologically wooly places whose belief systems can accommodate just about any interpretation of the Good Book."[6] Such religion, broadly defined, has included a wide variety of perspectives, though its adherents are typically white, working class, and with only a high school education, whose interests are often locally focused. To the extent that such voters may have drifted rightward in their cultural politics, it is, this author suggests, because they have "no political leadership whatsoever. . . . Only right-wing politicians appealing to their religious prejudices and ignorance on behalf of big money pay any attention to them."⁷ And the appeals to such voters, this author claims, are often based in "fear of human beings culturally unlike themselves," including gays, leading to efforts of the early-twenty-first century to ban same-sex marriage.⁸

Of course, these efforts to ban same-sex marriage failed with court decisions clearing the way for it. But, after a century in which issues of sex and religion have divided U.S. voters, the de jure resolution of this issue has not removed the division. One reason for this, R. Marie Griffith writes, is that both proponents and opponents of gay rights see "opposition to homosexuality and opposition to feminism [as] hand in glove."⁹ The two issues had become intertwined over time, and both threatened traditional patriarchal authority. As I noted in my earlier research, such authority often might defer to influences of leading women in a congregation, but it remains prevalent. Hence, adherents of these groups see decisions such as *Obergefell* as not only going against some Biblical strictures, but also threatening long-held social organizing principles. Similar battles continue to rage elsewhere. Recent presidential campaigns, Griffith claims, have reinforced many of the fissures that had been growing. Donald Trump, in this view, won the presidency "not in spite of his attitude toward women but because of it."¹⁰ At the same time, Democrats may be forgoing the votes of many white working-class women by neglecting cultural issues, such as harassment from men, which can cut across class lines.

Across the nation, culturally conservative views are in many ways receding, and with them, some traditional religious structures. In the past two decades, for example, opinion on same-sex marriage has reversed, with a large majority now supporting it.¹¹ As such views have changed, some scholars have cited the linkage of conservative politics with religion as leading to decreased adherence to U.S. churches. A growing body of research has noted, if not abandonment of faith, then abandonment of many of its previously dominant structures. One of the first works on this topic documented the rise of the "nones," those who still professed belief in God but outside that expressed in churches. To be sure, other trends have likely affected U.S. religion, both in broad terms and among local Baptists. Michael Hout and Claude Fischer, in documenting the rise of the "nones," note that younger people are delaying marriage and parenthood, leading to smaller families formed later; they argue these factors reduce specific religious preferences or the need for them altogether.[12] But they also find politics to be a significant influence. Political moderates and liberals have increasingly expressed no particular religious preference, while preferences among political conservatives have remained unchanged.

One of the latest works on religion and politics takes this analysis further, finding a "secular surge" among non-religious voters. Rather than just abandoning religion, many voters have come to express increasingly secular views. This, in turn, David E. Campbell, Geoffrey C. Layman, and John C. Green claim, can lead to increasing polarization in U.S. politics, with less-educated and less-affluent "religionists" at one end and more educated and more affluent "secularists" at the other.[13] Such a split could divide Democratic leaders from their more traditional working-class voters as well as from more religious black and Hispanic voters.

Three elements might temper such a split and its implications. First, the rhetoric of successful national politicians straddles the secular and the religious. Barack Obama was the first president to mention nonbelievers in an inaugural address. Yet, the Democratic National Convention address four years earlier that first placed him in the national spotlight was, as Kevin M. Kruse notes, replete with religious themes.[14] While there is a history since the New Deal of using the phrase "one nation under God" to foster conservative politics, some uses of religion in U.S. politics today can be so anodyne as to lose meaning, or at least lead to uses that may not have been foreseen by those fostering them.

Second, in some places of the nation, cultural divisions and the receding of many forms of religious authority may be less evident. While "White Christian" influence may be declining, as Robert P. Jones writes, white Protestants remain majorities in Alabama, Kentucky, Tennessee, and West Virginia, among others, as Jones also notes.[15] The concentration of such populations in these states may mask the decline of their influence elsewhere. Indeed, by 2014, Alabama, Kentucky, Tennessee, and West Virginia were among the last seven states where majorities opposed same-sex marriage. The story of Kim Davis, the county clerk who refused to issue same-sex marriage licenses, shows the power but later declining influence of such attitudes even in eastern Kentucky. Davis, though outside the specific traditions

I studied, did cite Biblical beliefs in her refusal.[16] She received local backing in her refusal, including, initially, from the Kentucky governor.[17] Ultimately, though, such licenses were issued, the governor retreated, and Davis, after switching to the Republican Party, lost re-election.[18]

Third, those seeing a "secular surge" in U.S. politics, and links between nonreligiosity and support for Trump, draw on sources that may show a more nuanced relationship between religiosity and politics, especially in the regions I studied. Trump's earliest support, Campbell, Layman, and Green write, came from "those who are clearly not committed to Secularist beliefs, but they are also not committed to the conventional practices of organized religion."[19]

As evidence, they cite J. D. Vance's recent personal reflection on the region. Of his maternal grandmother, Vance writes: "[Hers] was a deeply personal (albeit quirky) faith. She couldn't say 'organized religion' without contempt. She saw churches as breeding grounds for perverts and money changers. And she hated what she called 'the loud and proud'—people who wore their faith on their sleeve, always ready to let you know how pious they were . . . By [her] reckoning, God never left our side. He celebrated with us when times were good and comforted us when they weren't . . . the theology she taught was unsophisticated."[20] This contrasts with Vance's father's Pentecostal church with more structure and strictures. It was one able to provide more support in communities undergoing social disruption and economic dislocation but unable to brook theological or political dissent. Vance's grandmother was able to accommodate a wide variety of eclectic political and religious beliefs, while being disconnected politically. As Vance notes, the lack of trust in any but the most rudimentary institutions can also lead to susceptibility to myriad conspiracy theories, which spread more easily through electronic communications. Later, Vance would claim that "Church is increasingly something that is relatively confined to upper-income, well-educated people."[21]

Neither nonreligionist attitudes nor faith appealing to those of the upper classes reflects precisely the Baptists I studied. Still, such attitudes show the contours of the world they have navigated. Their origins were often in reaction to monied missionary interests of the time. Theirs is a personal faith that seeks to apply Biblical events and interpretation to their local lives.

Theirs is a theology often summarized in about a dozen sentences, including belief in an inerrant Bible. And adherents may even attend church infrequently, given many of their churches meet only monthly.

In sum, the Baptists of my original work appear in many ways to be a distinct part of U.S. religion with unique lessons on politics, even as related scholarship has expanded. Their sectarian characteristics and interests reflect many continuing concerns and interests of conservative Christian churches, emphasizing Biblical authority and interpretation while placing them in some unexpected places as well. I turn next to some indicators of how these churches, and the communities where they are embedded, have changed in recent years.

Local Baptists of the Middle and Uplands South and Their Communities

While the approach of the original research was not possible to repeat, there are some available indicators on how these Baptists and their communities have changed. Among these are changes in numbers for some associations, broader social and economic changes in their communities, and political indicators, both in national and local contexts.

My original work included more than fifty associations in six different groups. These groups had concentrations in the middle and uplands South, but also congregations in places where residents of these regions had moved.

The lack of centralization of these groups, while a defining characteristic, also makes tracking trends among them difficult. The Old Regular Baptists in 1990, for example, numbered 15,218 members (and an estimated 19,257 adherents, including children) among 17 different associations.[22] Replicating the count of these associations was not possible. Nevertheless, details from three associations whose data are available online show change. Two of these are concentrated within the traditional Old Regular Baptist heartland of eastern Kentucky and West Virginia. The other is concentrated among Ohio counties where migrants of an earlier generation had moved.

The Indian Bottom Association of Old Regular Baptists has been one of the oldest and larger associations of the group. Founded in 1896, in 1990 it had 1,337 members in 26 churches.[23] The Sardis Association of Old Regular

Baptists is also one of the oldest associations of the group. Founded in 1893, in 1990 it had 1,195 members in 29 churches.[24] The Northern New Salem Association is one of the younger associations of the group. Organized in 1957 from churches whose members had been affiliated with the New Salem Association but who had migrated north, in 1990 it had 847 members in 24 churches.[25] Together, these three associations accounted for 22 percent of all Old Regular Baptists enumerated in 1990.

Between 1990 and 2000, these three associations roughly held their own in these communities, as Table 0.1 shows. Indian Bottom gained through growth in some of its existing churches as well as through creation of new churches and acceptance of churches from elsewhere. Sardis and Northern New Salem both had some losses, though these were small compared to what followed.

Table 0.1
Churches and Members of Select Old Regular Baptist Associations, 1990–2020

	1990	2000	2010	2019–2020[a]
Indian Bottom				
Churches	26	44	45	43
Members	1,337	1,941	1,852	1,561
Northern New Salem				
Churches	24	25	24	22
Members	847	719	540	329
Sardis				
Churches	29	29	27	24
Members	1,195	992	748	492

NOTE: [a]As of July 2021, 2020 is the most recent year of statistics available for Indian Bottom and Northern New Salem, while 2019 is the most recent year available for Sardis.

In the first two decades of this century, all three of these associations have lost members. Indian Bottom lost nearly a fifth of its members, and Sardis and Northern New Salem lost more than half.

The losses were greatest in Northern New Salem. This is unsurprising given two facts. First, this association has been concentrated in Ohio, which traditionally has accounted for about half its members, and Michigan, which has accounted for about a third. The association arose, as noted, because of migration. In its new northern home, it encountered more religious diversity than is evident in the counties where these churches organized. A recent county-level analysis of religious diversity, for example, found that 12 of the 15 Ohio and Michigan counties where Northern New Salem has churches also have greater levels of religious diversity than the average U.S. county and greater still than the average county in the Old Regular Baptist heartland.[26] In most of these counties, a recent analysis found "white evangelical Protestants" comprise less than 30 percent of the population, in contrast to the Old Regular Baptist heartland where such Protestants typically account for a majority of the population. Put another way, members of the Northern New Salem Association encountered a much different landscape than is prevalent in the areas where they originated.

Second, migration from the traditional Old Regular Baptist homeland to northern states has diminished from a flood to a trickle. While an enormous number of persons left central Appalachia for elsewhere, particularly Ohio and Michigan, from the 1950s to the 1970s, this migration diminished as opportunities also declined. Country music popularized this lesson. Dwight Yoakam sang that "readin', writin', and Route 23," the traditional road from eastern Kentucky north to Ohio and Michigan, was as likely to lead to "a world of misery" as to "the luxury and comfort a coal miner can't afford."[27] Steve Earle, in turn, proclaimed in a song called "Hillbilly Highway" that the destination of migrants from the region had shifted from Detroit to Houston.[28] As migration diminished, so, apparently, has Northern New Salem.

Yet Indian Bottom and Sardis also suffered losses in their traditional homelands. This is evident when comparing their numbers with those of other leading religious bodies (Table 0.2).[29] While most Sardis members in 1990 were in Pike County, Kentucky, and Mingo County, West Virginia, by 2019 Sardis had less than half the members in these counties than it had in 1990. Furthermore, while Sardis lost members in these counties, other leading religious bodies there, including the Southern Baptist Convention, the United Methodist Church, and the Church of God (Cleveland, Tennessee) either had more modest losses or even gained members during this time. (County-level data for other religious bodies except the Southern Baptist Convention in 2019 was not available at the time of this writing.) At the same time, religion in these counties, even if not diverse, is diffuse. In 2010, the five leading evangelical Protestant bodies—the Southern Baptist Convention, the Church of God (Cleveland, TN), the Churches of Christ, the National Association of Free Will Baptists, and the Christian Churches and Churches of Christ—in these four counties claimed adherents totaling more than 20 percent of the population.[30] A recent estimate of individual religiosity in these counties estimates that more than 50 percent of the population is "white evangelical Protestant."[31] These data suggest that while most of the population in these counties is of similar religion, most adherents of this religion are in smaller religious bodies, or no religious body at all. From this, we may surmise that even if the particular religious bodies that are the focus of this work have declined, the influence of similar religious bodies may not have.

Indian Bottom has also lost members in its core counties, though not to the extent of Sardis. It also suffered fewer losses in Letcher County, Kentucky, one of its two core counties, than in Knott County, Kentucky. In 1990, more than 80 percent of Indian Bottom members were in these two counties; by 2020, less than half were. Nevertheless, while both these counties lost population in the 1990s, both Indian Bottom and the Southern Baptist Convention, the largest religious body in them, gained members. In the first decade of the twenty-first century, as total population losses here continued, both Indian Bottom and the Southern Baptist Convention lost members, with Indian Bottom losses being fewer in Letcher County than in Knott County. From 2010 to 2020, Indian Bottom continued to lose members, though not as much in Letcher County, the home of its long-time moderator.

The persistence that Indian Bottom has had in Letcher County is intriguing. Its moderator is active in county government, including a controver-

Table 0.2
Members of Sardis and Indian Bottom Old Regular Baptist Associations in Select Counties, 1990–2020

	1990	2000	2010	2019–2020
Knott County, KY				
Indian Bottom	425	578	383	286
Southern Baptist Convention	2,011	2,584	2,416	2,228
"White Evangelical Protestant"[a]				7,300
Letcher County, KY				
Indian Bottom	674	678	533	478
Southern Baptist Convention	2,858	3,541	3,061	2,924
"White Evangelical Protestant"[a]				11,600
Pike County, KY				
Sardis	605	505	392	316
Southern Baptist Convention	6,787	8,197	8,811	7,873
United Methodist Church	1,496	1,676	1,353	
"White Evangelical Protestant"[a]				29,900
Mingo County, WV				
Sardis	339	234	116	74
Church of God (Cleveland, TN)	1,207	1,372	1,285	
Southern Baptist Convention	1,276	1,253	1,114	1,143
"White Evangelical Protestant"[a]				12,300

NOTE: [a] This is an estimate based on a survey. Public Religion Research Institute (PRRI), "The 2020 Census of U.S. Religion," July 8, 2021.

sial effort to build a maximum-security federal prison there.[32] Proponents touted the $444 million expenditure and promise of prison jobs. Opponents noted that federal prison jobs, because of the skills and experience they require, rarely go to local residents most in need of employment. The county has been and remains in dire straits: economic census data indicate local employers only offer about 3,000 jobs for a working-age population of more than 18,000. At the same time, American Community Survey data show the county has a proportion of college-educated residents less than half that for the nation, raising the question of what jobs local residents might hold.

Regardless, the point for this work is that the moderator's involvement in the prison project does not appear to have affected the standing of the association in the county. Indeed, there appears to have been no specific religious overtones to the prison dispute. The moderator appears to have couched his support for the project in terms of jobs and lack of other opportunities. The project ultimately failed when the Trump administration rejected it, citing research claiming that prison growth may impede rather than stimulate economic growth in rural areas.[33] The thwarting of the prison project little affected Trump's standing in the county, as he won 79 percent of its votes in 2020.[34]

OTHER COMMUNITY CONTEXTS

One of the most dominant political themes in these communities, as in other rural communities, has been the overwhelming support for Donald Trump. Any accounting of politics in these communities must recognize this, but focusing too much on it can cause one to overlook other local political adaptations. While documenting the evolution of these counties toward overwhelming support for Trump, I also discuss other recent political events there, particularly in areas that had not historically been Republican leaning.

In examining clusters of counties where these Baptists are most prevalent, I had found in the mid-1990s that their support for Democratic presidential candidates ranged from 35 to 65 percent. Among the most Democratic were the Old Regular Baptist concentration in eastern Kentucky, southern West Virginia, southwestern Virginia, and the largely overlapping concentration of United Baptists in eastern Kentucky and southern West Virginia.

The 17 counties of overlapping United Baptist and Old Regular Baptist territory shown in Map 0.1 illustrate well the conditions in which many

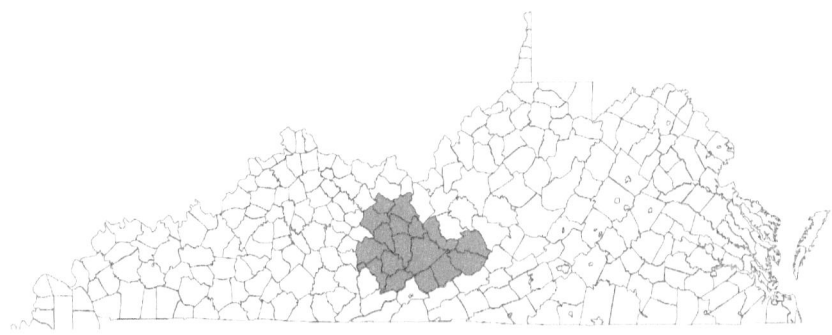

Map 0.1 Seventeen Core Counties with Historic Concentrations of Old Regular and United Baptists.

of these Baptists find themselves as well and the challenges of their communities.[35] Some analyses consider these counties to be among the most distressed places to live in the United States. One analysis, for example, cited 2 Congressional districts (Kentucky's fifth district and West Virginia's third) as being the 2 worst in the nation for resident well-being.[36] Another placed 5 of these counties as among the 25 worst in the United States based on poverty, education, and life expectancy.[37] All 17 are also considered to be economically distressed, whose fortunes have lagged with those of the regional coal industry.[38]

Since 2000, these 17 counties have lost population at about the same rate that the rest of the nation has gained population. Among these counties in 1990, Old Regular Baptists claimed 14,818 adherents, and United Baptists claimed 12,152.[39] Three other similar Baptist groups—Enterprise Baptists, Primitive Baptists, and Central Baptists—claimed 6,401 adherents combined. Altogether, these five Baptist groups claimed 33,371 adherents—nearly as many as the 36,991 that the Southern Baptists claimed. Since then, we do not, as noted, have statistics on all the associations that comprised Old Regular Baptists, United Baptists, and similar Baptists.

More recent statistics indicate the Southern Baptist population has increased, though its influence still may not be as pervasive as those of other, similar but smaller populations. In recent decades, the Southern Baptist population has never exceeded 10 percent of the population in these 17 counties. At the same time, the population of these counties appears to remain predominantly "white Evangelical Protestant," albeit concentrated outside leading "Evangelical Protestant" bodies.

While the discussion here must remain speculative given the nature of the data, it may still be instructive. In 2010, the Religion Census of the Association of Statisticians of American Religious Bodies (ASARB) found "Evangelical Protestant" bodies reporting their data claimed 81,833 adherents in these core counties—or less than half the "white Evangelical Protestant" population that would be estimated there in 2020.[40] Across the nation, enumerated "Evangelical Protestant" bodies in the ASARB Religion Census claimed 50,013,107 adherents—or more than the "white Evangelical Protestant" population that would be estimated in 2020. There are many reasons these numbers are not strictly comparable. "Evangelical Protestant" bodies may have nonwhite members. (They do exclude "Black Protestant" bodies that might otherwise be considered "evangelical.") Time likely changed religious adherence in this region and across the nation. Nevertheless, the point is that these statistics do provide some rough indicator of "Evangelical Protestant" experience outside commonly considered churches in this region. This would include both churches such as Old Regular Baptist and United Baptist that have not been included in the ASARB Religion Census since my count of them in 1990 and still other unique local churches.

Beyond their unique religious environment, these counties remain overwhelmingly single-race non-Hispanic white, while the rest of the nation has become more diverse (Table 0.3). Their populations are aging: most persons there are older than 40, while most of the national population is younger than 40. Household and family structures are about the same here as elsewhere, with children typically living in families headed by a married couple.

Socioeconomic indicators are not encouraging (Table 0.4). Educational attainment is low. The proportion who did not graduate high school is about double the proportion that did not graduate from high school nationwide, while the proportion with a bachelor's degree is about a third of the rate nationwide. Labor-force participation is lower and unemployment higher than both rates nationwide. Among those who do work, employment in

Table 0.3
Demographic Characteristics in Seventeen Core Counties with
Historic Concentrations of Old Regular and United Baptists[a]

	Core counties	USA
Total population		
2000	409,876	281,421,906
2020	354,116	331,449,281
Change (%)	-14	18
Religious Affiliation		
Old Regular Baptists, 1990	14,818	19,257
United Baptists, 1990	12,152	68,187
Southern Baptist Convention, 1990	36,591	18,940,682
Southern Baptist Convention, 2010	38,564	19,896,975
"Evangelical Protestants," 2010[b]	81,833	50,013,107
"White Evangelical Protestants," 2020[c]	185,600	46,400,000
Single-race non-Hispanic white (%)		
2000	97	69
2020	94	58
Population by age, est., 2019 (%)		
Under 20	23	25
20–39	23	27
40–59	28	26
60+	26	22
Own children in families, % headed by married couple, 2019	69	70

NOTES: [a]Statistics are from the 2000 and 2020 decennial Census, the five-year average of the American Community Survey, the ASARB "Religion Census," and the PRRI "Census of U.S. Religion." [b]In ASARB Religion Census, 2010. [c]Estimated, 2020.

Table 0.4
Socioeconomic Characteristics in Seventeen Core Counties with Historic Concentrations of Old Regular and United Baptists, 2019

	Core counties	USA
Educational attainment, age 25+, 2019 (%)		
Did not graduate high school	24	11
Bachelor's degree or higher	12	33
Labor force, 2019 (%)		
Age 16+ in labor force	41	64
Civilian unemployment rate	10	5
Industry for civilian employed (%)		
Agriculture, forestry, fishing and hunting	1	1
Mining, quarrying, and oil and gas extraction	7	1
Construction	6	7
Manufacturing	6	10
Wholesale trade	2	3
Retail trade	13	11
Transportation and warehousing, and utilities	6	6
Information	2	2
Finance, insurance, real estate, rental, leasing	4	6
Professional, scientific, management, administrative, waste management	6	12
Educational services, health care, social assistance	31	23
Arts, entertainment, recreation, accommodation, food services	7	10
Other services, except public administration	4	5
Public administration	6	4
Worked outside county of residence (%)	34	28
Poverty (%)	27	12

mining, education, and social services is higher here than elsewhere. Workers here are more likely to work outside their county of residence. (Such commuting, and other means to support access to middle-class jobs in this region, have been the subject of a recent regional country music hit.[41]) The lower levels of educational attainment and employment have led to poverty rates more than double those for the nation.

From 1980 to 1996, these regions regularly voted at least 60 percent Democratic for president. Since then, they have become overwhelmingly Republican for president (Table 5). But, on further examination, a mixture of material and cultural interests, rather than strictly cultural interests, may have fueled this transformation. And variation below the presidential level particularly indicates local interests can still be salient.

In presidential elections, this group of counties went from majority Democratic to majority Republican in 2008. One analysis of presidential elections returns in the region that year attributed the change to issues of race,

Table 0.5
Percentage Democratic Vote for President in Seventeen Core Counties with Historic Concentrations of Old Regular and United Baptists, 1996–2020, Compared with National Vote

Democratic for president	Core counties (%)	USA (%)
1996	61	49
2000	55	48
2004	52	48
2008	41	53
2012	27	51
2016	19	48
2020	19	51

guns, other cultural issues, and coal.[42] One political strategist suggested that Democrats in the region were appealing on issues of class, which would appeal to some, and Republicans on issues of culture, which could appeal to all. Still, within this group of counties, it may be difficult to overstate the long-term importance of the decline in the coal industry. The industry in the region had been declining since the mid-1990s. Coincidentally or not, this decline accelerated after Obama's election, as did the prospects of Democratic presidential candidates in the region. Figure 0.1 shows the percentage Democratic for president since 1996 in these counties, as well as coal production in this time.[43] From 1996 to 2016, the percentage of these counties voting Democratic, and coal production, both decreased to about one-fourth of their former level. In counties where educational attainment continues to trail that of the nation, this likely represented the disappearance of many economic opportunities, as well as of declining union organization, and adverse consequences to the Democrats that were not evident before the decline.

One analysis of recent presidential campaigns points to Hillary Clinton's statement at a town hall meeting that "we're going to put a lot of coal miners and coal companies out of business" as a catalyst for Trump's overwhelming

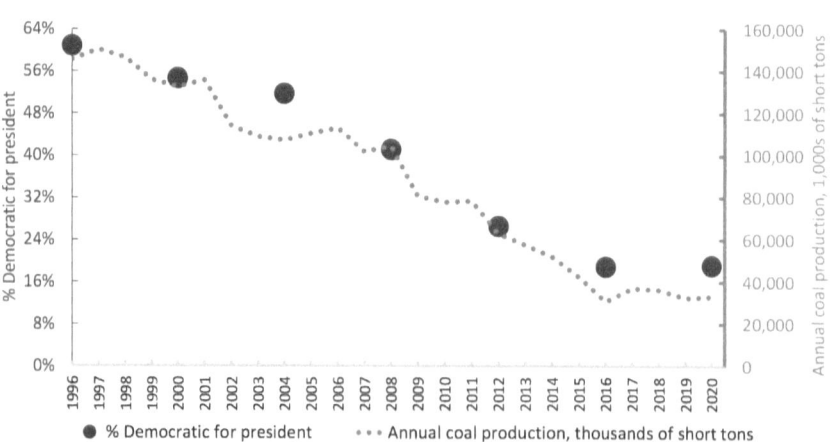

Figure 0.1 Democratic Presidential Vote and Coal Production in Seventeen Core Counties with Historic Concentrations of Old Regular and United Baptists, 1996–2020.

support in the region.⁴⁴ The comment, reportedly made as an observation of market changes that the coal industry could not combat, shifted presidential politics in the region to place the economic interests of many voters to the same side as their cultural interests. Though the Trump administration did not appreciably increase coal production or jobs, even Democratic lawmakers conceded "Eastern Kentucky 'probably still looks at it as if he tried.'"⁴⁵

On local levels, politics in these counties remain more mixed. As of mid-2021, Democrats control most of the county governments in this region, often elected without opposition. And in Magoffin County, Kentucky, the focus of a chapter in the original research, local politics can still draw more attention than national politics. The number of voters in the county executive general election in Magoffin in 2018 exceeded the number of presidential voters there in 2016 or 2020. Of course, the local success that Democrats still have in some of these counties may reflect the power of incumbency or the long time it may take for changes in national politics to reach local levels. Still, some elements of Kentucky state politics in recent years may demonstrate how local concerns can offset other political trends.

In 2015, Republican Matt Bevin became only the third Republican to be elected governor of Kentucky since World War II. In winning election, he won eleven of the twelve Kentucky counties in the Old Regular Baptist and United Baptist core area. As governor, he supported many cultural issues that were seemingly popular in this region, including laws limiting abortion access and permitting the carrying of concealed handguns without permits. He also, however, supported issues that do not appear to have been as popular in these counties. These included a "right-to-work" law, reductions in teacher pensions, and the addition of work requirements to the state's Medicaid program, which had been expanded in 2013 under his predecessor, Steve Beshear.⁴⁶

Bevin's actions drew predictable opposition from Democrats, but they also spurred a fellow Republican to challenge him in the primary. In announcing his gubernatorial campaign, Robert Goforth, a Republican state senator, while touting his own opposition to abortion and support for gun rights, also vowed to oppose what he called Bevin's "corporate-first agenda."⁴⁷ He also opposed diversion of public education funding to charter schools while promising "to unite Kentucky instead of catering to big corporations" and "to have a people-first agenda."[48] Goforth strengthened his appeal to these counties by selecting his running mate, the Republican county attorney of Lawrence County.

A candidate who proved to be still more popular in these counties was Rocky Adkins. Adkins was a Democratic state representative who hailed from the same county as Kim Davis and whose district overlapped a portion of the counties that I examine here. In his campaign, Adkins emphasized "kitchen-table" issues," focusing on "rural communities, which he says have been forgotten by state government and pummeled by larger economic forces."[49] Similarly, he supported increased support for education and infrastructure, "fair wage[s]," and greater health-care access. He was, however, "dogged" at primary debates regarding his stances on "social issues," such as his support for a bill banning abortion after eleven weeks. In Jefferson County (Louisville), he won only 10 percent, compared to 39 percent in the rest of the state.

Though neither Adkins nor Goforth won their party primaries, they were, by substantial margins, the most popular candidates in the counties I examine here. Adkins won more than 70 percent of Democratic primary ballots in these counties, and more than 50 percent of the combined Democratic and Republican primary ballots there. Goforth won more than 50 percent of Republican primary ballots in these counties, and nearly 15 percent of the combined Democratic and Republican ballots there. Put another way, candidates spurred to run by opposition to Bevin's economic policies received support from about two in three voters in these counties on primary election day.

In the general election campaign, Bevin won most of these counties, but Andy Beshear, the Democratic candidate for governor, as well as outgoing attorney general and son of Steve Beshear, made substantial gains relative to the Democratic gubernatorial candidate in 2015. Altogether, Beshear won five of these twelve counties, and gained voter share in all but one.[50] Among these counties, Beshear was stronger where the proportions of the uninsured population were highest before Medicaid expansion under the governorship of his father; he ran six percentage points better in the six counties that had the highest rates of uninsured than he did in the other six counties of this region.

Of course, most persons in these counties still choose to have no more than minimal political involvement. While the number of ballots cast in presidential elections in has increased in recent years, it still remains below that for the nation as a whole. In 2020, 54 percent of the voting-age population in these counties cast a presidential ballot, while 61 percent of the voting age population nationwide did so. Put another way, one of the most basic acts of political participation, voting, remains more sporadic here than it does nationwide.

Yet when voting, those in the core counties of Old Regular and United Baptists may consider their more immediate and local needs than is often realized. This emphasis on location is not just related to the issues decided at the ballot box but also ensuring contests at the ballot box are cleanly decided. While, as I noted in my original research, some broad efforts at fundamental reform in Magoffin County had faltered, some efforts at more basic reform have evolved. In one recent election, for example, ministers sought to discourage vote buying, long a rampant problem in the county, by citing Biblical teaching to obey lawful authority and against exploitation of the poor.[51]

Past, Present, and Future Contexts

Since the original publication of this work, other research has helped place these Baptists in a broader context. Though cultural issues are important to them and their communities, so are more material concerns. Like other voters, those in these communities respond to appeals made to them. To be sure, these appeals are bounded by "cultural" issues, but other issues can be salient, especially when cultural issues are effectively settled within a community.

The limited current evidence on these groups suggests that, like other groups elsewhere, they are losing adherents at varying rates. Yet, within their own communities, particularly where their leadership is integrated with others, they may sustain themselves. Though one of their leaders became involved with a controversial project in his home county, this does not appear to have affected his standing or that of his church.

Both past evidence and a limited amount of more recent indicators show these Baptists to be on something of a middle ground in the current U.S. religious landscape. They are not tied to an ascendant secularism, but neither are they tied to an assertive and affluent evangelical Christianity. How long they can stay in that middle ground, particularly in an era of polarization that does not revolve around their unique interests, is unclear.

Given the limited ecological indicators above, it is difficult to draw strong conclusions on the present and future of these groups. Nevertheless, I suggest that these Baptists continue to approach their communities and the politics within them more practically than we may realize. At the national level, their preference for Republican candidates may not be driven by cultural issues as much as by profound economic shifts, the effects these shifts have had on their communities, and the frustration that follows. The decimation of the coal industry in their core areas likely wiped out not only union miners but also many related industries supporting the mines. On more local levels, continued support for Democratic candidates may reflect not just established community patterns but also more immediate interests such as access to health care. Finally, of course, these Baptists and others in their communities may choose to remove themselves from the political arena. One reason for this, of course, is the characteristics of their communities that make political participation difficult. Yet another is the scandal which may influence politics in these communities, and in turn reflect poorly on church members.

In concluding my original research, I noted that changes in broader politics and local circumstances can reshape the politics of these groups. In particular, I noted that these Baptists "present an intriguing mix of traditional cultural concerns and evolving local adaptation." This continues to be the case. While cultural concerns may appear predominant in these communities, more material concerns, even if less visible, influence them as well. Within this context, the politics of these Baptists, like their faith, may remain adaptable in some ways, even if strictly bounded by others. But how long such adaptation can persist, or even how long these churches may remain, is open to question.

Acknowledgments

I again thank all those I mentioned in my previous acknowledgments. Without their input and guidance, this book would not have been printed, much less reprinted.

I thank as well Keith Harper, editor of the America's Baptist series, and, once again, Scot Danforth, director of the University of Tennessee Press. I was flattered, of course, by the opportunity they gave me to revisit this work so many years later. They helped me devise a plan to bring the work up-to-date. They were patient and helpful when personal and professional circumstances delayed this longer than I had anticipated.

I also thank Art Farnsley of IUPUI for two things. First, his generous review of my original work for Sociology of Religion expressed succinctly the lessons that I sought to share. Second, when this opportunity arose, he helped me identify much of the research in the new preface. Both helped in drafting the new preface.

This work originated with my work on the Religion Census of the Association of Statisticians of American Religious Bodies (ASARB). I thank my ASARB colleagues for two things as well. First, they serve as continuing inspiration for me in considering the state of American religion. Second, two of them, Dale Jones and Richie Stanley, helped me with the statistics on religious bodies I present in the new preface.

The dedication page expresses inadequately the debt I have to my family.

Notes

1. Bethany Moreton, *To Serve God and Wal-Mart: The Making of Christian Free Enterprise* (Cambridge, Mass.: Harvard Univ. Press, 2009).
2. Darren Dorchuk, *From Bible Belt to Sun Belt: Plain-Folk Religion, Grassroots Politics, and the Rise of Evangelical Conservatism* (New York: W. W. Norton, 2010).
3. Dorchuk, 11.
4. Dorchuk, 100.
5. Joe Bageant, *Deer Hunting with Jesus: Dispatches from America's Class War* (New York: Crown, 2007).
6. Bageant, 162.

7. Bageant, 82.
8. Bageant, 91–92.
9. R. Marie Griffith, *Moral Combat: How Sex Divided American Christians & Fractured American Politics* (New York: Basic Books, 2017).
10. Griffith, 318.
11. Pew Research Center, "Attitudes on Same Sex Marriage" (https://www.pewforum.org/fact-sheet/changing-attitudes-on-gay-marriage/, May 24, 2019).
12. Michael Hout and Claude S. Fischer, "Why More Americans Have No Religious Preference: Politics and Generations," *American Sociological Review* 67 (2002): 163–190, https://doi.org/10.2307/3088891.
13. David E. Campbell, Geoffrey C. Layman, and John C. Green, *Secular Surge: A New Fault Line in American Politics* (Cambridge, UK: Cambridge Univ. Press, 2021).
14. Kevin M. Kruse, *One Nation Under God: How Corporate America Invented Christian America* (New York: Basic Books, 2016).
15. Robert P. Jones, *The End of White Christian America* (New York: Simon & Schuster, 2016).
16. Mike Wynn, "Clerk 'Sought God' on Marriage License Issue," Louisville *Courier-Journal,* July 21, 2015, https://www.courier-journal.com/story/news/local/2015/07/21/marriage-license-suit-vs-clerk-back-court/30319757/.
17. Steve Bittenbender, "Kentucky Governor Orders Clerks' Names Removed from Marriage Licenses," Reuters, Dec. 22, 2015, https://www.reuters.com/article/us-kentucky-gaymarriage/kentucky-governor-orders-clerks-names-removed-from-marriage-licenses-idUSKBN0U52BJ20151223.
18. Will Wright, "Kim Davis, clerk who refused to sign marriage licenses for gay couples, loses to Democrat," Lexington *Herald-Leader,* Nov. 6, 2018, https://www.kentucky.com/news/politics-government/article221121745.html.
19. Campbell, Layman, and Green, 172.
20. J. D. Vance, *Hillbilly Elegy: A Memoir of a Family and Culture in Crisis* (New York: HarperCollins, 2016).
21. Kelsey Dallas, "God Plays an Important Role in Hillbilly Country, but not in the Way You'd Expect," Salt Lake City *Deseret News,* Sept. 3, 2016, https://www.deseret.com/2016/9/3/20595303/god-plays-an-important-role-in-hillbilly-country-but-not-in-the-way-you-d-expect#god-is-an-important-part-of-life-in-the-appalachian-region-of-the-u-s-but-not-in-the-way-youd-expect-says-author-j-d-vance.
22. Martin B. Bradley, Norman M. Green Jr., Dale E. Jones, Mac Lynn, and Lou McNeil, *Churches and Church Membership in the United States, 1990* (Atlanta, GA: Glenmary Research Center, 1992).

23. Statistics for the Indian Bottom Association are taken from annual minutes books published on its webpage at https://oldregularbaptist.com/about/minute-books/.
24. Statistics for the Sardis Association are taken from annual minutes books posted by the Pike County (Ky.) Public Library District at http://www.pikelibrary.org/Linkpages/sardisminutes.htm.
25. Statistics for the Northern New Salem Association are taken from annual minutes books published on its webpage at http://northernnewsalem.com/.
26. See Public Religion Research Institute (PRRI), "The 2020 Census of U.S. Religion" (July 8, 2021), https://www.prri.org/research/2020-census-of-american-religion/.
27. See lyrics as posted to https://www.lyricsmode.com/lyrics/d/dwight_yoakam/readin_rightin_rt_23.html.
28. See lyrics as posted to https://www.azlyrics.com/lyrics/steveearle/hillbillyhighway.html.
29. Statistics for other religious bodies in this table are from Bradley et al., 1992; Dale E. Jones, Sherri Doty, Clifford Grammich, James E. Horsch, Richard Houseal, Mac Lynn, John P. Marcum, Kenneth M. Sanchagrin, and Richard H. Taylor, *Religious Congregations & Membership in the United States* (Nashville, TN: Glenmary Research Center, 2002); and Clifford Grammich, Kirk Hadaway, Richard Houseal, Dale E. Jones, Alexei Krindatch, Richie Stanley, and Richard H. Taylor, *2010 U.S. Religion Census: Religious Congregations & Membership Study* (Association of Statisticians of American Religious Bodies, Kansas City, MO: 2012).
30. Grammich et al., *2010 U.S. Religion Census.*
31. PRRI, "The 2020 Census of U.S. Religion."
32. For background on this proposal, see, among others, Sam Adler-Bell, "Appalachia vs. the Carceral State," *New Republic*, Nov. 25, 2019, https://newrepublic.com/article/155660/appalachia-coal-mining-mountaintop-removal-prison-fight; Elwood Cornett, "Prison Detractors Should Say How They Would Bring Jobs to Letcher County's Unemployed Coal Miners," Lexington *Herald-Leader*, May 2, 2018, https://www.kentucky.com/opinion/op-ed/article210254554.html; and Sylvia Ryerson, "Prison Progress?", *The Daily Yonder*, Feb. 20, 2013, https://dailyyonder.com/speak-your-piece-prison-progress/2013/02/20/.
33. For more on the limitations of prisons in economic development, see Robert Todd Perdue and Kenneth Sanchagrin, "Imprisoning Appalachia: The Socio-Economic Impacts of Prison Development," *Journal of Appalachian Studies* 22 (2016): 210–23, https://doi.org/10.5406/jappastud.22.2.0210.

34. Election statistics here and below are from Secretary of State or Elections Division offices for each state.
35. These 17 counties are Breathitt, Elliott, Floyd, Johnson, Knott, Lawrence, Letcher, Magoffin, Martin, Morgan, Perry, and Pike in Kentucky; Buchanan and Dickenson in Virginia, and McDowell, Mingo, and Wyoming in West Virginia.
36. Gallup, Inc., and Healthways, Inc., "State of American Well-Being: 2013 State, Community, and Congressional District Analysis" (2014), https://cdn2.hubspot.net/hub/162029/file-610480715-pdf/WBI2013/Gallup-Healthways_State_of_American_Well-Being_Full_Report_2013.pdf.
37. Samuel Stebbins and Michael B. Stauter, "These Are the 25 Worst Counties to Live In. Did Yours Make the List?" *USA Today* and 24/7 Wall Street (March 13, 2019), https://www.usatoday.com/story/money/2019/03/13/worst-places-live-us-counties-ranked-poverty-life-expectancy/39163929/.
38. Will Wright, "Income Falls in Several Appalachian Kentucky Counties as Coal Fails to Bounce Back," Lexington *Herald-Leader,* June 26, 2019, https://www.kentucky.com/news/state/kentucky/article231937238.html.
39. Bradley et al., *Churches and Church Membership in the United States, 1990.*
40. Details on the 2010 enumeration of religious bodies are from Grammich et al., *2010 U.S. Religion Census.* "White Evangelical Protestant" population estimates for 2020 are from PRRI, "The 2020 Census of U.S. Religion."
41. See the performance of "Magoffin County Cadillac" at https://www.youtube.com/watch?v=XONH_afIk60, including the introduction by the performer, "Laid Back Country Picker," also known as David Price, a Lawrence County, Kentucky, social studies teacher. In it, Price praises both American-made cars and the "fine union boys" from Magoffin County who use their "Cadillacs" (decommissioned police cruisers) to carpool to jobs around the region.
42. David Sutton, "The 2008 Presidential Election in Appalachia: Reading from the Margins." Appalachian Journal 36 (2009): 188–98, http://www.jstor.org/stable/40934503.
43. Coal production statistics are from U.S. Department of Labor Mine Safety and Health Administration, "Mine Employment and Coal Production," https://www.msha.gov/mine-employment-and-coal-production.
44. Bill Estep and Liz Moomey, "Trump Promised to Revive KY Coal. He Didn't, but He's Still Expected to Win 'Huge.'" Lexington *Herald-Leader,* September 17, 2020, https://www.kentucky.com/news/politics-government/article245657425.html.
45. Estep and Moomey, "Trump Promised to Revive KY Coal."

46. Katie Reilly, "How Republican Governor Matt Bevin Lost Teachers and Lost Kentucky," Time, Nov. 7, 2019, https://time.com/5719885/matt-bevin-republican-kentucky-teacher-protests/.
47. Bruce Schreiner, "Kentucky Lawmaker Challenging Bevin in GOP Primary," Associated Press, Jan. 8, 2019, https://apnews.com/article/26da2f180bb54bfe9e65a1b68ab89062.
48. "What to Know about Robert Goforth in the 2019 Kentucky Governor's Race," Louisville Courier Journal, May 13, 2019, https://www.courier-journal.com/story/news/politics/elections/kentucky/2019/05/13/robert-goforth-bio-2019-kentucky-elections-governors-race/1188162001/.
49. "What to Know about Rocky Adkins in the 2019 Kentucky Governor's Race," Louisville Courier Journal, May 13, 2019, https://www.courier-journal.com/story/news/politics/elections/kentucky/2019/05/13/rocky-adkins-bio-kentucky-governor-races-2019-election/1189259001/.
50. Bill Bishop, "Where the Vote Shifted in Kentucky from 2015 to 2019," *The Daily* Yonder, Nov. 8, 2019, https://dailyyonder.com/where-the-vote-shifted-in-kentucky-from-2015-to-2019/2019/11/08/.
51. Bill Estep, "Ministers Push Candidates to Sign Pledge Against Vote Buying in Magoffin," Lexington *Herald-Leader* (October 29, 2014), https://www.kentucky.com/news/politics-government/article44518923.html.

ACKNOWLEDGMENTS

Chronologically, I owe my first thanks to Lou McNeil, former Glenmary Research Center director. Lou was quick to recognize some of the shortcomings of past church-membership studies published by Glenmary, and he encouraged (and funded) me in an attempt to improve the accuracy of *Churches and Church Membership in the United States 1990* among peoples and an area I have known all my life, the United Baptists and Old Regular Baptists of eastern Kentucky. That project led both to the enumeration of other, similar groups and, eventually, to my further observation that study of these Baptists could offer new insights into American religion, politics, and society. For the first push along the way, I thank both him and the Glenmary Research Center. I also thank his successor as director of the center, Sister Mary Priniski, O.P., for the opportunity to continue serving the Catholic Church in its mission to rural America, which has also been an opportunity to improve my knowledge of the areas I analyze in this work.

Howard Dorgan, H. Allan Gleason, and Chester Young were all instrumental in the initial enumeration project that eventually gave birth to this manuscript. Young was particularly generous in helping me conduct a systematic count of many small Baptist groups, including those I present in this work. Dorgan and Gleason very considerately shared their extensive knowledge of these groups and offered much helpful advice on enumerating them for *Churches and Church Membership in the United States*. Years after that project, they helped me again by reading some of the last drafts of this work and by guiding me past pitfalls into which I otherwise would have fallen.

The Commission on Religion in Appalachia (CORA) in Knoxville, Tennessee, helped me in two minor but significant ways. First, the knowledge I gained in preparing the *Appalachian Atlas* for the CORA served me well in studying Baptists concentrated in areas of concern to the CORA. Second, I am grateful to the CORA—and in particular to the Reverend Jim Sessions, the former executive director of the CORA—for some of the information I present in the fourth chapter of this work. A story Sessions shared with me about a unionization effort in an East Tennessee mine confirmed many suspicions I had about politics among some of these Baptists, and a large file the CORA staff had compiled and generously loaned for my use helped me flesh out Sessions's story.

A previous version of this manuscript was my doctoral dissertation in political science at the University of Chicago. I again thank my dissertation committee—Michael Dawson, J. Mark Hansen, Martin Riesebrodt, and Gerald Suttles—for the help they gave me. I also acknowledge the help of Ted G. Jelen of the University of Nevada at Las Vegas, particularly in helping me link my research to the burgeoning literature in political science on religion.

The University of Tennessee Press, of course, has my gratitude for many reasons. I am grateful for the persistence of Joyce Harrison in explaining each stage of the consideration and publication process to me. Stan Ivester took over where Joyce left off by making sure my questions were answered by the right person. Kay Jursik was patient in helping me present the best graphics and design I could, while Scot Danforth was even more patient in handling my editing questions. I am also grateful for the comments of Samuel S. Hill and Charles H. Lippy in their reviews of my work for the press. Like many of the individuals I mentioned above, they helped me see my work in perspectives I had not considered. I appreciate the gentle admonitions they made in placing my work correctly among other studies of broader phenomena, a placement their comments helped me better understand. I think their lessons here may have finally helped me understand what others before them have tried to teach me.

My grandparents, James Arthur and Virgie Ressie Lykins of Edna, Magoffin County, Kentucky, tolerated my visits and curiosity about their faith and their community always with a warm welcome and usually with nothing short of good humor. I again thank those who did so much to support this research in its prior, dissertation form, including my parents, Clifford and Betty Grammich, and my wife, Kathleen. I am also grateful for the diversions my son, James Patrick, has provided to this and other work, diversions that I hope have helped me recognize the ultimately important things.

Finally, and most important, I owe many thanks to those whom I visited and interviewed for this work. For reasons I explain fully in this work, I cannot name them, but I will always remember them. They have more reasons than most to suspect outside interest in their lives, but for reasons best known to them they chose to trust me. I hope that I have done nothing to betray their trust and confidence and that maybe I even repaid it in some small way.

My only regret in sharing the credit for whatever good comes of this work is that doing so emphasizes all the more my responsibility for any remaining shortcomings.

Politics and the Bible: An Introduction

What are the political consequences of a religion claiming to be based on the literal interpretation of a sacred text? The story of some local Baptist churches in the middle and uplands South that claim to follow the literal word of the Bible for all elements of their faith and practice suggests that they can be as varied as the needs of local members. The common theme of such politics is not of any consistent, pervasive ideology. Rather, they follow many strands from broad concerns of preserving the traditional family, particularly its patriarchal authority, of constraining excessive worldliness, and of adapting traditional themes to modern circumstances. Framed by these concerns, these Baptists' broader political participation is typically sporadic and focused locally.

Churches emphasizing a supposedly literal reading of the Bible for all elements of faith and practice make up a deceptively broad family. At first glance, such churches seem to constitute a common family of "literalists" or "fundamentalists." Nevertheless, there is a wide variety of practice among them. I will show how the particular Baptist population I study, comprising Central, Duck River and Kindred, Old Missionary, Old Regular, Eastern District Primitive, and United Baptists, differ in their own ways. They are not identical to those most commonly called fundamentalist, for they are not rationalists or rabid textualists in applying their creed to their lives.[1] They are devoted more to personal purity than to moral or evangelistic conquest.

What these Baptists have in common with fundamentalists and others of similar faith is that their common claims of a biblical basis overlay a rich array of adaptations and interpretations serving differing needs of individuals and congregations. All share common concerns for defending the traditional family and for restraining excessive worldliness, but beyond this vague agenda they are free to adapt their theology to local conditions. All churches adapt as the needs and social conditions of adherents change, but among those relying on a literal Bible, this adaptability grows with increasing emphasis on the sufficiency of local authority for biblical interpretation. Religion with such emphasis can be adapted to local needs and conditions more quickly and more often under the influence of laity most affected by social, economic, and political changes.

This work will show how changing needs for local religious authority affect the political influences of biblically oriented religion featuring such authority. Their faith gives adherents sharing a core of traditional concerns a means of seizing local religious authority for their own use. This authority cannot cover all needs over all time, since it remains concerned with traditional, patriarchal family authority, regardless of broader community changes.

Martin Riesebrodt is most explicit about the presence of traditional patriarchy among fundamentalists. His findings, I believe, apply to others claiming faith based on the literal interpretation of a sacred text. In an effort to find a comparative standard for fundamentalism, Riesebrodt examines it as a religiously inspired protest movement, including a defense of a supposed tradition and culminating in a radical patriarchy, by urbanites facing modern upheaval in the United States during the 1920s and in Iran during the 1960s and 1970s.[2] There are many differences between the groups Riesebrodt studies and those I study. He studies urban Americans of the 1920s; I study predominantly rural Americans of the 1990s. Yet both groups have adopted similar solutions to the problems they face, i.e., an emphasis on traditional, patriarchal family authority.

Nancy T. Ammerman expands upon the theme of reshaped traditions in accounting for Christian fundamentalism. She writes, "Fundamentalist movements are organized efforts to shape the future of a people in light of a past that is seen through the lense[s] of sacred texts and authorities traditionally available in the culture."[3] While the population that concerns Ammerman constitutes a more formal movement, traditionalism is not a concern limited to those most closely identified with fundamentalism. Among adherents of a more common "folk" religion without institutional structures, cultural conservatism and traditionalism often guide adherents in search of the "old-time" ways.[4]

Behind this traditionalism, churches and adherents with literal biblical beliefs find themselves in a variety of social and economic circumstances. These circumstances elicit a matching variety in their politics, from cultural conservatism to economic populism to a shunning of politics to still other responses. Analyzing the adaptation of their theology to local conditions shows how populations lacking political resources of their own can develop them on their own. H. Richard Niebuhr writes, "Theological opinions have their roots in the relationship of the religious life to the cultural and political conditions prevailing in any group of Christians."[5] I contend this is particularly true for those "Bible believers" with coexisting desires for local secular authority and local religious authority.

The Bible is remarkably ambiguous in many ways. It relies upon examples, parables, and other stories more than on general religious laws. It contains many contextualized rules that, if taken in isolation, contradict one another. Those claiming to base their faith on a literal reading of the Bible may share a simple, common theology, but biblical ambiguity allows them to draw profoundly different political lessons from their religion. This is because when they use the Bible for argument, they may select passages to strengthen a political argument rather than to maintain theological consistency.

It is difficult to reduce Christianity completely to simple, elementary rules whose meaning remains unchanged across time and place. The political meaning of Christianity is often vague because the religion focuses on supporting individuals across time, and not on exalting societies.[6] Much of what Allan Gleason says about "prooftext" use of the Bible also applies here. When specific Bible verses acquire special meaning and uses, they become biblical prooftexts. Gleason notes that those most likely to use prooftexts in casual conversation often put into them a great deal of special meaning.[7] He adds that prooftext use is more common among those who place an inerrant Bible at the center of their theology. I would add that those using prooftexts are likely to do so to shape theology to local circumstances and to give them special, localized meanings.

In emphasizing the adaptive possibilities open to creeds based on "literal" sacred texts, I do not overlook the common secular characteristics of adherents. Much scholarly attention is given to the increasing affluence, social status, and political participation of such Protestants in the United States, but many remain, like those I study, on the margins of society. They typically comprise lower-income families whose educational and geographical backgrounds place them near the margins of modernity or on the borders of the "mainstream."

Such Protestants are more likely to be southern, non-metropolitan, and have less education and lower incomes than the general population. The National Opinion Research Center–General Social Survey (NORC–GSS), for example, finds that, among non-Hispanic white Protestants in the United States claiming to believe in a literally true Bible and belonging to a church classified as fundamentalist in doctrine, 51 percent were both raised and currently live in the South, compared with 29 percent of all respondents; 68 percent live outside the one hundred largest metropolitan areas of the nation, compared with 48 percent of all respondents; 13 percent hold a bachelor's or higher degree, compared with 24 percent of all respondents; and such Protestants have lower median incomes than those reported for all respondents.[8]

Like all such marginal peoples, these Protestants face special problems or conflicts in adjusting to modern life, particularly those conflicts that challenge patriarchal family authority or require means for participation (e.g., affluence) that they often lack. When they come into conflict with those who hold overlapping economic, political, and ecclesiastical authority hostile to their interests, they often seek their own sources of religious authority. This is often the only authority open to local control, since such Protestants typically lack economic or political power of their own. The religion has uses for the community as well. Throughout the world there is little to attract unattached males to economically depressed places like those where these Protestants predominate. A religiously sanctioned exchange of formal (and sometimes actual) male authority for disciplined behavior by males as household providers often ensures community stability as few other social institutions can.

The politics of these Protestants, including their basic decisions about political participation, vary by the margins on which they find themselves. For some, marginality is declining as affluence is increasing. Those with increasing affluence may adapt their religion to improving local conditions by shaping religious commands to justify their new wealth and increased consumption, or to bridge the gap between their traditional faith and cosmopolitan expectations, or to offer support for other means of affirming their social and economic mobility.

It is the adaptation to local circumstances by those who do not want to be constrained by church history or a detailed theology or a systematic tradition of commentary that most interests me. Those claiming the sufficiency of local authority to interpret literally a sacred text can make many of their religious rules say what they want them to say. They likewise shape social and political commands based on these pliable rules.

This work is hardly the first to examine the political participation and attitudes of those who would believe in a literal Bible. Past research has presented a wide range of findings on a similarly broad range of groups. The Baptists I study, like different groups in other studies, have their own singular characteristics. I will examine these and the particular effect they have. Because those I study are relatively unknown, and because there is little documentation on them, I will show, for the benefit of the reader not familiar with them, how they relate to similar groups in previous research on religion and politics.

Links to Biblical Literalists in Research on Politics and Society

These Baptists share many characteristics that Sidney Verba, Kay Lehman Schlozman, and Henry E. Brady identify as increasing political participation among adherents. Verba, Schlozman, and Brady identify three characteristics of Protestantism that provide political socialization for those unable to gain it elsewhere. These are Protestantism's typically small congregation size, emphasis on congregational rather than hierarchical organization, and greater opportunity afforded to lay participation in liturgy and church matters.[9] All are pronounced in the churches I study. Verba, Schlozman, and Brady add that low-church Protestants such as Baptists, fundamentalists, Pentecostals, and other evangelicals are likely to practice civic skills in church and hence have greater political participation than their economic and other social characteristics would predict.[10] These findings are a needed antidote to past emphases on the "otherworldliness" of such populations. Too much emphasis on them, however, can lead us to neglect how that which helps give such religion its appeal, its emphasis on individual and local community concerns, can sometimes impede political participation.

Some scholars note growing ties between such Protestantism and political conservatism. Nancy T. Ammerman contends fundamentalists avoid worldly contact whenever possible, mobilizing only when "they perceive that the issues with which they were concerned . . . had to be wedded to a political agenda" opposing abortion rights, gay rights, women's rights, socialism, and atheism at home and abroad.[11] The fundamentalists Ammerman studies are those who emphasize evangelism, biblical inerrancy, premillenialism, and separatism in their faith. As such, we can expect them to differ from those who do not share all four of these characteristics, including the Baptists I study. The logic, for example, of premillenialism, a doctrine that holds that Christ will return after the rapture of all believers and before the final tribulation, compels a different attitude toward the world than postmillenialism and its belief in a progressive conversion of the world before the Second Coming. Many of the Baptists I study hold premillenial beliefs; a few hold postmillennial beliefs. Few on either side emphasize such beliefs, much less apply them to their politics. What is more apparent among them is the concern they share with Ammerman's fundamentalists for some broader issues, e.g., gay rights, which rarely affect individuals directly in their faith communities; their attention to such issues often arises from concerns about the effects of the broader culture upon individual families.[12]

Other scholars have pointed to the growing links between faiths based in literally interpreted sacred texts and more active political support for conservatism, or even anti-democratic politics. Bruce Lawrence, in seeking a crossnational standard of fundamentalism, goes so far as to claim that the movement serves as "an affirmation of religious authority as holistic and absolute . . . demand[ing] that . . . dictates derived from scripture be publicly recognized and enforced."[13] Within the United States, an analysis of political socialization by theologically conservative churches found that they instill political conservatism in their adherents beyond what could otherwise be predicted from personal commitment to traditional values.[14]

Those who link conservative theology and conservative politics usually point to the concerns of traditional morality held by adherents of the former. A typical description of such religion and its political implications is that of "white Protestant conservatives," including the Baptists I study,[15] offered by Wade Clark Roof and William McKinney. They write that "white Protestant conservatives" share "a traditional religious and cultural outlook . . . and evangelical doctrines emphasizing the necessity of a conversion experience, the authority of the Bible and the importance of a moral life, freed especially from such barroom vices as drinking, dancing, and card playing . . . the posture of conservative Protestantism continues to be shaped by its confrontation with modernity . . . [it] resist[s] the encroachments of modernism and secularism ... by holding to literalistic orthodox Christian doctrines, a view of the Bible as inerrant, and a metaphysic that assumes reality is inhabited by both physical and spiritual beings."[16]

"White Protestant conservatives" and the Baptists I study share many of the characteristics of "white evangelical Protestants," as Lyman Kellstedt and John Green use the term. Kellstedt and Green classify the Southern Baptist Convention, American Baptist Churches USA, and the Baptist General Conference as "white evangelical Protestant" bodies, as opposed to "white mainline Protestants."[17] Although they do not classify every extant Baptist church in their scheme, they place none outside "white evangelical Protestantism." White evangelical Protestantism, Kellstedt and Green note, has its origins in sectarianism. They write that "sect movements generate diversity within denominational families by seeking separation from the broader culture. These movements tend to produce conservative denominations or nondenominational churches with a conservative ethos: an acceptance of individuals based on commitment to narrow values specific to a cultural tradition. Fundamentalism, neoevangelicalism, and charismatic renewal are examples of recent sectarian movements among Protestants."[18]

We can consider such religion to be "agentic"—that is, individualistic—as Peter L. Benson and Dorothy L. Williams use the term. An "agentic" religion holds that "God's work is done mostly through individual persons, and persons relate individually and directly to God."[19] In studying religious attitudes among members of Congress, Benson and Williams find "agentic" religion to be linked with opposition to general government spending, foreign aid, hunger relief, abortion, and government protection of civil liberties, and with support for military expenditures and legislation protecting free enterprise and the rights of private property.[20] They attribute these concerns to the interest of agentic religion in preserving individualism and the links between individualistic religion and individualistic politics.[21] Benson and Williams note many hazards of extrapolating from their study of a very elite population to the general public. They add that agentic and individualistic themes cut across denominational traditions, with many theologically "conservative Protestants" having more concern salvation of the community than that of the individual alone.

I would add that it is not clear why religion that focuses on individual or local needs logically leads to conservative politics that do not change over time or across communities and their social and economic circumstances.

Among the mass public, it is not clear why such religion, by itself, must lead toward or away from any political activity. The recent concentration of much political science literature on the greater political participation of theologically conservative Protestants is understandable, given past neglect of this topic, but it can cause us to look past many questions of political participation and its context in local communities. Like most Americans, most of these Protestants either do not vote or vote only in presidential elections and otherwise infrequently participate in politics. A focus on electoral behavior, while helpful to understanding the drama of national elections so attractive to academic and journalistic observers, overlooks many more basic questions of political attitudes and participation.

For theologically conservative Protestants who are politically active, on many issues there are no clear linkages to theology. An evangelical minister who said, "I don't believe there's a biblical position on the Panama Canal," provides a particularly pointed example of this.[22] Ambiguity between political and theological conservatism is most noticeable on economic issues. A study of economic attitudes among "fundamentalists" found "no evidence that the logic of fundamentalism drives people toward a particular view of the economy, much less particular economic policies."[23] Another scholar notes that in the Bible one can find indignation at economic inequality as well as passages that could be interpreted as direct affirmations of capitalism.[24]

Changing Sources of "Bible-based" Politics

Though biblically based religious adherents with differing economic views today appear united on many social issues, it is evident that the social issues which concern them change over time or circumstance. Some of those I study, for example, oppose slacks for women, while the rest have accommodated this change but resisted others. The same is true for other "Bible-based" groups.[25] In one, the story of Noah is taken as a command to provide more environmentally conscious stewardship of God's creation.[26] This example is unusual in that no other group with similar theology appears to have made such an interpretation, but that reflects precisely my argument. Those who wish to make a particular religious interpretation for whatever reason—whether because they are concerned about the environment or because they perceive that with changes in women's apparel comes a threat to patriarchal family authority—are more free to do so within this tradition than they are in more formal churches. Dissenters could hardly reproduce the Evangelical Lutheran Church of America or the Church of England, much less the Catholic Church and its papal authority. But establishing new churches and rules supporting the laity in changing circumstances is much easier in a tradition in which a hoary joke is often heard: two Baptist ministers stranded alone on an island start separate churches within a week.

I am concerned with what those two Baptist ministers might do on the mainland. I contend that to the extent that they rely on a faith emphasizing a literal Bible and the sufficiency of local authority to interpret it is the extent to which they will find the freedom to adapt many pliable commands to local circumstances. My concerns are under what local conditions will such a religion activate political participation, and, once activated, how such a religion affects political attitudes in varying local circumstances. I am concerned about what might be called a more "thick description" of local communities can tell us about how the same religious influences on politics can act differently in varying communities.[27]

In interpreting such political differences, we do well to follow the advice of H. Richard Niebuhr, who recognizes economic, historical, and social differences in theology. He writes that

> theological opinions have their roots in the relationship of the religious life to the cultural and political conditions prevailing in any group of Christians. This does not mean that an economic or purely political interpretation of theology is justified, but . . . that the religious life is so interwoven with social circumstances that the formulation of theology is necessarily conditioned by these . . . Back of the divergences of doctrine one must look for the conditions which make . . . one [or an]other interpretation appear . . . more desirable.[28]

Niebuhr's advice is meant to account for differences in basic theology between denominations. But it is also sound in accounting for differences in theological interpretation and action within the same denomination, even those with the most elementary theology.

Consider three preachers among the Baptists I studied. One lives in Alabama, another in Tennessee, and the third in Virginia. The Alabama and

Tennessee preachers personally know and live within 150 miles of each other and belong to the same small denomination of approximately 13,000 adherents. The Virginia preacher lives within 200 miles of the Alabama preacher and 350 miles of the Tennessee preacher. Like them, he lives in a relatively homogeneous rural area of the South. He is of a different denomination, but shares the others' theology.

Their religious similarities far outweigh their geographic differences. All three preach a religion grounded in a literal interpretation of the King James Bible. They share many social and religious views, including traditional views of sex roles and opposition to missions, seminaries, and professional clergy. Yet they are quite different in the political lessons they draw from their common theology.

The Tennessean is an archetypal member of the religious right. He and many of the members of his congregation distrust the secular world and its media. They rely on Pat Robertson's Christian Broadcasting Network (CBN) and other similar sources for their news on public affairs. Robertson and other prominent preachers who share his political and theological conservatism have inspired this preacher and some of the members of his congregation to become more actively involved in cultural issues, such as opposition to abortion rights, opposition to gay rights, and, in the 1990s, opposition to their fellow Baptist, Bill Clinton. They do not view their opposition to Clinton as opposition to a fellow Baptist, for they do not regard the president as a true Baptist. This preacher told me, "If Bill Clinton were a member of one of our churches, he would have been excluded long ago."[29]

The Alabamian is reserved in his politics. He is wary of any worldly involvement. He turned down a promotion to foreman at work because he thought it would bring him into worldly conflict unseemly for a preacher. One of his few public passions is support for his labor union. He believes labor unions have biblical and economic justification. He told me that "labor unions have done a lot of things I don't agree with, and the people I work with know I don't agree with them and I won't take part in them. But the labor union is also the best thing to ever happen to a man who has to work on a job like mine and who has to provide for his family by working at a place like I do."

The Virginian is also a labor union member. Unlike the Alabamian, he actively supports the broader politics of organized labor. A Clinton supporter, his politics are opposed to those of the Tennessean. As for whether Clinton could belong to his church, he told me there would be no objections if the president, like every other person "legitimately" baptized, would give an evidentiary testimony "that he felt beyond a reasonable doubt that God had saved him by His grace."[30] Clinton's baptism in a Southern Baptist church, though by immersion as these churches require, would not suffice for inclusion. His stands on abortion and gay rights, though abhorred by this preacher, do not suffice for exclusion.

Social, economic, and community differences among these preachers help explain their political differences. The Tennessean, a math teacher at the public high school in his county, is the best educated and most affluent. He represents a relatively new but increasingly common phenomenon: affluent southern fundamentalism. The Alabamian enjoys a comfortable living from his job and his eighty-acre farm. He understands how his labor union supports his economic standing and stability. The Virginian is also aware of how organized labor supported his standard of living while he was working and now in his retirement. Many of the churches in his denomination are in nearby sections of the Appalachian coal belt, which are staunchly Democratic and militant in support of the United Mine Workers of America and other unions.

Their theological similarities remain strong. In addition to being Baptist, all three share certain tenets: a belief in the King James Bible as the unerring Word of God; an emphasis on the ancient origins of their "true" faith; a belief in salvation vaguely between the doctrines of predestination and of free will;[31] an emphasis on personal, experiential knowledge of salvation; a simple style of congregational worship; a distrust of centralized church authorities; and a stress on the sufficiency of local authority for religious interpretation and the autonomy of the individual congregation to exercise that authority in its own community.

In searching for a theme in common to the politics adherents draw from this religion, we should not focus on its conservatism but on its traditionalism. This includes its antimodern concerns, or those of science, technology, rationality, or progress, or more generally social emancipation made in the name of rationality and the social and economic challenges this poses, particularly to those, like many of the Baptists I study, on the margins of society. Despite being viewed as pathetic and ignorant by much of the modern world, such persons can enjoy a comfortable life on low but stable incomes in the face of modern upheaval, provided they are able to safeguard family life through repressing consumer impulses and ensuring males become disciplined household providers in a community sustained by supportive peers. Within this traditionalism, much adaptation to local circumstances is made possible by religious ambiguity. The sources of this ambiguity include the variety of practices that the Bible can justify and the sectarian nature of much of conservative Protestantism.

The most common secular claims of such religion across social and economic circumstance are a defense of tradition, particularly the patriarchal family, and a restraint on consumerism and pronounced worldliness. Beyond these claims, this religion does not comprise a uniform force shaping the social and political attitudes and practices of the faithful, but can serve as a means to help adherents meet varying secular needs.

One of the great attractions of this religion is the variety of justifications it allows in interpreting sacred commands and texts to meet local needs. This variation gives literalists the flexibility to shape sacred commands to local circumstances, unencumbered by disagreeable or distant religious or secular "experts" more prevalent in hierarchical churches. This faith typically develops upward from the ground of the laity. Adherents take full advantage of the ambiguities of their text and newfound traditions in a local shaping of the faith.

Religious Structures and Regionalism

The sectarian characteristics of this religion, particularly those featuring control of, by, and for local communities, emphasize flexibility in adapting traditional religion to modern politics. This flexibility has limits. It must take into account broad concerns with living a moral life, and it is shaped by many antimodern concerns. But by linking sectarianism with that form of Protestantism most reliant on a literal Bible and local authority, a whole new array of possibilities for political activity becomes apparent. These possibilities range from otherworldliness to political activation for traditional causes to religious justification for populist or redistributionist causes.

Politics, Sectarianism, and Denominationalism

The insistence that conservative Protestantism leads to conservative politics carries with it certain assumptions about sectarianism. These hold either that sectarianism is otherworldly or that it is concerned more with moral than economic affairs in the public realm. Such assumptions do not take into account the variation evident in sects as described by Ernst Troeltsch, Max Weber, Richard Niebuhr, and Werner Stark.

Troeltsch's discussion of sects has been among the most influential among analysts of sectarianism. Sects, Troeltsch writes, are "comparatively small groups ... aspir[ing] after personal inward perfection ... aim[ing] at a direct personal fellowship between ... members."[32] Some Baptists I study have shared "indifferent, tolerant, or hostile" attitudes toward the world, "since they ha[d] no desire to control and incorporate" worldly concerns and aspirations.[33] Others, however, have exhibited a broad variety of political activity and attitudes.

Weber attributes to Baptist sects only a few stable positions that influence their political attitudes and activity. He writes, "A strict avoidance of the world, in the sense of all not strictly necessary intercourse with worldly people, together with the strictest bibliocracy in the sense of taking the life of the first generations of Christians as a model, were the [characteristics] of the first Baptist communities, and this principle of avoidance of the world [has] never quite disappeared so long as the old spirit remain[s] alive."[34] For Weber, sects are often marginal groups unable to exert influence over the state.

The Baptists I study take "the life of the first generations of Christians as a model," but this does not always lead to a "principle of avoidance of the world" among them. Weber himself provides evidence of the changing relationship between Christianity and the secular realm when he discusses the four types of attitudes found in ancient and medieval Christianity towards the state. All four of these are evident in some form among "Bible-based" Protestants today, though the numbers conforming to each has changed over time.

In ancient Christianity's weaker days, believers' attitudes toward the public weal were 1) of the state "as the dominion of anti-Christ," or 2) of "complete indifference ... and hence passive sufferance ... entail[ing] active compliance with all ... obligations imposed by the state ... which did not directly imperil religious salvation."[35] As Christianity became ascendant, believers were more likely to regard the state with 3) "recognition as somehow being desired by God," or as 4) "an indispensable instrument for the social control of reprehensible sins and as a general condition for all mundane existence pleasing to God."[36] As Christians, including some Baptists I study, become more able to exert influence over the state, many desire to use it for their own ends.

H. Richard Niebuhr's discussion of differences between sects and churches on structures, ethics, and doctrines is more precise on the modern political influence of sects. Differences between church and sect members, Niebuhr writes, stem from birth, with members being born into the church but having to join the sect. He adds, "Churches are inclusive institutions . . . emphasiz[ing] the universalism of the gospel . . . [the] sect [is] exclusive in character . . . appeal[ing] to the individualistic element [and] likely to demand some definite type of religious experience as a pre-requisite of membership . . . attach[ing] primary importance to the religious experience of its members prior to their fellowship with the group. It frequently rejects an official clergy, preferring to trust for guidance to lay inspiration rather than to . . . expertness."[37] The Baptists examined in this work likewise reject a professional clergy and avoid the constraints of outside "expertness" through pronounced emphasis on the autonomy of local congregations, with only the barest minimum of religious authority exercised by bodies (with their own decidedly local characteristics) above the individual congregation.

Niebuhr is most pointed about the economic origins of sectarianism, writing that the Protestant sect typically arises among the outcast, as a "religious revolt of the poor, of those who were without effective representation in church or state," who form dissenting bodies "in the only way open to them, on the democratic, associational pattern."[38] The church, by contrast, is dominated by prevailing political, economic, and cultural interests, and "must represent the morality of the respectable majority, not of the heroic minority."[39] Niebuhr does not see in sectarianism and the "religious revolt of the poor" a turning away from the world as much as a re-engagement with the roots of Christianity. He writes, "The rise of new sects to champion the uncompromising ethics of Jesus and 'to preach the gospel to the poor' has again and again been the effective means of recalling Christendom to its mission."[40]

Werner Stark's analysis of the religious sect and the political party emphasizes why a "revolt of the poor" would in one circumstance turn to religion and in another turn to concerted secular political action. For Stark, the key to whether the "spirit of revolt" is expressed in "metaphysical-religious" terms or in "physical-practical-political" terms "would seem to lie in the relative hopefulness or hopelessness of the situation when considered with a view to possible reform. If reform is a distinct possibility, a political party rather than a religious sect will arise; if reform is, or is judged, a virtual impossibility, a religious sect rather than a political party will appear. Much depends on the concrete conditions in which a class or sub-class finds itself."[41]

However otherworldly a sectarian response may appear to be, Stark says, it is not necessarily a final, irrevocable withdrawal from the world. Instead, the radicalism of sectarian religion can translate to secular radicalism. He writes:

> It would be wrong to see the radical party in politics only as a competitor and killer of the radical sect in religion: it is as much to be regarded as its child and continuator. The typical sect bears in itself, but thinly disguised, the future form of the typical party.... In other words, [radical sects] propagate the principles of a radical democratic reform. The left, as can be seen, is always the left, whether it prays or plots, whether it is too weak to fight and turns utopian and religious, or strong enough to fight and turns realistic and political.[42]

Stark makes explicit that which Weber implies. Weber sees Christianity generally changing its attitudes toward political power as it is more able to use the public weal for its own ends, but he is ambiguous on the specific ability of sectarianism to do so. Stark is not. Sectarianism to him is otherworldly only to the extent that adherents perceive they have no chance to vie for public authority. As they become able to do so, they become less otherworldly.

A wide range of political implications for religion based in sectarianism is now apparent. Those implications do not just take the form of a withdrawal from the world. Even when adherents appear otherworldly, sectarianism can still prepare them for a more active and worldly means of advancing political interests. The extent that the Baptists considered in this study are the products of sectarianism is the extent to which they are open to the many differing influences, both worldly and otherworldly, that can run through sectarianism.

Sectarianism may be the most informative of existing social science definitions to describe the Baptists I study, but it is not ideal. Troeltsch and Niebuhr, for example, both emphasize the short-lived nature of sects. Most of the "sects" I study have persisted for nearly two centuries.

In time, many sects "come to be dominated by the most successful ... and begin the gradual accommodation to the world."[43] Some of the Baptists examined in this work have become successful, and their religion and politics have changed accordingly. They have trod the road Weber maps, from considering the state with indifference to considering it as an instrument to make all life pleasing to God. Others have become more closely allied with "churches," such as the Southern Baptist Convention, but later found reason to reemphasize their sectarian independence rather than continuing down the road toward "churchly" instead of sectarian religion. Most find reason to reassert continually their sectarian independence.

Bryan R. Wilson offers sectarian categories that serve as means to describe these Baptists in reference to broader populations. Wilson differentiates between four types of sects in explaining why some endure and some transform into denominations.[44] The Baptists I study share many characteristics of traits he identifies as "conversionist" and "introversionist." Among their "conversionist" traits are reliance on a literally true Bible as the only guide to salvation, emphasis on a conversion experience, and hostility to clerical learning and to modernism.[45] Among their "introversionist" traits are "reliance on inner illumination," a theological emphasis such that "doctrine is of lesser importance in what the letter has surrendered to the spirit," and opposition to most evangelism.[46] Wilson argues that "conversionist" sects are most likely to transform into denominations, while "introversionist" sects are more likely to persist as sects.

Though I would argue that these Baptists are more "sectarian" than "denominational," some of the denominational characteristics identified by David Martin apply to them as well. Martin writes that in denominations "the underlying principle [emphasis in original] of organization is . . . the priesthood of all believers. Authority is conceived as resting collectively in the whole religious body. . . ."[47] Those Martin identifies as denominational come to realize their "genuine stake in the present social order."[48] Such religion, he writes, typically draws the "lower middle class . . . with an appeal for the independently situated type of worker, the earnest self-improving artisan, and to the business man in so far as he is not swallowed up in the collectivism of late monopoly capitalism."[49]

Such religion is not of individualism run amok, but of the peculiar blend of individual and collective tendencies evident throughout the United States and the British Commonwealth. It is one of stable, working people, like the Baptists in this work. It is adaptable to some individual needs, but flourishes only "where social change proceeds at a steady pace" or where sudden, drastic adaptation is not needed.[50] Likewise, while many Baptist churches I study have their origins in economic conflict and turmoil, we will see that they now adapt best where social change is less drastic.

Sidney E. Mead identifies two characteristics shaping Protestantism in America which apply to these Baptists, particularly their growing inability to adapt to rapid social change. These include "the 'sectarian' tendency of each . . . to justify its peculiar interpretation and practices as more closely conforming to those of the early church," and "the voluntary principle."[51]

The "sectarian" tendency stems from an antihistorical basis, which in turn has roots in the Protestant desire to appeal over church tradition of the first millennium of Christian (that is, Catholic) history and go straight to the Word. This ploy, which undercuts all intervening traditions between Christ and modern times, also had the effect of "limit[ing] the restrictions placed on the ardent men and women who were engaged in building churches in the new land" of America.[52]

Despite its individualistic nature, voluntaryism helps curb sectarian impulses. It does not lead to an individualism or adaptability that is completely unbounded. Rather, it becomes "a leaven in the mind and practices of the religious groups, conditioning their development . . . [tending] to push tangible, practical conditions to the fore . . . the center of a denomination, as of any other voluntary association, is a tangible, defined objective to which consent can be given."[53] Once this tangible, defined core is achieved, denominational leaders have been reluctant to consider anything that might be divisive in their churches. Thus, rather than resulting in continuing adaptation, voluntaryism yielded a core with "a kind of massive and stubborn stability, inertia, and momentum of its own . . . [which is] likely to become evident especially in periods of internal stress or external threat. . . ."[54]

The same is often true of these Baptists. Many congregations originated in the need to adapt church authority to local uses. Adaptability persists, but is increasingly constrained by an enduring commitment to traditionalism. The traditionalism of these Baptists now prohibits radical changes to their mores, even where they may be needed or at least should be considered. We shall see, for example, how their commitment to localism and patriarchal family authority, while continuing to serve many secular needs, affects their ability to counter external threats to an eastern Kentucky county where these Baptists predominate.

Sectarianism and Regional Religion

Many cite sectarian influences in arguing the links between conservatism and southern religion. Wilbur Cash claimed that a southerner, when "beset with difficulties beyond his control and comprehension . . . tended, like his father before him in the early days of the nineteenth century and in Reconstruction time, to retreat into other-worldliness and, in the solace and hope he found there, to resign himself to his lot in this world. . . ."[55]

A more recent study of the prospects for populism among southern blue-collar workers contends the Bible-laden southern ethos inhibits worldly involvement by teaching that

> the problems of this world are unimportant compared to the promises of the afterlife. Such a belief leads men fatalistically to accept their economic and social conditions and pursue spiritual rather than material goals . . . religion [may] promote political interest in the enforcement of the moral codes rather than economic issues. Men who are preoccupied with the laws regarding the sale and consumption of alcohol and the public availability of pornographic materials are easily distracted from pursuing political strategies of economic self-interest . . . [southern] religion . . . [also] promote[s] social and economic conservatism [by opposing federal actions tainted as socialist or remotely interfering with beliefs]. . . .[56]

Others dispute both the historical and religious bases for political conservatism among southern whites, particularly those, like many of the Baptists I study, in the uplands South. J. Morgan Kousser notes lower-class whites in racially homogeneous uplands counties have not been as consumed with the grim racial politics that led to reactionary politics elsewhere in the South.[57] V. O. Key Jr. documents the "natural political cleavage between lowlands and hills" dating from before the Civil War, isolating those in the uplands in opposition to the more conservative interests of the wealthier lowlands.[58] A recent study of economic attitudes among southern white "evangelical" Protestants found that "only a minority are, by nature, across-the-board political conservatives . . . Southern white Evangelicals are more likely to favor governmental intervention in the economy than are Southern non-Evangelicals."[59]

The growing literature on religion in the Appalachian South has been leery about using the term "sectarianism" to describe it. Deborah Vansau McCauley is most pointed in her objections to the use of "sectarian" to describe "Appalachian mountain religion." McCauley's work is a valuable resource for this study for many reasons, including being one of the few to consider some of the same churches I do. Much of her opposition to the use of "sectarian" to describe these churches stems from her justified objections to the focus of some past social scientists on how "such churches epitomize a subculture of poverty . . . [and] pointed . . . to such churches as the premier example of . . . sectarianism run amok."[60]

McCauley is particularly scornful of those who would classify "Appalachian mountain religion" as "the religion of the poor." Such an interpretation, she says, is "pernicious, insidious, and condescending."[61] McCauley performs a valuable service in documenting the ideological baggage, particularly that of liberation theology, which weights an interpretation of such religion as "the religion of the poor." Yet it would be inaccurate to interpret the comments of Niebuhr, among others, of nearly seventy years ago as an endorsement of the uses and abuses of liberation theology today.

However "pernicious" it is to be poor or to be perceived as such, there are, unfortunately, few words more accurate than poor to describe the economic conditions of some areas in which the churches we both study are. Among the 88 poorest counties of the nation (from a total of 3,141), as measured by per capita income in the 1990 census, for example, 17 are in Appalachian Regional Commission (ARC) counties of Kentucky.[62] The combined 49 Kentucky ARC counties had a per capita income less than 60 percent of the national level.[63] This work does well to avoid the mire of ideological debates accompanying modern study of "*the* religion of *the* poor" [my italics], but it would be foolish to ignore altogether the severe economic challenges where many of these Baptists are concentrated.

Jeff Todd Titon's study of an Appalachian Baptist church in Page County, Virginia, offers a more nuanced interpretation of economic changes and how they affect indigenous churches of the region. Much of what he says is applicable to the Baptists I study. He writes, "Each time the outside world intruded . . . mountain farmers were victimized. The overriding conclusion is inescapable: mountain history and tradition taught the mountain families that interaction with the outside world was risky and that household and kin-network self-sufficiency was the best strategy. . . . Little wonder that the[ir] religion . . . emphasized the distance between the church community and the outside world."[64]

The literature on indigenous "Appalachian" churches illustrate many of the characteristics of those I study, but not all. The Baptists I examine are both more narrow and more broad than the groups McCauley studies. These Baptists provide a more narrow topic in that they do not encompass the variety of religious expression McCauley examines. But they provide a broader topic in that they are present in a different geographic region than the one McCauley studies, being concentrated not just in the highlands, but also in other parts of the middle and upper South. Analyses of "popular" southern religion and of "folk" religion, while describing religious phenomena beyond the geography of these Baptists, are closer to their religious essence.

Samuel S. Hill was among the first to make a systematic study of "popular Southern religion." It is, he claims, "best delineated as a medley of revivalistic and fundamentalistic strains."[65] Although many scholars, including Hill, in recent years have increasingly emphasized variety rather than homogeneity in southern religion, much of what Hill originally identified as popular southern religion applies to the Baptists I study, including the effects of a relatively late frontier history, of a historically rural character, and of frequent cultural insulation. These have helped give the churches I study a static quality in their structures, but is not one that has prohibited any adaptation whatsoever.[66] Rather, there has been a tension between inherited structures, which once clearly met secular needs but now resist some changes, and a tradition, as well as a continuing practice, of shaping religious authority to meet local needs.

Many of the characteristics William Clements identifies in the folk church applies to the Baptists I study. In addition to sectarianism, the other characteristics of a folk church Clements identifies that apply at least in part to these Baptists are a general orientation toward the past, scriptural literalism, informality, emotionalism, egalitarianism, and the relative isolation of churches.[67] Politically, Clements writes, "The difference between folk religion and official religion is seen as being based on their respective relationships to the power structures of the complex societies of which they are a part. Unlike official religion, folk religion does not have the support of the society's official secular institutions—its government, economy, technology, education, art. Official religion is official because it is inextricably bound to those institutions which comprise the society's power structure."[68]

In understanding how broader religious influences can affect such a group, I would draw some attention to "syncretism," or "the process of fusing two different religious ideas or systems which are usually analogous."[69] Clements limits discussion of this phenomenon among folk churches to "period[s] of acculturation when the religious system of the dominant society is recast to be acceptable to the dominated society,"[70] but I suggest similar processes occur both between these Baptists and their surrounding environment, and between these Baptists and more prevalent churches of similar beliefs. Clements acknowledges the possibility for such a relationship, writing "folk religion is 'nonestablishment' rather than 'antiestablishment,' for while official institutions do not support folk religion, folk religion is not necessarily in ideological opposition to those institutions. . . . It differs from official religion only in its lack of association with the society's power structure."[71]

Examples of a "syncretic" adoption of broader social mores among the Baptists I study have occurred in both social and religious mores. Some, for example, have changed a few elements of traditional sex codes to accommodate the greater presence of women in the workplace. Others have developed attitudes prevalent in more prominent churches with beliefs in a literal Bible, thus incorporating what they see as most acceptable in more dominant churches. This is clear in the case of the Tennessee preacher cited above who relies on Pat Robertson for news and views. All the groups I study make their adaptations in response to local circumstances, though they are not always able to make such adaptations as rapidly or as broadly as local circumstances change. The extent to which these churches have adapted acceptable practices of other churches, whether "fundamentalist" or "Appalachian" or "southern" or "folk" churches, helps show the extent to which analysis of these Baptists has implications for other Protestants.

Review and Preview

This work explores the boundaries of political participation and attitudes stemming from religion for a population of local Baptists in the middle and uplands South. These Baptists claim the sufficiency of local authority to interpret the local Bible for all elements of faith and practice. In this they are similar to many other Protestants, but their claims to follow a literal Bible mask a variety of adaptation of sacred commands to local circumstances. The ability to shape supposedly universal commands to local circumstances, free of the constraints of a centralized church bureaucracy or a systematic tradition of commentary, is one of the chief appeals of such religion. Within a broad concern for tradition, particularly the authority of the patriarchal family and a concern with the effects of pronounced worldliness, Protestants who base their religion on a literal interpretation of the Bible are free to interpret their sacred commands to suit local circumstances. Adaptability increases with greater stress on the sufficiency of local authority to interpret the Bible. It is made possible by the vagueness of the Bible and its many ambiguous rules. I am most concerned with what community influences on "Bible-based" religion can activate or inhibit political participation, and what effects such religion has on political attitudes.

Those relying on local interpretation of the Bible and making local adaptations do so within a concern for traditionalism, particularly a concern for patriarchal family authority. This concern can still serve many secular needs for them, but it can also hinder their ability to adapt their religion to meet other needs. Tension between their traditionalism and their local community concerns, on the one hand, and their economic needs and broader community challenges, on the other, inhibits them from making their religion a pure agent of their worldly needs and aspirations.

Both the adaptability of such religion and its limits are particularly evident among Baptist sectarians of the upper South. These Baptists have more pronounced sectarian characteristics than are typical among other similar Protestants, but sectarianism itself, and its waxing and waning, is essential to understanding changes in religion and politics, particularly among such Protestants. The tension among these Baptists between their concern for tradition and the demands placed upon them by their modern social and economic conditions is an underlying theme of this work. I will explore this tension in four subsequent chapters, followed by a concluding chapter summarizing the implications of this work for the study of politics among broader populations.

The first chapter demonstrates the large historical themes of politics common to these and similar, broader groups. Some groups are most concerned about confrontation between traditional and modern life and use their religion to justify social practices assisting or sheltering the transition to modern life. Others confront changes in social and economic status. Those unable to partake of a consumer society use their religion to develop virtues of discipline and austerity. The growing numbers who have experienced upward social and economic mobility confront different problems, namely, how to justify and portray their consumption, or how to bridge the gaps between their tradition and the more cosmopolitan world of which they are more and more frequently able to partake. This history of national trends in local settings does not show consistent political themes, but continual adaptation to social and economic conditions prevalent at a given time, with little regard given to the past, both among the particular population I study and among other, similar populations. If reference is made to historical precedent, it is done so as "case law" that either arose with past splits in the church or that emphasized sectarian independence from centralized church bureaucracies.

The second chapter turns from how broader themes play out in particular settings to consider more local characteristics of the particular population I examine. This consideration includes how local issues arise among them and are handled by local adaptation. This chapter examines the individual characteristics of each group I study, and how their common features lead to a variety of adaptations. It is worth emphasizing that these Baptists fiercely maintain religious distinctions among themselves. While their distinctions may matter for building political coalitions, what is most important about this divisiveness is that, when faced with too great dissonance or disagreement between local needs and church commands, these Baptists can and do seize local religious authority, which makes recourse to the same sacred source, but allows differing conclusions on the implications of sacred commands.[72]

The third chapter examines the effects of local labor union mobilization on these Baptists' politics. This is one place where their adaptation is most effective, particularly in "syncretically" adapting the goals of such organizations into their own. Some scholars suggest that fundamentalists neither have nor desire social organization outside the church.[73] This is not always true for other believers of a literal Bible. Church-related organizations are the leading form of social participation for many, but many also belong to an organization with at least some secular purpose. The NORC-GSS finds non-Hispanic white Protestants with literal biblical beliefs who belong to a "fundamentalist" church are more likely (51 percent) than the general public (33 percent) to belong to another church-related organization.[74] Yet nearly half (48 percent) of this population (compared with 61 percent of the general public) belongs to an organization with at least some secular purpose (e.g., a political organization or fraternal society).[75] Most strikingly, one in eleven households in this population has a labor union member.[76]

Where secular organizations, rather than the church, become the social space of politics—as they often do among labor union members—the demands of the secular organization become the primary influence on members' politics, regardless of their religion. The Baptists I study are in some of the few places where both labor unions and Protestantism based on a literal Bible both flourish. The story of labor unions among them shows how religion can be interpreted to support economic goals. This interpretation can lead their politics in ways we might not expect. In an exceptional case, these Baptists used their tradition to generate support for a local coal mine unionization effort that was greater than that offered by the usual supporters of organized labor in Catholic and mainline Protestant hierarchies. The story of labor unions among these sects also shows how concern for tradition sometimes places limits on their politics.

These limits become more clear in the fourth chapter, which examines recent politics in an eastern Kentucky county. This county is one of the few places where these sects are dominant, comprising most enumerated church adherents. Its politics in the 1990s was dominated by a proposed landfill, which was to accept more trash each day than all Kentucky produces. A grassroots environmental movement stymied construction, but also uncovered the limits religion places on county politics. The movement's leadership is predominantly female, which has caused some resistance to it. It has shifted its attention from stopping the landfill to reforming the county government that had permitted the landfill to be built in the first place. The movement's accomplishments occurred without the help of these churches, who feared that political activism would threaten the community they fostered.

Many of the characteristics, particularly decentralization, which give this religion its appeal hinder it in bringing about more complex collective goals for county residents. Churches with centralized bureaucracies that might hinder local adaptation find within these same bureaucracies help to achieve secular collective goals. These are resources the sectarians I study do not possess. Any effort by them to achieve secular collective goals would threaten the collective goal they have managed to attain, that of building a relatively stable community in a severely deprived area. This story will show the difficulties these sectarians have in organizing for collective goals, how one collective goal can threaten another, what this says about modern reasons for bureaucratized authority, and the continuing tension between effective politics and a socially effective religion, a tension as old as American politics itself.[77]

The fifth and final chapter discusses how this study points to new elements to consider in the analysis of politics among similar groups. I consider in particular what lessons these Baptists offer on the political aggregation among other religious groups, on the "crisis" of and paradox in southern religion, and on more general points relating to the routinization of charisma in organizations, which can have political effects. We will see that the same elements that give an adaptable religion its appeal are the same that make it difficult to use for political purposes. We will also see that religion with sectarian roots can have many social and other noneconomic benefits that have not been considered. This work will show that the strength or weaknesses of sectarian characteristics can affect the political variety open to these Baptists, as well as their willingness to engage in politics. Their "sectarian" goals can become valued in themselves, and not just as agents to an economic goal or some other secular goal. Sectarian goals can affect adherents and their congregations in different ways. The more sectarian adherents are, the more variety there is to their politics. At the same time, the more sectarian they are, the less likely they are to pursue broader political goals, lest they lose the collective good their religion helps them attain. The means these groups use to preserve their founding spirit, as well as the unique place they find in American religious life between sectarianism and denominationalism, affect their place in politics and society in distinct ways and point to new lessons for the study of religion and political behavior.

CHAPTER 1

National Themes in Local Settings

There are four broad characteristics the Baptists of this study share with other populations more widely studied in fundamentalism or southern religion. These include 1) the ambiguity of their sacred text and its adaptability, free of external expertise, to local circumstances; 2) an emphasis on traditions ensuring family stability by making male discipline a condition of formal male authority; 3) the use of religious adaptability to address economic concerns, including both local struggles against outside economic interests, and, in recent years, to justify newfound affluence; and 4) the tension arising between traditionalism and the adaptability of the religion, particularly as economic conditions change but social traditions do not.

These strains are not present in all variants of this religion, but they are among the most common ones that activate or shape political behavior and attitudes. Their history demonstrates that many of the adaptations to changing social conditions that we can observe today have occurred repeatedly in the past. This religion develops precedents for the future only in exceptional circumstances, such as when they involve a rift among members or when they especially emphasize the adaptation of theology to local needs and circumstances. The history of religion ironically demonstrates the ahistorical nature of its political influences and adaptability.

Three political themes are most evident in prior research on similar groups. These are:

1) Concern with the confrontation between traditional and modern life.

We have much historical evidence on how confrontation between traditional and modern life affects biblically based Protestants, thanks to prolific literature on "fundamentalism" and "modernism." Such Protestants confronting cosmopolitan influences have turned to their religion to justify social practices that assist or shelter transition to modern life.

2) Economic threats. Economic threats to these Protestants are a clear, though often overlooked, historical basis for their political mobilization. Most notably, the populism of William Jennings Bryan drew together freeholders who shared his faith and who faced threats in the loss of credit and the decline of farm prices. Bryan strengthened the link between fundamentalism and populism by opposing the use of "Darwin's teachings . . . to bolster political and social conservatism in the form of Social Darwinism."[1] Within the South, "the sectarian revolt at the turn of the century was clearly a parallel movement" to Bryan's populism.[2] Even before this, the South had a deep history of economic divisions reinforcing religious divisions, with the poor turning away from cosmopolitan and toward local, biblically oriented religious authority.

3) Changes in social and economic status. On one side, those Bible believers unable to partake of "the good life," as defined by having material possessions, must develop the virtues of discipline and austerity, or more general virtues in opposition to a consumer society. On the other, the growing number who have experienced considerable occupational mobility and corresponding increases in income confront the problem of how to portray their consumption. The newly affluent often engage in a conservative politics that seeks to justify wealth.

The Baptists of this study and other related Protestants most readily coalesce around cultural traditionalism. This occurs not only in their cultural politics, but also in their economic politics. Those engaging in redistributionist politics use themes of cultural tradition to justify either actions they say will preserve the strength of the family and of other institutions dear to them, or practices that shelter the family and its authority from cosmopolitan standards. Adherents who practice politics of affluence also use themes of cultural traditionalism to justify their wealth, often through the church institutions they foster.

The politics of such religion occasionally founders on economic themes. This is not surprising given the differing interests of the many poor and the increasing numbers of rich who practice such religion. Poor and rich adherents of biblically based Protestantism sometimes use their religion for different economic themes in their politics. The less affluent have resented church establishments, their monetary demands, and the wealthy interests that support them. The most affluent inadvertently subject their churches to the same economic, "church-sect" tension that spawns them. Economic influences of such religion may work at crosspurposes with traditional concerns.

Below I examine, first, the cultural concerns of such religion, and the themes these give to the Baptists of this study and other similar populations, and, second, the variation economic themes cause. In reviewing cultural and economic politics among these groups, I focus on the general themes of such politics and how the religion was used to meet the challenges these themes could pose.

CULTURAL POLITICS

Noted Historical Occurrences

Cultural traditionalism is one of the most recurring and recognized themes of politics among these sectarians and others basing their faith in a literal interpretation of a sacred text. We find cultural conservatism, or a reclamation of what were once supposedly cultural standards, in the ascetic sects that are among the spiritual ancestors of the Baptists in this study. Troeltsch traces the rise of the Anabaptist movement to the abandonment of "the real Christian ethic" by dominant denominations and their appeal to "the secular ethic of Natural Law."[3] The first Baptist movement "laid particular emphasis upon certain elements which had originally formed part of the spiritual ideal of the Reformers, which, however, under the stress of circumstances, had become ... compromise[d] with secular civilization."[4]

American fundamentalists of the early twentieth century also sought to reclaim a cultural ideal in the face of upheaval that challenged their communities. George Marsden writes, "Fundamentalists ... experienced the transition from the old world of the nineteenth century to the new world of the twentieth century wholly involuntarily ... they not only experienced a sense of alienation, but felt called to a militant defense of the old order ... [we might] picture fundamentalists sheltered behind their ideological ghetto wall, with the wall itself as heavily fortified as the very wall of Zion."[5] The ideals that early-twentieth-century fundamentalists sought to recover may have differed from those that Troeltsch identifies, but the strain of cultural reclamation remains. For many this cultural reclamation represented innovations matching the needs of practitioners in a specific time and place.[6]

Cultural reclamation has been a theme in the recent resurgence of religious politics of Protestant traditionalism. Among issues driving it in recent decades have been "the anti-Catholic/anti-Kennedy vote of 1960, early opposition to the civil rights movement throughout the 1960s, the emergence of the social issue agenda in the 1970s, the embrace of this agenda by the Republican party in the 1980s, and the mobilization efforts of the Christian Right in the late 1970s and early 1980s."[7]

Even as cultural traditionalism affected such politics in recent decades, undercurrents of economic populism have remained. Barry Goldwater in 1964 won traditional Protestant areas where William Jennings Bryan had his greatest support several decades earlier.[8] Goldwater's traditional Protestant supporters were concerned about federal power and school prayer, but, in contrast to their candidate, they did not differ from the general population on economic issues.[9] Four years later, concern over distant federal power and changing cultural standards helped George Wallace win support from many of these same voters.[10] Some odious cultural issues fueled support for Goldwater and Wallace, but support for them among culturally traditional Protestants was more complicated than reactionary racial politics. Under Wallace, for example, Alabama was one of the most liberal states in the South on economic issues.[11]

Eight years later Jimmy Carter's appeal to traditional white southern Protestants further demonstrated the dual themes in their politics. Carter's 1976 effort was the last presidential campaign to appeal to both cultural conservatism and economic populism. There is some danger in overemphasizing Carter's attractiveness to this population. It is true that "many secular commentators . . . assigned to [traditional white southern Protestants] a disproportionate role" in Carter's victory, particularly since Gerald Ford actually won the white South in 1976.[12] The disillusionment that "evangelical activists" expressed about Carter in 1980 further demonstrated the limits of his appeal to this population. The more important point, however, is that Carter was able to address quite legitimately both traditional religious sentiment and populist economic grievances.[13]

Furthermore, the two most explicitly "Bible-based" major presidential candidates of recent years, Pat Robertson and Jesse Jackson, easily blended both themes of cultural traditionalism and economic populism. Allen D. Hertzke writes that, while Robertson was most strongly identified with cultural conservatism, he included many radical economic proposals in his campaign, while Jackson, more closely identified with economic populism, also called for greater adherence to biblical codes of behavior.[14]

Still, since Carter's election, the issues most noticed among culturally traditional white Protestants have been those of cultural conservatism. There are two reasons for this. One is the failure of any national campaign to embrace both economic populism and cultural conservatism. The other, which I address later, is the increasing affluence of many in this white Protestant population. Among the cultural issues most noticed among this population in recent decades have been women's rights, gay rights, and textbook controversies.

Two analyses of textbook controversies in the upper South demonstrate some of the processes of culturally conservative politics in the face of cosmopolitan influences among regions and groups similar to those studied in this work. An analysis of a West Virginia textbook controversy found that it was rooted in "status politics."[15] Religious adherents in an area where their "cultural fundamentalism [had been] dominant" feared the rise of an educational program representing "urban heterogeneity, consumer-oriented affluence, and the pervasive drive of rationalization in all spheres of life."[16] A critique of another uplands South textbook controversy found that it stemmed from an attempt by local biblically based adherents "to maintain local religious traditions in the face of the community's increased incorporation into the social network of mass society."[17]

These community analyses are helpful in studying those most like the Baptists in this work because of their focus on local challenges and issues. These studies demonstrate the resistance of "Bible-based" Protestants to the introduction of new cosmopolitan standards in traditional communities, where these Protestants perceive that the cultural "war" has encroached increasingly on their home turf. Yet they leave unexamined why some Protestants may not mobilize even in the face of these perceived cultural threats.

This work explores some additional evidence on what community influences will activate cultural politics for such adherents, as well as why they may not turn to politics, even when they perceive broader cultural challenges. These reasons often stem from their desire to hold onto the one collective good they can provide for adherents—a stable, supportive community. The increasing conflict between cosmopolitan authority and local interests in these areas has not always led to culturally conservative political activism. What is evident is episodic political activity. Many are either politically inactive or active in ways that contrast with the recent religious right.

I do not suggest that findings on increased conservatism and political activity among similar populations are wrong.[18] I do suggest that the groups I study demonstrate how such populations may or may not become politically active or rally for conservative causes because of their cultural concerns. For the population I study, there is an attraction to religion that has little to do with the broad worldviews fostered by fundamentalist leaders such as Ralph Reed or establishments such as the Christian Coalition, and that difference can logically lead to a variety of political responses, including the lack of a response.

Cultural Concerns among Baptist Sects of the Upper South

To be sure, if there is one set of political issues that can unite all the Baptists I study, it is cultural issues such as opposition to abortion in nearly all cases,[19] to gay rights, and to full sexual equality. To a lesser but nonetheless widespread extent, many oppose women having any role outside the home. They also oppose the sale of alcoholic beverages and the extension of gambling through lotteries and casinos, subjects of referenda which have occurred in many of these churches' communities in recent years.

Their current opposition to gambling, liquor, and other "barroom vices" has historical ironies, given that the antimission movement that helped spawn these groups has its roots in Jacksonian politics, which viewed with suspicion outside missionaries who would bring abstinence from such "vices" to the South in an effort to "reform" the region.[20] This point demonstrates the ahistorical nature of many of these Baptists' claims to moral authority, even those claims that one might most expect today of them. A more sympathetic interpretation might hold that modern gambling, particularly as it has grown through government-run lotteries that prey on the poor, and alcohol consumption, which now rarely entails consumption of locally brewed products but rather products from distant corporations or occurs in places (e.g., taverns) that can pose threats to the family, have required these Baptists to adjust their attitudes accordingly. Despite their agreement on many current cultural issues, there is not much organized political activity among these Baptists on such issues. Sectarian resistance to politics and a need for maintaining harmony in the congregation help reduce activism for cultural conservatism.

One Old Missionary Baptist preacher told me what his congregation does politically is of little interest to him, and he himself has little interest in politics. He said, "I don't get heavily involved in politics. I don't feel like I could minister to my whole congregation if I did. I think I would segregate myself from some of them if I got too heavily involved in politics. I don't try to form anybody's political views. I try to teach our people to do what's right regardless of what their politics are. Stand for what's right, and if it goes against your politics, just grit your teeth and keep standing for what's right."

Those who do practice politics are not predictable in what they emphasize. Two Old Missionary Baptist preachers, who belong to different parties and know each other personally and know the preacher quoted above, provide contrasting examples. Cultural conservatism drives some of their politics, but pragmatic concerns play larger roles.

The Democrat is a Kentucky highway supervisor. Since Democrats have held the Kentucky governorship for all but four years since World War II, his choice of parties is prudent. Nevertheless, he told me that he is a Democrat because "both sides of my family raised me to be a Democrat, and that's what I am." He put a Clinton/Gore bumper sticker on his truck, which it still sported when we met, and he volunteered for Clinton's campaign because he "thought we needed a change in our government." This was a remarkable ideological commitment in a county where Clinton won only about one-third of the vote in his two presidential campaigns.

His religiously based social attitudes place limits on his Democratic politics. He opposes efforts "to allow homosexuality in the military." He is not naive about this; he says, "I know it's there and it's always been there, but I just don't think it ought to be opened up." He refused to support Martha Layne Collins when she was the Democratic nominee for governor in 1983, because he "just do[es]n't believe" a woman should hold executive office. He "feel[s] like the church ought to take a more active part in politics and on the abortion issue, homosexuality, the lottery system, and casino gambling."

Yet he also says he will not personally try to persuade any members of his congregation to take a more active political role on these issues. He is reluctant to become more actively involved with campaigns led by religious right leaders, both because he disagrees with them on many theological and political issues and because he doubts any preacher ought to be involved with politics as much as Pat Robertson and Jerry Falwell are.

The Republican lives in an adjacent Tennessee county. Like the Kentucky Democrat, he claims family influences to be the main force shaping his politics. He has won county elective office, but downplays politics in church. He told me, "There's no politics in my religion . . . the political world is not even remotely connected with true religion in my thinking." Instead, he tells a poignant story about why he ran for assessor:

> I did not run to become politically involved. I've had a pretty hard [economic] tussle pastoring churches like this. You can see the salary they pay me,[21] and there's no way I can live on that. I had to look at something. . . . I have to be careful in the jobs that I take, because I've got to work for someone that understands when I need off for a funeral I've got to go. In this office I've got good employees that help me, and when I need to be at a funeral or a wake or revival they can take care of the work.

When some members of his church said "a preacher don't need to be involved in politics," he responded, "I need a better-paying job. My home's not paid for. I should retire if I was able, but I'm not financially able. That's the only reason I ran for assessor." This preacher was in his sixties at the time of our interview. His jobs before becoming assessor included an unsuccessful venture in real estate and work with a construction company which did not have the flexibility that would permit performing his pastoral duties at any time.

He mentions topics like "abortion, gay rights, and things like that" in his sermons, issues "that old-time Baptists don't believe in," but he also says, "When we come into church, there is no party. I've got good friends, even some of the deacons here, who are strong Democrats. What they do outside is their business. I know men here who voted for Clinton, but that don't affect their worship here, not in the least."

Part of his caution in pushing a cultural conservatism tied to Republican politics may stem from the unique political geography of his county. It is adjacent to the home county of the two Albert Gores, and his county cast a healthy 1992 majority for the presidential ticket that listed Bill Clinton and its neighbor. Four years earlier, the county had cast nearly two-thirds of its votes for George Bush over Michael Dukakis. Four years after the 1992 election, while giving a slight plurality to Bob Dole, it did not give a majority to any presidential candidate. Given such volatility, downplaying partisan politics is a sound way to preserve congregational harmony, and a typical example of modifying the cultural concerns of this religion to local conditions.

Some of these Baptists are willing to become involved in church-directed politics, but they are selective about the issues on which they will campaign. One preacher, for example, said he feels his position as a minister gives him leadership authority he should use on behalf of the community. When I asked him on what types of issues he would wield his influence, he mentioned "temperance" issues. He does not believe that his church should "have any special programs set up" to consider political issues or the actions that should be taken on them.

On volatile issues, his association ducks formal pronouncements. On abortion, they have taken no stand, and he has not been active in antiabortion politics. He explains, "ninety five percent or more of our people do not believe in advocating abortions. But we do not go out in marches or things of that kind. Our people would not go out to abortion clinics to walk picket lines or hurl insults or destroy property." This attitude parallels that of these Baptists who belong to labor unions. Many support organized labor in general but not militant union activities. This preacher supports broad cultural conservatism but not the movement's militancy. Again and again, one hears these preachers and church members saying they will avoid anything bringing "reproach" upon the church. The lack of broader ecclesiastical structures that give these Baptists greater flexibility in adapting their religion to local circumstances also appear to prevent them from exercising broad influence, lest they bring scorn upon themselves from secular elites or others with greater organizational resources.

Not all are reticent about linking their cultural conservatism with broader politics. The West Tennessee preacher whom I mentioned in the introduction, a Duck River Baptist, is a striking example. He says, "More of our people [are now] actively against" gay rights and abortion rights. He told me, "We're becoming more active against them just as the SBC [Southern Baptist Convention] is." He sees the SBC and other fundamentalist denominations as an appropriate model for his church's secular activity.

He applauds the efforts religious right leaders make in upholding "Christian" culture and standards. His comments on secular and religious media show this: "A lot of our people rely on Christian commentaries on world events, because we've gotten to the point not many of us trust the news media anymore. So I think a lot of us have looked to them to filter out and make some meaning out of all that is going on. I don't know if all of us would support the political ambitions of these preachers, and I don't know how many of us would vote for Pat Robertson as president or Jerry Falwell, but I dare say that most of our people have at least listened to them or to CBN."

Despite his ambitions, he admits that neither his church nor his association will likely become a local vanguard for the religious right. He recognizes that he is more involved in politics than most Americans, and still more than most members of his church. He says that while he is a conservative Republican and most members of his church are very conservative, there are also liberal Democrats who are in good standing in his church and who will neither leave nor be pushed out. A visitor to his church will find cars sporting bumper stickers for Democratic candidates, including Clinton and Gore. Because of the partisan division within his church, he says most political energy tends to be spent on "safe" doctrinal issues, such as whether an individual is qualified for the ministry, or on widely varying interpretations of biblical prophecies and how they apply to modern times.

Even when a preacher of these Baptists is committed to expanding the scope of cultural conservatism to broader conservative politics, there are limits on its practice. What could help achieve a broader activism inspired by cultural conservatism is an increase in affluence similar to that which the Duck River Baptist preacher quoted above has undergone. Increases in affluence have accompanied corresponding changes in attitudes toward the church's work in the world and attachment to broader causes. I return to this theme in discussing economic influences among these Baptists. Without such affluence, or without many other means to help bring stability to their communities, these Baptists avoid whatever they perceive may threaten either their vulnerable position in the community or the sense of community the church itself fosters.

Effects and Limits of Culturally Conservative Politics

Nearly all these Baptists share culturally conservative values, as well as opinions on such issues as abortion rights, gay rights, and women's rights, held by the leadership of the religious right. Yet there are several factors that inhibit their participation in broader conservatism.

Some avoid any political activity. This is either because they do not believe in engaging in such worldly endeavors or because they do not want to risk a split within their churches. All the preachers quoted above recognize varying partisan viewpoints within their congregations. Some preachers participate in politics only for the most pragmatic of reasons, and they emphasize the worldly necessity of their participation to those who question their involvement.

Wariness of worldly action affects even those who do engage in politics. Many will campaign for local prohibition, an issue which is closely contested but rarely provokes public strife. They shun the political limelight when it comes to more bitterly contested issues like abortion. Opinion on liquor sales and abortion rights is similar among these Baptists; nearly all are opposed to both. But since conflict over abortion rights often provokes public strife, these churches will not take part in public opposition to abortion. They avoid bringing "reproach," or scorn from secular elites, upon themselves.

There are some whose cultural concerns lead them to greater contact and alliances with leading figures and organizations of the modern religious right. But there is an inherent tension in such efforts. By tying themselves more closely to such figures and organizations, they become more "church"-like. These groups' histories lie in a rejection of ecclesiastical authority. Even if Pat Robertson, Jerry Falwell, and Ralph Reed are more palatable to their tastes than previous "church" leaders, such leaders still represent a formally trained clergy and an ecclesiastical establishment. Many Baptists I interviewed mention these leaders negatively; some cited political reasons, but most cited ecclesiastical reasons for this dislike. If these Baptists were to decide they wanted to follow the religious right, they would confront the momentous challenge of renouncing their own tradition of local authority, derived free from the standards such as those of seminaries or Bible schools that are associated with such religious establishments.

If they remain true to their sectarian traditions, they cannot adopt the ecclesiastical establishments that Falwell, Robertson, or Reed represent. If they accept such ecclesiastical establishments, they can become the object of the same forces that once animated their religion, namely, forces of protest against religious establishment. Cultural conservatism of a religious establishment will not cause schism among them, but issues of broader conservatism, particularly economic conservatism (or, more precisely, of classic economic liberalism), could.

This means that sectarian influences among them inhibit the development of cultural traditionalism into broader conservative politics. Some scholars have argued that sectarian influences often lead adherents to act contrary to their economic interests. Here, sectarian influences, particularly those that lead adherents to shun the world and its intense conflicts, lead some of these Baptists to ignore their cultural interests in broader politics. That which gives their religion its appeal, its localized nature, is that which inhibits its use in broader political movements.

Nancy T. Ammerman provides an excellent example of how broader "fundamentalist" communities can adapt the same biblical passage either to support or constrain worldly activism. She writes that there has never been a question about whether fundamentalists would be active in their world, but rather "how they define, at any given moment, what constitutes the world in which they are to be active. In some times and places, that world has barely extended beyond immediate family and small congregation. In other times and places, the call to follow God takes the believer into marketplace, school, government, and foreign affairs."[22] The ambiguous verse she cites here is II Chronicles 7:14, which states, "If my people, which are called by my name, shall humble themselves, and pray, and seek my face, and turn from their wicked ways; then will I hear from heaven, and will forgive their sin, and will heal their land."[23]

Depending on how they view their world, North American fundamentalists are able to follow one of two different versions of interpretation for this passage. Ammerman writes, "The first version expresses the intentions of a pious remnant, people who criticize the corruption of their age and who resist it by their own defiant piety and belief. The second version expresses the determination of a people seeking to bring about the cultural repentance that will avert disaster. The first version directs attention inward; the second outward. It is all the same story, but the meanings attached to its characters and plots change as it is told and retold in response to the changing panorama of daily events."[24]

Viewing the world with an eye toward their economic position leads many of the Baptists in this work to support political candidates who hold positions against their cultural interests. Economic concerns drive their politics in a different direction than their cultural traditionalism does. Cultural conservatism can set an initial direction for much of their politics, since it presents the only set of issues that unites them. But it competes with other influences on their politics, as well as some remaining reluctance to engage in "worldly" affairs. In this context, the only thing surprising about populist politics among them is that such politics can still occur without the accompaniment of cultural traditionalism.

ECONOMIC POPULISM

Historical Occurrences

"Bible-based" Protestantism does not react solely to cultural issues. In fact, sects of this tradition have arisen more often in response to changing economic class structures, and accompanying changes in religious establishments, than over concern with changing cultural standards. This has been particularly true in the South. The antimission movement among both these Baptists and other, similar groups was one of the earliest American instances of class conflict leading to religious changes, particularly those emphasizing local authority in biblical interpretation.

The antimission movement in the South, whose spirit still animates the Baptists examined in this work (as I will discuss in the following chapter), helped uncover class fissures and resentments, particularly among poorer adherents who were more likely to rely on local biblical interpretation for the tenets of their faith. Bertram Wyatt-Brown notes that "most antimissionists did not belong to the ruling elite whose attitudes have shaded modern perspective . . . antimissionism was one expression of a confused internal cleavage between the folkways of the poor and their social betters. . . ."[25] Among the "Hard-Shell" Baptists more directly related to those I study, antimission sentiment "represented in extreme form a fear of any modification of scriptural truth *as the Hard-Shells understood it* [my emphasis]."[26] From this perspective, antimissionism was, in part, an effort to maintain local control over churches in the face of new, external political and economic powers seeking religious powers as well.

Antimissionism had broad appeal among similar other groups in the South, including those more likely to emphasize the parallels between new church establishments and other trends threatening local authority over disputes of biblical interpretation. Wyatt-Brown finds southern antimissionism beginning "with the post-war depression of 1819. Backwoods opinion was running strongly against the Bank of the United States, the eastern establishment, and local southern and western creditors in the towns and cities. When John Taylor, a Baptist preacher of Clear Creek, Kentucky, published his *Thoughts on Missions* in 1820, it produced a widespread response."[27]

Taylor was proud of the self-sufficiency of his church work, as well as his own self-sufficiency through farming. He had many scriptural objections to the growth of church structures, but he also worried that, with the rise in local areas of larger church structures, "community control would diminish, while alien, unreachable powers in distant cities imposed a new tyranny. Taylor had deep forebodings that a new aristocracy was emerging in America, one that was subverting religious action to a spirit of commercial, northern imperialism."[28] With the rise of Jacksonian politics, regional and national politics reinforced economic and religious fault lines.

The effect of populist politics on similar Protestantism was limited neither to the South nor to mere reaction against wealthy interests. The politics of William Jennings Bryan is a vivid example of the fusion of a "Bible-based" Protestantism to an active, rather than reactive, economic program. Bryan saw no conflict between populism and the cultural traditionalism of fundamentalism, and he linked them together until the end of his life. On the eve of the Scopes trial, he said, "People often ask me why I can be a progressive in politics and a fundamentalist in religion. The answer is easy. Government is man made and therefore imperfect. It can always be improved. But religion is not a man-made affair."[29] Bryan's biblical orientation was at least as grounded in politics as it was in religion. It was a religion he followed in reaction to theories viewing "man as having his present state 'by the operation of the law of hate—the merciless law by which strong crowd out the weak' . . . he preferred to believe that 'love rather than hatred is the law of development.'"[30]

Bryan's religion was one of opposition to powers, even those often viewed as more enlightened, that were hostile to common persons.[31] Garry Wills points out that Bryan, in opposing Social Darwinism, was in many ways more enlightened than his critics, particularly his tormentor, H. L. Mencken. Mencken used Darwinian teachings and the writings of Friedrich Nietzsche, inspired by Darwin, in particular to justify repression of women, blacks, Jews, and other socially weaker peoples, practices that horrified Bryan. An additional point here is that the religion Bryan exemplifies was not a means of repression, but a resource, however flawed, in the fight by weaker peoples against repression of one sort or another.

Some scholars question how well Bryan represented populism; one historian dates the death of the movement to the moment the People's Party adopted Bryan's free silver platform and candidacy.[32] The significance for religion and politics of Bryan's career, however, lies not in his monetary policy, but in how he fused his traditional religious beliefs with progressive politics. Prior to Bryan, the only explicitly political actions biblically oriented Protestants made as a group were "on such traditional evangelical concerns as temperance and opposition to gambling."[33] With Bryan's example, many "extended their political interests to include broader social and economic issues."[34]

Bryan's politics were paralleled in the South. One historian goes so far as to claim that the parallel movement was "perhaps the first time in southern history [that] the region experienced a grass-roots rebellion by the truly economically and religiously dispossessed. For some southerners ... conscience demanded [religious] secession."[35]

Socialist ministers in the Southwest recognized the uses of biblically oriented religion in advancing their politics, using "camp-meeting fervor and a Fundamentalist idiom to create a 'Socialist Gospel' that transformed secular socialism into a millenarian and transcendent faith in the possibility of reform."[36] J. Wayne Flynt adds that in the "intellectual ferment" of the early 1900s, as social and economic problems were increasingly noticed, southern ministers joined those "who were attending the University of Chicago, studying rural sociology, attending conferences on social reform, and reading books" with an eye toward taking stronger action to curing the ills of society.[37]

Most of these ministers had not shed their traditionalism, for they did not accept liberal theology and its "'higher criticism' of scripture, its attempt to rationalize science with religion, and its humanism," but they were more "receptive to the new and more relevant gospel message."[38] Many of their resulting efforts, particularly their "campaigns against prostitution and Demon Rum often have been dismissed as pietist attempts to enforce private moral standards in the entire community," but they also led to further efforts throughout the first part of the century against child labor, the convict lease system, lynching, and for support for health services, and many other welfare, educational, and economic reforms.[39] All originated in local concern for social and economic conditions and were carried forth in the face of occasional opposition by more distant church authorities.

Such politics continue to influence the attitudes of many "fundamentalists" and others with similar biblical faiths. One analysis of fundamentalists' economic attitudes found them to be "actually *more* [emphasis in original] liberal than others," concluding, "William Jennings Bryan 'seems a more apt personification of Protestant Fundamentalism than does Jerry Falwell.'"[40] Today fundamentalists with differing economic interests offer the spectacle of "selective retrieval . . . picking and choosing . . . from some earlier . . . stages in one's own sacred history."[41] On economic issues fundamentalists typically "have no difficulty advocating any . . . economic orientation . . . with reference to their . . . written authorities . . . consensus . . . among fundamentalists and evangelicals on [economic questions] i[s] more than likely . . . the working of external [rather than internal] religious forces . . . fundamentalists . . . appropriate economic concepts [by] picking and choosing [with] little attention to an item's original source . . . using everything they can . . . to further their religious [and social] agenda."[42] Likewise, other forms of "Bible-based" Protestantism, which often have their origins in economic conflict, are malleable to the economic needs of adherents as these needs change over time and circumstance.

Economic Populism among Baptist Sects of the Upper South

Economically based schisms have often animated the groups I study. Some of these sects originated in lower-class resentment of church establishments. The same antimissionary forces that swept through the Jacksonian South gave rise to many of these Baptists. Economic conflict has been behind many of the theological questions which often have vexed them.

Antimission sentiment surfaced as a theological question, but always had broader economic implications in the South, particularly in those areas which were "far from the increasing flow of trade . . . [and] cash exchanges, [in] areas . . . isolat[ed] from the market [and] sparsely settled."[43] Much of the antimission sentiment arose in reaction to the "foreignness" of "ecclesiastical agencies [which] may have been the first extra-local presence" to enter many of these areas.[44] Poorer farmers resented the "dunning by itinerants" for causes beyond the local area addressing problems "also alien to the neighborhood."⁴⁵ The missionaries, having accepted the patronage of the wealthy, "also received a reputation for class consciousness not belied by their criticism of 'ignorant' people living in 'a state of moral degradation.'"⁴⁶

Baptist sects in "isolated areas" first rejected but then accepted "benevolent societies" when both the definition and the class backing of such "benevolence" changed. The history of the conflict over benevolence and its resolution shows both the flexibility of these Baptists' religion and the limits they have in relating to larger church establishments.

At first the conflict over "benevolence" appeared to be strictly theological. Missions were the primary work of benevolence. One pro-mission church history claims that the sects of this work, like other Baptists, initially supported such work, noting, "Benevolent enterprises, for advancing the Redeemer's kingdom, and bettering the condition of man, received the hearty approval of the early Baptists of Kentucky. From the organization of their first churches and associations, down to the year 1815, a period of more than thirty years, there appears no dissent from the spirit and practice of missions. . . . An Anti-Missionary Baptist was unknown, in Kentucky, previous to the year 1815."⁴⁷

These Baptists, however, like other poor Protestants, would come to resent the economic and social interests behind missionary societies. They saw those supporting such efforts as those who "had gone 'out from us because they were not of us.'"⁴⁸ Their preachers offered "bitter . . . satires against missions, Sunday-schools, Bible societies, Colleges, Protracted Meetings and [learned] preachers."⁴⁹ Mangling Paul's admonition on schism to the Corinthians, they denounced "the Missionary *scheme,* the Bible Society *scheme,* the Sunday-school *scheme,* and all other benevolent *schemes*" [emphases in original].⁵⁰

Class lines ran through this conflict. A pro-missionary historian charged that antimission doctrine "harmoniz[ed] with covetousness."⁵¹ These Baptists in turn claimed that "they were the original Baptist denomination," maintaining the true faith in the face of desertions by those who had been tempted away from the original emphasis on local authority and autonomy by a new desire to lord it over others through benevolent societies.⁵² Maybe the antimissionary preachers denouncing "schemes" were not making a malapropism. The rise of such schemes had, in their opinion, led to a schism with the original faith, even if only a "single item of forming and contributing to benevolent societies" was primarily responsible for the schism.⁵³

Arguments over benevolence have risen repeatedly among these Baptists, with their tone and outcome changing as the definition of benevolence changed. Benevolent societies were of particular concern to Old Regular Baptists in the 1870s. The New Salem Association concerned itself not only with the "benevolence" of church missions, but of all "secret or open," religious or political, societies. Not all Old Regular Baptists agreed on this concern, with some splitting over this expanded opposition to "benevolence."

The question of secret orders and their compatibility with the Baptist faith were an issue in forcing Kyova Association, which remained steadfastly opposed to such orders and to labor unions, from other Old Regular Baptists. Old Regular Baptist doctrine on such issues (which I will discuss in greater depth in the next chapter) gradually accepted such groups as they saw both the need for them and the increasing malleability of such groups to local control. When I asked one preacher why "secret orders" came to be accepted, he said it was because Old Regular Baptists now realized "secret orders have never done damage to the Baptist faith. They have never interfered with the doctrine of salvation by the grace of God or the practice in general of the Baptist people because they are organizations formed to help poor people survive, have homes, and have their children get an education. All those Baptists who have opposed it never really had experience where they needed these groups."

As the question of "benevolence" came to focus more on groups which were of, by, and for local residents, these sects accommodated them. Fraternal groups performing charitable works or community service under the leadership of local members have found greater acceptance among these Baptists than outside ecclesiastical uplift agencies ever could.

Some are still concerned about secret orders, but their concern appears to be more genuinely religious than economic. One preacher told me he is opposed to Masonry because he believes it is "very New Age, a religion in itself, almost like a cult."[54] Still, he recognizes many members of his church belong to Masonic lodges, and his feelings on Masonry appear to be religious rather than camouflage for some hidden economic agenda.

These Baptists participate in non-church organizations to advance their economic interests. Like William Jennings Bryan and others of similar faith, they often use the themes of their religion to justify their economic views. As individuals and in non-church groups, these Baptists will use religious themes and resources in confronting economic threats. As one scholar writes,

It was Ollie Combs, a member of the Old Regular Baptist Church, who sat down in front of and stopped the bulldozers trying to strip her land, who was carried off to jail, and who later testified before the Kentucky legislature to bring in the first strong strip-mine regulations in Kentucky. This bill was called the "Widow Combs" bill. Dan Gibson, an Old Regular Baptist elder, stopped the strippers on his stepson's land, and he and Mrs. Combs were important members of the Appalachian Group to Save the Land and People. The Reverend Otis King, a Missionary Baptist preacher from Harlan County, electrified viewers of the NET film, "Appalachia: Rich Land, Poor People," with his evangelical denunciation of absentee ownership and the rape of Kentucky....[55]

But just as they are reluctant to have their churches take direct action on many cultural issues, they are reluctant to have their churches take direct action on economic issues or other worldly concerns. They "believe... that the church is not of this world" and should be kept "unspotted from the world."[56] Likewise, many are reluctant, for religious, economic, and historical reasons, to have outside churches take action for them. Yet many remain ready and willing to act through secular means by and for their own behalf.

THE POLITICS AND RELIGION OF AFFLUENCE

Historical Occurrences

Despite the roots of many "Bible-based" Protestant bodies in the economic interests of poorer adherents, more affluent bases for their economic politics are emerging. This is a relatively new phenomenon among those I study, but one which has affected them in the past, and one which is now widespread among other similar groups.

Income conservation remains a common need of such Protestants, but increasingly it is not a need for all. A growing number of low-church, biblically oriented Protestants with rural or small-town backgrounds in this century have experienced occupational mobility and corresponding increases in affluence. Because of their previous poverty, they have been raised to consider consumption sinful. They confront problems of how to portray their consumption properly or how to apply the standards with which they have been raised in more affluent settings. The Promise Keepers movement appears to be one example of those who emphasize patriarchal family authority trying to find new ways to apply the old standards. At an opposing grotesque and materialistic extreme, other efforts can reflect those of Jim and Tammy Bakker, who barely disguised entertainment and consumerism in a thin veneer of joyous religion. The most political consequences of the effort to bridge affluence and traditional faith appear to arise when newly affluent adherents share their new wealth with religious institutions of similar faith, tying themselves more closely to these institutions' conservative leadership, who in turn justify their followers' newfound affluence.[57]

This upward mobility uncovers a contradiction—as old as ascetic Protestantism—among the adherents of such faith, which can lead to alteration and regeneration. The ethics of such religion often inspire adherents to succeed in a capitalist economy. Yet their success generates the conditions that first caused ascetic Protestants to form sects in a revolt against economic interests of the established ecclesiastical order.

Max Weber first drew attention to the success of this "Protestant ethic" in producing successful members of a capitalist economy, and how it leads to its self-destruction. The most faithful adherents of this ethic, Weber writes, often rose "from a lowly status" to riches only "to repudiate the old ideals" which first inspired their religion.[58] The whole history of asceticism "is in a certain sense the history of a continual struggle with the problem of the secularizing influence of wealth."[59] Weber also notes that salvation religion has a special appeal to the privileged.[60] If privileged classes require anything of religion, it is "psychological reassurance of legitimacy."[61] A happy, privileged man, Weber writes, "is not content with the fact of his happiness, but desires something more, namely the right to this happiness, the consciousness that he has earned his good fortune, in contrast to the unfortunate one who must equally have earned his misfortune."[62]

From this perspective, biblically oriented Protestantism, as an ascetic religion, becomes more than a means of attaining worldly success. Its adaptive possibilities allow it to become the means of justifying worldly success. Those who, by industry and frugality inspired by their religion, attain riches, are able to justify them by continuing to adhere to a religious ethic which emphasizes industry and frugality as the means not just to eternal salvation but to worldly salvation as well. Rather than emphasizing otherworldliness and rejection of worldly goods, the original sectarian spirit here changes so as to not only accept worldly riches but to justify them.

The bridging of the gap between rich and poor under such religion has been difficult to achieve. This was because the new affluence of wealthier members led away from the theological traditionalism of poorer members. One of the earliest and most noteworthy bridgings of this gap in the twentieth century has been within the Southern Baptist Convention (SBC). Roger Finke and Rodney Stark, in their broader argument on how strict religion leads to church growth, cite the SBC as an example of how to avoid liberalization, which had previously accompanied increasing affluence in other religions nearly invariably and which alienated poorer adherents.[63] The point for my discussion is not what leads to church growth so much as that traditional religion this century has found a formula to survive—and even thrive—in the face of tension caused by affluence through renewing its emphasis on the laity and their concerns for tradition. Growing emphasis on local control has led to continued reliance on religious tradition.[64]

Many "Bible-based" Protestants, including Southern Baptists and other similar "evangelicals," have achieved dramatic gains in social and economic status during the past half-century.[65] Those who have been able to accommodate both theological traditionalism and newly affluent members may affect American politics profoundly. This is because increasing affluence has led them to increase their political activity, to acquire more of an interest in both socially and fiscally conservative Republican politics, and to strengthen their ties to the Republican Party when the party advocates governmental aids for church institutions built by newly affluent adherents.[66]

The key to understanding how theologically traditional Protestantism affirms affluence and continues to hold poorer adherents is in understanding its maintenance of a traditional theology. When more affluent churches previously divided along economic lines, a split between the theological traditionalism of poorer adherents and the theological liberalism of institutions supported by affluent adherents was often behind the schism. The genius of the modern alliance between traditional religion and broader conservative politics has been the maintenance of a theological traditionalism that affirms affluence while continuing to attract poorer traditionalists. There are limits to this accommodation between the interests of rich and poor, but they have not yet been reached in the largest churches of theologically traditional Protestantism, much less among Baptist sects of the upper South.

Politics of Affluence among Baptist Sects of the Upper South

Many of the Baptists I study have neither need of nor opportunity for a religiously based politics of affluence. They are concentrated in parts of the rural South that trail both the nation and nearby metropolitan centers in most social and economic indicators. Furthermore, while few Protestant churches prior to this century managed to join both poor and affluent under the same traditional theology, these Baptists have a particularly pointed nineteenth-century history of rejecting any such efforts.

They are not, however, completely barren for analysis of affluence and traditional religion. While the influence of wealth is still only in embryonic form among them, it has affected them in the past, particularly in their response to denominational agencies representing affluent interests.

The rise of and splits within southern evangelicalism have had themes of affluence throughout, themes which usually repelled these Baptists. Southern evangelical Protestantism had been like the churches of this study in attracting those shut out by established orders in which ecclesiastical, economic, and political power overlapped. It succeeded so well that those aspiring to greater economic and social status in the movement also gained political power. The movement helped create a new economic class, which built its own religious establishments such as schools and ecclesiastical governments.

Less fortunate dissidents, resentful of the airs of these new establishments, presented themselves as "common folk exploited by people intent on improving their social position" through religion.[67] The conflict between them and the new establishment of the religion which had originally attracted them was one between "parochial and cosmopolitan, community and society, locality and nation."[68] The dissidents sought to recapture the local authority and autonomy that had been part of the original appeal of southern evangelical Protestantism. When that failed, they split off into sectarian groups, including some of those I study.[69] In some cases, churches refused even to affiliate with an association, "preferring a lonely but proud existence apart from the controversy and discontent of the world."[70] This spirit remains among the Baptists examined in this work.

In recent years, the effects of increasing affluence among these groups, though not as visible as it is among churches such as the SBC, has been evident among a few of them in four ways. These include the following: 1) acquisition of churchly accouterments, raising concern among some about abandonment of simpler ways; 2) dropping of the most traditional dress and behavior codes, which accompanies the desire of adherents for two-income families and the affluence they bring; 3) the fostering of modest church institutions; and 4) more general effects of the growth of a more cosmopolitan and affluent membership.

The most symbolic battles involving modern affluence in these groups are over their worship style, or how far to go in modernizing services, such as whether to break the taboo against musical instruments (typically by purchasing a piano) or to drop the most traditional ordinance of foot washing. Typically those churches away from these groups' traditional geographic areas will first purchase a piano for their services. While a piano is a first concession to affluence and, indeed, is impossible to obtain without some money, those congregations that buy them are careful not to encourage, in the words of one preacher, "a jam session" in church. Nearly all these churches shun musical innovations beyond the introduction of a piano or an organ. One rural northwest Indiana congregation, which used to be of this tradition, left in part over a desire to have more "spirit-filled" services, including music with amplified instruments.[71]

While the introduction of a piano or an organ for service music may seem a trivial innovation to an outsider, it can still cause resentment. One association nearly split over the introduction of pianos into some of its churches. This near-schism, a preacher told me, was accompanied by concerns that the church was also leaving behind other elements of simplicity. Even the adoption of a new hymnal can cause concern among such congregations, both for their higher cost and for any elements, such as suggested prayers and responses, which might "reek of officialdom" and therefore be considered "man-made" and hence "could not yield a Spirit-led liturgy."[72]

Traditional sex codes have served an economic purpose in some of the poor, core areas for these sects, e.g., those in eastern Kentucky. Such codes do not have to be enforced all the way down to dress codes, as they sometimes are, to ensure their economic purpose, but by ensuring that men are disciplined household providers and women have an honored and significant role within the home, they ease competition for the few available places at work outside the home. Under these codes, no job outside the home can be considered (or denigrated) as "women's work," and men are to take any job they can find.

As the need for this economic purpose has changed, these codes have changed somewhat. Away from the poorest core regions, there are more jobs available for both men and women, and women want their share. These additional jobs help adherents achieve affluence unknown in their poorer, traditional homes. The sex codes that have an economic rationale in the poorest regions make less sense in areas where women are more likely to be in the workforce. Women in a metropolitan workforce are less likely to conform to archaic codes of dress and behavior that are better suited for poor areas of agriculture and mining, which offer few places for women outside the home. As a result, though the churches remain male-dominated, women's roles and dress codes become less closely prescribed.

This is particularly evident in the case of Central Baptists and Eastern District Primitive Baptists, both of which have seen considerable migration from surrounding rural areas to the more prosperous Tri-Cities metropolitan area of East Tennessee. Central Baptists attribute their relaxed dress and their sex codes to an emphasis on the "new" codes of the New Testament rather than the "old" codes of the Old Testament. Some others have even offered innovative ways to ensure the "old" Deuteronomic dress codes sanction some modern behavior, noting, for example, that if slacks are designed for the feminine form, then they are women's apparel, and not men's. In each case local authorities have shaped the interpretation of sacred texts to meet changing local needs.

Many of these churches now permit some role for women in church governance, such as being a church clerk or treasurer. Women remain far from equal in these churches. But the more important point is that the traditional sex codes that serve economic purposes are modified when economic needs change, or when members desire the affluence that a woman's outside income can bring into the home.

An additional modification of these Baptists' attitudes rising with their affluence is evident in their limited support of missions and charities operated by the church. The most notable of these is the Central Baptist orphanage. A desire to establish the orphanage was the chief stimulus to creating the Central Baptist Association. As they adopted the comparatively cosmopolitan standards of the Tri-Cities area, Central Baptists wished for more established forms of charitable expression. Such forms are not available in the Eastern District Primitive Baptist Association, from which Central Baptists separated. Interpreting the creation of the orphanage strictly as an act to justify wealth is unfair, but among its effects has been to provide an outlet for the newfound affluence of Central Baptists. The orphanage indirectly encourages greater striving for riches by Central Baptists so they can support the orphanage. It provides a means to tie adherents more closely to church establishment through its support, and it can even tie Central Baptists to a particular political party or program to the extent that such a party or program will support such church-related establishments.

Others among these Baptists have more modest church establishments, such as summer youth camps. These provide a modest outlet for expressing affluence by association members, just like the Central Baptist orphanage does for members of that association. More typically, many of these Baptists now offer informal support for missions. Their support may be restricted by a requirement that a mission have indigenous leadership, or it may be limited to missionaries they know personally, but it still exists.

Many others support neither missions nor other church-related activities, but I would not suggest this denotes they have no interest in organizing, much less supporting, charitable ventures. During the 1950s, for example, several Old Regular Baptist associations sponsored an orphanage. It failed after the associations backing it became involved in a doctrinal fight over issues not related to the orphanage. The individualist ethos of Old Regular Baptist bodies may prevent such ventures within the tradition from being long-lived. A scholar of the tradition writes, "It seems fair to say that the Old Regular associations proved incapable—at least in this instance—of making such a joint venture work."[73] Perhaps one of the reasons for the success of the Central Baptist home is that only one association operates it, while there are several associations among Old Regular Baptists, which often have only tenuous relations to one another. The tenuous nature of relationships among the associations that make up these Baptists, even those of the same tradition, are a hindrance to practicing a religiously based institutional politics of affluence.

Some of these local Baptist preachers see members' increasing affluence and argue that a greater spirit of giving and of church establishment among them would actually continue, rather than contradict, the spirit of earlier days. One ambitious preacher in a prosperous exurban area near Nashville told me:

> We haven't preached tithing, and it kind of frustrates me somewhat that we haven't. It's something that I've prayed about and I think we need to do it. Because we haven't done it we don't have the capabilities financially to do much mission work in our community or anywhere else.... To be fair to the pastors before me, and the preachers and the people before me, most of our churches came out of rural areas. They may have been giving almost 10 percent. They may have been kicking in a couple of bucks every week, and they may have made, at most, a few thousand dollars per year on the farm. But what's happening today is we've still got a couple of bucks being passed in and we're not able to grow financially.... It's work, but I think there's blessings in bringing the goods to the storehouse.

Another preacher, the high school teacher of rural West Tennessee who was introduced above, is most conscious about linking his social and economic position, which is above that of his parents, with broader movements of religion and politics. He sees his upward mobility as giving him a duty to be "more involved than most of our people are" in broader politics. He feels compelled to lead his people in a broader cultural conservatism because of his religious and secular position. He is more affluent than a majority of his congregation and of southerners generally. While he is very young—twenty-five at the time of my first interview with him—to be moderator (or leader) of the association, with justification he attributes his rise in the association to his "leadership skills and abilities," particularly in comparison with many of his fellow preachers. He has a political sophistication lacking in many of his church's members. Because he feels a duty to be "very involved" in supporting his "very conservative" beliefs, he promotes the establishments of theologically conservative preachers such as Robertson or Falwell, though he is circumspect about supporting their political ambitions.

Those who would tie their church's ambitions to a broader movement of religious and political conservatism are a minority among these sects, but their numbers could grow. This is particularly true among those who have moved to more affluent southern metropolitan areas, as the Central Baptists have. The migration among these groups to northern industrial areas has slowed, and those leaving the core rural areas of these Baptists are now more likely to move to southern metropolitan centers such as Atlanta, Nashville, or the many small- to medium-sized metropolitan centers in the Carolinas and throughout the upper South. There, they often encounter a southern political culture that emphasizes "belie[f] in the primacy of individual, not governmental, responsibility for . . . well-being," and where those aspiring to social mobility adopt such attitudes.[74] Where an individualist emphasis combines with the maintenance of sectarian traditionalism, a religious politics of affluence can work to ensure continuation and growth of traditional religion, including its establishments.

Much "Bible-based" Protestantism in the twentieth century has succeeded in joining rich and poor by emphasizing traditional theology among all, rather than seeing its more affluent adherents foster ecclesiastical institutions that adopt theological innovations that alienate poorer members. This emphasis on theological traditionalism by both rich and poor can gloss over economic differences, though it cannot do so forever. As noted by one scathing liberal Protestant critique of those who claim that "conservative" churches, or those with "traditional" theologies, are the "winners" in the nation's religious economy, those churches most prospering are those who say, "join us, buy us, read us, identify with us, we who have access to the [Republican] White House . . . who have all the Miss Americas and the whole National Football League, who have BMWs and a nice return on our ('sacrificial') tithe investment, and who have peace of mind and health and wealth. That hardly sounds like stigmatization or the effectual preaching of hellfire."[75]

Traditional Protestants in the increasingly affluent metropolitan areas of the South may not notice the irony. But the Baptists of this work cannot escape it. They are most strongly tied to rural areas with some of the deepest pockets of poverty in the nation and have only scattered acquaintance with the increasing affluence of the metropolitan South. Conceivably, of course, affluence could reach the industrialized hinterlands of many of these sects, if not their most impoverished areas. Yet until there are signs of its doing so, or until these churches are no longer predominantly rural but metropolitan—and neither prospect looks likely in the near future—these churches will have to continue to negotiate the tension Richard Niebuhr identifies between, on the one hand, sectarianism's continual emphasis on the ethics of Jesus and its appeal to the poor and, on the other, the more affluent strains of traditional Protestantism, which are beginning to touch their most successful members.

SIMILARITIES AND DIFFERENCES IN THEMES OF RELIGION AND POLITICS

The themes of cultural traditionalism, economic populism, and increasing affluence are evident both among the sects of this study and in similar, broader populations. These themes do not operate identically among all such groups at all times. The qualitative evidence from the sects I study suggests some issues worth examining further to understand how these themes vary.

Cultural traditionalism is a driving force in the political, religious, and social attitudes of these Baptists and other similar groups, but there are limits to its practice. The same elements of this religion that inhibit political activity in general also inhibit the militant practice of traditional politics among these groups. They will likely never favor abortion rights, but neither will they join in the most militant protests against those rights. These Baptists have many reasons to fear scorn from a more sophisticated world and see no reason to bring reproach upon themselves through militant protests. Some cite their need to foster community among all their congregants as a reason to avoid culturally divisive politics.

Economic needs also drive their attitudes. Economic concerns over liberal expenditures for church establishments have long animated these groups. Economic concerns have continually shaped their theology, as their opposition to church establishments and the wealthier interests they represented first led some to an antimission theology viewing such works as religious folly, and later led more of them to accept worldly action when it was of more clear benefit to themselves.

The separation of cultural traditionalism from economic populism is, arguably, a relatively recent trend in American politics. The experience and attitudes of these Baptists show that a concerted campaign which joins cultural traditionalism and economic populism, however unlikely that may appear in American politics at present, would find a receptive audience among many traditional Protestants. Such politics may not be viable for a candidate seeking a majority of all voters, but they can play well among these populations. To the extent that a party of cultural tradition and economic conservatism (or classic economic liberalism) abandons the former, the more likely it may be to lose those among these Protestants who are repelled by the latter. This does not, of course, suggest the viability of cultural or economic conservatism or liberalism in a national campaign among both believers and nonbelievers. Nor does it address all the religious reasons this population may not choose to become involved in politics. It does show how treacherous political navigation can be in appealing to these populations. It also suggests that the absence of a prominent vehicle for the politics of cultural traditionalism and economic populism constitutes another obstacle for traditional Protestants who have many other obstacles to overcome with regard to political participation.

Many argue that some adherents of "Bible-based" Protestantism have acquired enough affluence to be attracted now by economically conservative politics. The implication is that economic conservatism could have even more appeal for this population than cultural traditionalism. This may increasingly be true for some of these adherents some of the time, but the nature of the religion suggests that it cannot be true for all of them all of the time. As long as this religion has sectarian characteristics, as long as it finds its origins in the religious protests of the poor, and as long as these are what give this religion its appeal, then it will find difficulty leaving behind forever the economic interests of the poor. For a time, it can paper over the differences between rich and poor by an appeal to cultural traditionalism. It can forestall a day of reckoning by pushing those elements of cultural traditionalism, such as patriarchal family authority, that may be most useful to those in marginal areas. But there is a limit to how well such ploys can work to join those of opposed interests in a religion that has roots in decentralized authority and the seizure of such authority when local interests dictate.

Throughout the discussion of this chapter's themes, we have seen how common themes are adapted to the particular time and place in which these adherents find themselves. As I suggested in the introduction to this work, localized adaptations are particularly evident in the population I study. In the next chapter I switch from focusing on national themes among national and local populations to a closer analysis of local themes among these local populations. This will include an analysis of the particular characteristics of the Baptists I study. Analyzing their particular characteristics will show further reasons for the adaptations, discussed in this chapter, they have made to national issues. It will also show how such characteristics lead to a more localized theology and politics than those considered in this chapter.

CHAPTER 2

Histories and Their Implications: Some Characteristics of Sectarian Baptists

My first experience with these groups came from my work on *Churches and Church Membership in the United States 1990 (CCMUS),* the only county-level church membership census in the United States.[1] I counted more than a dozen sects for that volume, and became increasingly interested in studying further the politics and communities of their adherents, particularly the political variation which became more evident to me as I became more familiar with them.

I focus here on those that I documented most completely and that shared the most common historical, religious, and social elements. It is difficult to fathom how those associations from similar sects that would not participate fully in the church membership study would differ from those that did participate. This is one reason I do not consider in this exercise many Primitive Baptists, who are quite like the groups I study and whose history is intertwined with them.

Correspondence I had with the clerk of a Primitive Baptist association illustrates this problem. While methodologically this instance is rather trivial, it helps show the variety of attitudes present in the same small association. In response to my query about the number of members in his association, the clerk questioned the purpose of a church membership study. David, he noted, invoked the wrath of God by taking a census of the Israelites.[2] Counting God's modern-day people would risk new tribulation. Besides, he added, a count was not needed since the number of true Christians is already in "the Lamb's Book of Life."

I eventually did get statistics for this clerk's association from another source, but the annual minutes bearing such statistics had surprising information. The moderator of this association, rather than being an otherworldly recluse, was the then-governor of Alabama, Guy Hunt, a Republican forced from office for using state planes for church business, allegations he was eventually cleared of. Hunt practices an aggressive politics of cultural conservatism. As governor, he "refused to haul down the Confederate Stars and Bars from the Capitol in Montgomery.... Like South Carolina's Strom Thurmond, he seems to have an uncomplicated but strong mind: he believes in a few fundamentals—the Christian religion and traditional values, patriotism and respect for the flag, free markets and economic growth—and charges straight ahead to further them."[3]

But what is the overall attitude toward the world among members of his association? Is it that of its longtime clerk, who would have nothing to do with a seemingly innocuous statistical research project? Is it that of its politically ambitious moderator? Or is it of somebody or something else entirely, which seemed a distinct possibility to me, since I had seen how association officers often have little effect on their members' secular attitudes? I thought it best for this project to concentrate on those denominations whose component associations cooperated with *CCMUS,* and not on those who did not want to aid *CCMUS.* This was because I presumed the latter would be even more reluctant to cooperate with and difficult to fathom on the more sensitive topics I discuss here.

I selected for this work groups that are most likely to appear in religious or regional reference works, hoping those wishing to verify or dispute my conclusions would not be completely at the mercy of my documentation. There were some similar sects I counted for *CCMUS 1990* that were complete but to which no other published academic reference could be found. Among these is the Interstate and Foreign Landmark Missionary Baptist Association, a denomination of approximately 18,000 adherents concentrated on the Gulf Coast from Pensacola to New Orleans, which, according to a minister of the association whom I did interview, descends from United Baptists who moved south from Kentucky and Tennessee. The groups I present in this work share many common elements of belief, doctrine, practice, and geography. They have some geographical differences, but these are not so great as to prevent meaningful analysis of them as a whole.

These groups do not exist as denominations per se. Rather, I define them by grouping of associations. Their congregations meet annually in association with neighboring churches of like faith and order. These associations are the only ecclesiastical authority they will recognize outside the local congregation. I use three guidelines to determine which associations to group together under the same label: an association's title, its correspondents, and whatever previous documentation may exist on it.[4]

The title of an association typically suffices for classifying it. For example, the New Salem Association of Old Regular Baptist and its churches are clearly Old Regular Baptist. Those whose titles do not clearly indicate classification usually can be classified by their correspondents. An association's correspondents are those associations (or, in some cases, unattached individual churches) that send letters of correspondence or delegates to its annual association meeting. We may view a group of mutually corresponding associations as an association of associations. Preachers of corresponding associations, like those of differing churches in the same association, can "share the stand," or jointly conduct services. Members of churches in corresponding associations, like members of differing churches in the same association, can partake of communion in any church of either association. Associational correspondence marks boundaries for these churches and their members similar to those made by denominational divisions elsewhere in American Protestantism. In a few instances, historical references help place scattered associations or churches.

This work analyzes six groupings identified by the above techniques: Central Baptists, Duck River and Kindred Baptists, "Old" Missionary Baptists, Old Regular Baptists, Eastern District Primitive Baptists, and United Baptists. After grouping and selecting the groups for this study, I conducted forty open-ended interviews among preachers of these sects. The number of interviews by group corresponds roughly with the size of the group, with the fewest interviews conducted with Central Baptists, the smallest of the groups, and the most with United Baptists, the largest. I interviewed thirty of the forty preachers in person, and the remainder by phone. Those interviewed by phone were generally those whom an informant recommended I contact for another viewpoint and whom I could not arrange to see during field visits. Interviews covered topics such as informants' views on the distinctiveness of their church, their own religious history, their other religious views, their social and political views, and their social and economic life outside church.

Since many of my interviews were with association moderators, I should briefly discuss their religious roles. Each association I study annually elects a moderator, who may be thought of as its leading, senior, or foremost minister. Moderators typically are older, respected preachers within the association who are re-elected for years. Some associations have elected younger moderators, and one association makes a practice of electing a new moderator every year, alternating between each geographic half of the association. Moderators are expected to keep peace within the association and are usually effective at the task, although their powers to enforce the peace are limited.

Most preachers cooperated as much as I could have expected, but some were reluctant to participate. To gain their cooperation, I assured them they would not be quoted by name, a protection that in fairness I extend to all. In addition to the preacher interviews, I conducted an additional twenty-five interviews with others, such as mainline preachers, labor union officials, and local community leaders, in my fieldwork for part of chapter 3 and all of chapter 4.

Furthermore, I visited twenty different congregations where I observed services and conducted additional short interviews with clergy and laity. Although United Baptists and Old Regular Baptists are the two largest groups I study, for personal reasons I concentrated my field visits away from their congregations. Nearly everybody in my mother's family is Baptist (notable exceptions include my mother, once a United Baptist but now a convert to Catholicism, and her two children), and most of the Baptists are Old Regular Baptists or United Baptists. My maternal grandfather is a longtime United Baptist church clerk, and of his three oldest sons one is a United Baptist association clerk, one is a "libertized" (i.e., probationary) Old Regular Baptist preacher, and one regularly serves as a delegate from his church to his Old Regular Baptist association meeting, as well as a delegate from his association to the annual meetings of corresponding associations. In other words, I thought it best to spend precious field resources—my wife and I alone paid for the fieldwork, as well as for every other aspect of this project except the original enumeration—away from churches I have known since birth. Nevertheless, my explicit fieldwork for this project included both interviews and field visits among each cluster of associations I could identify that maintain mutual correspondence.

Below I review in detail each of these groupings, including the history of those comprising the groupings, what can be gleaned regarding members' current social and economic characteristics, and some of what their preachers told me in interviews, with attention to local adaptations, in both religion and politics, on local issues confronting them. This review will point to common characteristics and variations that cut across ecclesiastical boundaries. This set of common characteristics in turn demonstrates the boundaries of religion and politics among these groups, how social and political concerns can sometimes affect their religion and how their religion can sometimes affect their social and political concerns, and some of the ways in which they reflect similar, broader groups.

Central Baptists

This grouping consists solely of the Central Baptist Association.[5] *CCMUS 1990* counted 35 Central Baptist churches and 4,031 adherents in 15 counties (see map 1).[6] Of all Central Baptist adherents, 3,277, or 76 percent, are in nine contiguous counties of Kentucky, Tennessee, and Virginia. These nine counties are centered near Kingsport, Tennessee, and the church's headquarters in Scott County, Virginia. A majority (56 percent) of Central Baptists are in four counties near the Tri-Cities area of East Tennessee. There are also Central Baptists in two northwestern counties of South Carolina and in the Indianapolis and Louisville areas.

The Central Baptist Association started in 1956 among churches formerly in the Eastern District Primitive Baptist Association. It has grown in patterns similar to those of the Eastern District Association, with a consolidation toward the Tri-Cities area of East Tennessee.

Central Baptists had two motives in forming. First, they sought a church with a "central" interpretation of the King James Bible, "varying neither to the right nor to the left." Some Central Baptists attribute their name to strictures from the Book of Joshua. After the death of Moses, God commanded Joshua to "be thou strong and very courageous, that thou mayest observe to do according to all the law, which Moses my servant commanded thee: turn not from it to the right or to the left, that thou mayest prosper whithersoever thou goest."[7] When Joshua himself had "waxed old and was stricken in age," he "called for all Israel," and passed on to them the command to "be ye therefore very courageous to keep and to do all that is written in the book of the law of Moses, that ye turn not aside therefrom to the right or to the left."[8]

The association's moderator told me that his churches are "fundamental,"

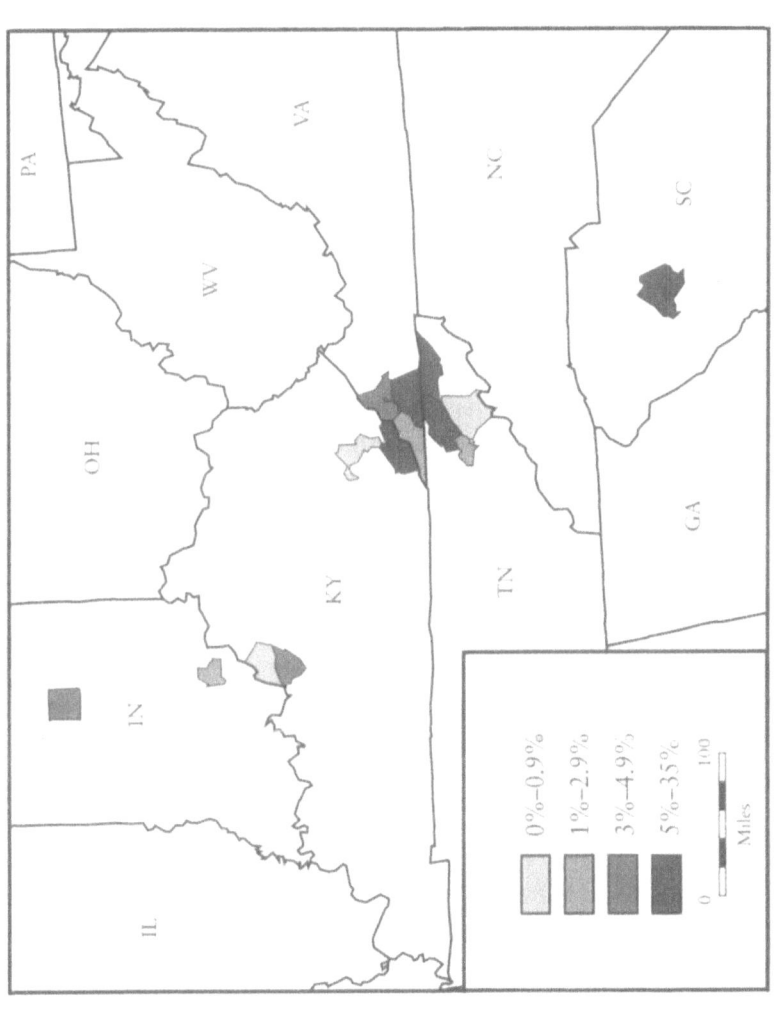

Map 1. Central Baptist Distribution by County, 1990.

that they "take the Bible literally," and that they let their "own study show them how to understand it." Central Baptists, he says, are "not really for a lot of the liberal viewpoints in today's society." Asked about the "liberal viewpoints" with which his members disagree, this culturally conservative supporter of labor unions (including his own) cites scripture prohibiting female ministers and ministers with more than one living spouse (i.e., divorced). All the groups I study prohibit divorce and remarriage among their ministers. Most cite I Timothy 3:2, which reads, "A bishop then must be blameless, the husband of one wife, vigilant, sober, of good behaviour, given to hospitality, apt to teach."

Central Baptists reject Primitive Baptist doctrine of individual predestination, but they believe "in election by grace according to the foreknowledge of God." This, the moderator says, means Central Baptists believe that the plan of salvation was foreordained, but individual salvation or damnation is not. He adds, "Nothing prevents the salvation of the greatest sinner on earth but his own voluntary rejection of Christ."

The second reason Central Baptists formed was to engage in works of charity and evangelization, which their Primitive Baptist forebears avoided. The association in 1956 started a home for homeless and destitute children. It continues to operate today and is the best-known Central Baptist ministry. The association also operates a summer youth camp.

Central Baptists are more accepting of ecclesiastical establishments than the other sects I study. They have a small headquarters and paid, full-time (nonministerial) staff. They provide mission support to indigenously led churches. Most of this support currently goes to a native Jamaican's church on his home island. They neither require nor prohibit higher religious training for their ministers.

They view themselves as more "progressive" than the Primitive Baptists they left. Since women cannot be preachers, they cannot be moderators and cannot run the association, but they have managed its financial affairs. Both the current treasurer and the chief fundraiser for the summer camp are women. Central Baptist rules of decorum prohibit women from speaking in church, but there are exceptions, their moderator says, for "case of conscience or . . . [of] circumstances that . . . may require it." The Eastern District Association has no such formal exceptions.

Central Baptists have a more permissive dress code than many of the sects I study. They attribute this to their emphasis on the "new" law of modest dress in I Timothy, rather than the "old" law of specific dress for the sexes in Deuteronomy. In the Old Testament Deuteronomy 22:6 commands that "the woman shall not wear that which pertaineth unto a man, neither shall a man put on a woman's garment: for all that do so are abomination unto the Lord thy God." In the New Testament I Timothy 2:9 simply commands women to "adorn themselves in modest apparel, with shamefacedness and sobriety; not with broided hair, or gold, or pearls, or costly array." This "new" law has the benefit of relaxing some traditional codes for those in the workplace, while also reinforcing emphases on frugality and the repression of excessive consumerism. This is a small but notable example of a locally oriented fundamentalist community adapting biblical commands to bridge the gap between their rapidly changing metropolitan environs and their own traditions.

Another indication of Central Baptist bridging of tradition and modern circumstances is the disregard of foot washing in some churches. Most of these sects have three "ordinances": baptism by immersion, foot washing, and annual communion. They take Jesus' example of washing His disciples' feet at the Last Supper and His command to the Twelve to do the same for each other[9] as a command to do the same before their annual communion. Among southern Protestants, foot washing is more prevalent among traditional, rural churches.[10] Among the churches I study that include foot washing, the practice, with sex segregation observed, serves as an emotional binding of the community.[11] A majority of Central Baptists still carry on the tradition, but as some congregations receive younger or more metropolitan members, they quietly drop the practice, which is identified more with rural churches.

The suspension of Central Baptists between rural customs and metropolitan life is clear in the demographics of their home communities. Few may confuse the Tri-Cities of Kingsport, Bristol, or Johnson City, Tennessee, with Knoxville, Memphis, or Nashville, much less New York, Chicago, or Los Angeles. Nonetheless, the four Tri-Cities area counties that are home to a majority of Central Baptists are distinct from the surrounding rural counties from which many migrated. This is clear in Census data on Scott County and the four Tri-Cities area counties where a majority of Central Baptists live (see table 1).[12]

The four Tri-Cities area counties grew in total population by nearly 50 percent between 1950 and 1980, although no growth has occurred in the 1980s. By contrast, Scott County, the denomination's headquarters and its original home, which is still home to more than one in eight Central Baptists

Table 1
Central Baptist Area Characteristics

	CENTRAL BAPTIST CORE COUNTIES (%)	SCOTT COUNTY VIRGINIA (%)	U.S. TOTALS (%)
Total Population (as % of 1990)			
1950	69	119	61
1960	77	111	72
1970	86	105	82
1980	100	108	91
1990	100	100	100
White	97	99	80
Under 18	23	22	26
Over 64	14	17	13
Males currently married[a]	65	66	57
Females currently married[a]	59	60	52
Did not graduate high school[b]	38	49	25
At least some college[b]	30	18	45
Civilian unemployed, 1990	6.6	9.4	6.3
Working mothers	64	51	68
Selected industry data			
Agriculture, forestry, fisheries	2	5	3
Mining	1	3	1
Manufacturing	34	32	18
Wholesale and retail trade	21	18	21
Other services	28	25	40
Selected occupational data			
Managerial or professional	19	12	26
Technical, sales, or support	27	21	32
Skilled craft, repair	15	16	11
Operator/assembler/inspector	15	18	7
Other labor	10	14	8
Voted Democratic for president[c]			
1980	41	47	42
1984	32	40	41
1988	34	42	46
1992	39	42	43
1996	39	41	50
Per capita income, 1989	$11,424	$9,100	$14,420

NOTES: [a] 15 years of age and older.
[b] 25 years of age and older.
[c] of votes for major candidates for president.

and eleven of the thirty-five Central Baptist churches, has lost nearly one-sixth of its population since 1950.

Those in the core counties have higher educational levels than those in Scott County. Unemployment in the core area is comparable to that of the nation, while that in Scott is higher. Working mothers are nearly as prevalent in the core as they are nationwide, but not so in Scott. Per capita income for the Tennessee counties is below the national level, but well above that for Scott. Median house value is also higher in the core counties, though below the national level.

Politically the Tennessee counties reflect modern southern conservatism more accurately than does Scott County. Both areas voted Republican in all five presidential elections between 1980 and 1996, but the core counties did so at higher rates.

As Central Baptists have migrated from rural southwestern Virginia to the Tri-Cities area, they have moved toward a more affluent, metropolitan, and Republican area. The relocation to the Tri-Cities area has placed a strain on some "old-time" Baptist traditions. Some in this small metropolitan area have discarded a few practices prevalent in surrounding rural areas, but in many ways they remain suspended between their rural, sectarian origins and more affluent, metropolitan influences. These influences are reshaping a church that in many ways remains profoundly traditional, but that has also allowed greater roles for women in running church affairs and that has drawn the church toward denominational works and establishments.

Duck River and Kindred Baptists

Duck River and Kindred Baptists, or the General Association of Baptist, comprise the Duck River Association, six kindred (or corresponding) associations, and one independent church.[13] These comprise 103 churches and 13,264 adherents in 25 counties of Alabama, Georgia, Kentucky, and Tennessee.

"Duck River and Kindred" is not a name commonly used by the group members themselves. Instead, they refer to themselves plainly as "Baptist," with only occasional references to the "General Association." In correspondence with the author, Allan Gleason, a geographer of religion who has also served as a United Church of Christ minister in the region, notes that some of these churches in Coffee County, Tennessee, have occasionally labeled themselves as "THE Baptist Church." The "Duck River and Kindred" label may have appeared first in U.S. Census Bureau counts of religious bodies in the early twentieth century. It has remained attached to the group in the few scholarly analyses of them ever since. The only ecclesiastical bodies Duck River Baptists recognize are, in declining order of importance, their own church, their individual associations, and the General Association.

Duck River Baptists have their origins in the Elk River Association, one of the first Baptist associations in Middle Tennessee, founded in the early 1800s.[14] Elk River Association was strongly Calvinistic, believing in predestination of individual salvation or damnation. Within it, there arose a less Calvinistic faction, more liberal on personal atonement and salvation. As this faction grew, its opponents became more Calvinistic. By 1825, the liberal faction organized the Duck River Association.[15]

In 1843, this splinter group itself split. Those straying even further from Calvinism and more toward free will doctrines left in a dispute over supporting missions, a publication society, and a denominational school, church works which make little sense to many who believe salvation or damnation is predestined.[16] Those left in the remnant opposing missions formed the nucleus of what are today Duck River and Kindred Baptists. This group reflects the theological journey of the other groups I study. They reject doctrines of individual predestination, but they will not support much evangelism.

Today, Duck River and Kindred Baptists are described as "liberally Calvinistic." A preacher explained "liberal Calvinism" to me by contrasting it with more orthodox Calvinism:

> Most of the Calvinistic, predestinarian Baptists don't invite sinners to repent. They just believe the elect will come to that knowledge and will make their public announcement and be baptized. Our people believe in calling sinners to repentance, but we don't believe that you can get saved anytime you get ready. The only time you can get saved is when God calls you.... We believe that through His foreknowledge God knew everybody that was going to be saved and everybody who's going to be lost. But we're not as strictly Calvinistic as others are in saying the elect will recognize it and that will be it.

Their call for sinners to repent remains local. They do not support foreign missions. A preacher endorsing indigenous leadership of churches told me,

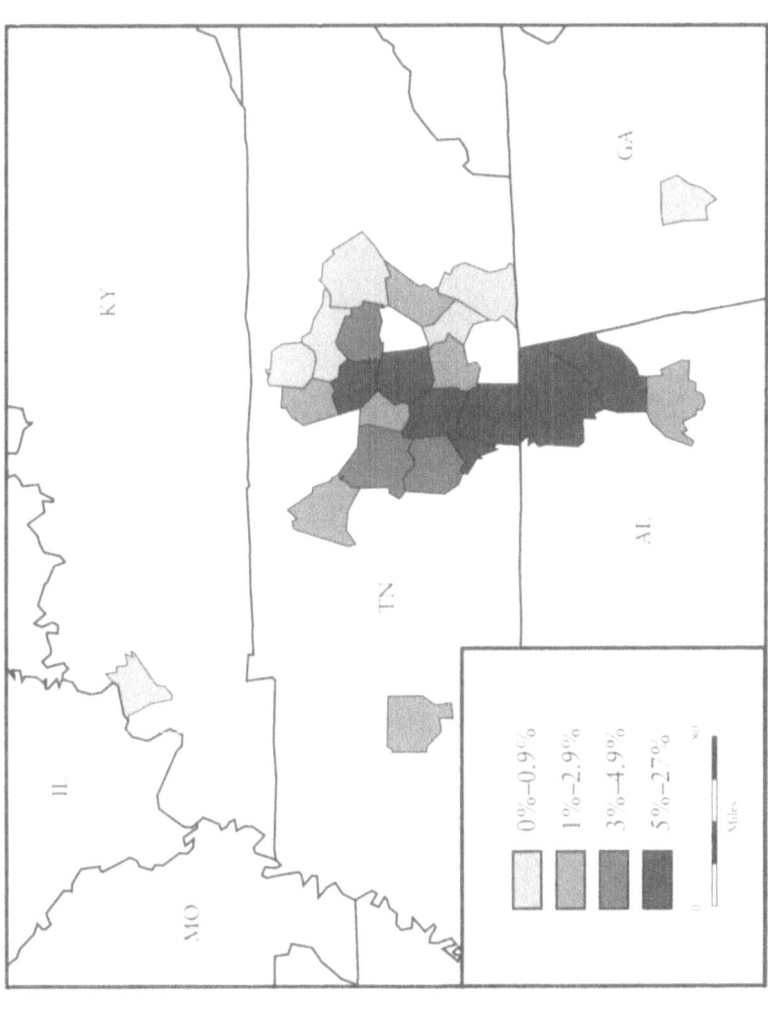

Map 2. Duck River and Kindred Baptist Distribution by County, 1990.

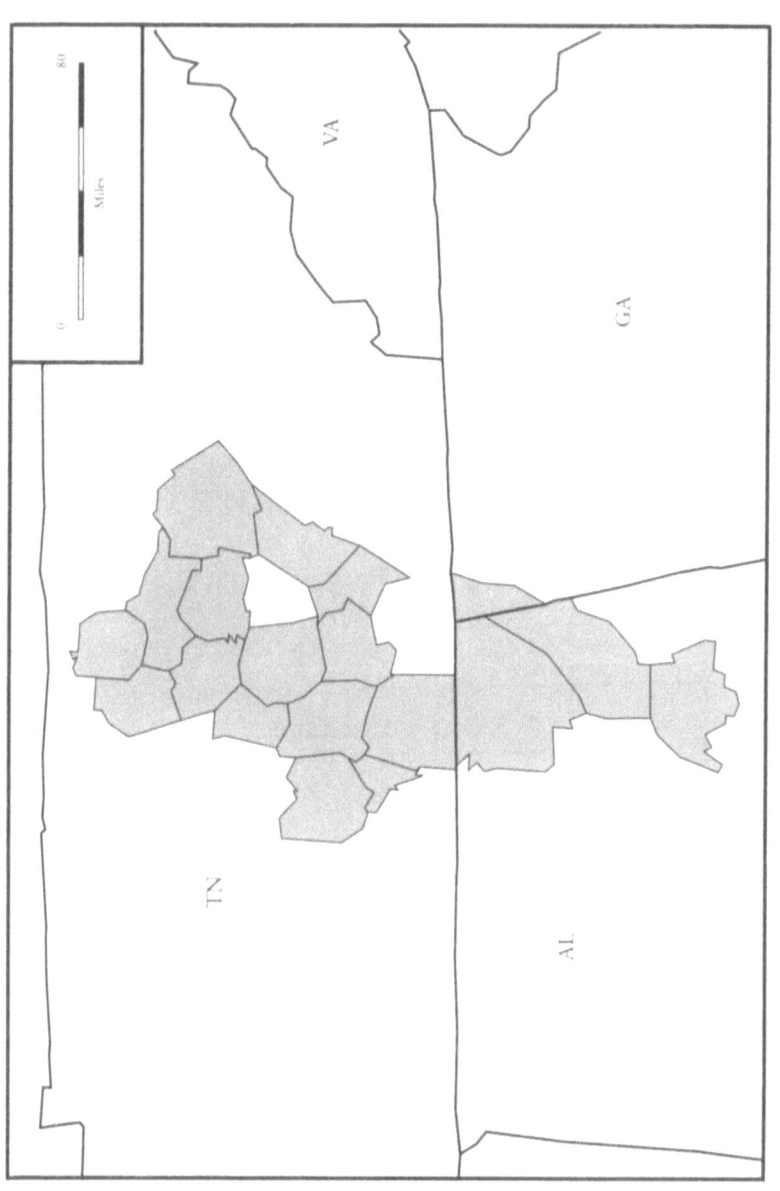

Map 3. Duck River and Kindred Baptist Core Counties.

"God can raise up a prophet in any land," and such a prophet raised up from within a foreign land would be more effective than a Duck River Baptist (or any other outside) missionary.

Duck River Baptists are among the more traditional groups among the Baptists I study. Most approve of musical instruments within church, but a few do not allow them, and none would tolerate anything beyond a piano or an organ for service music. They retain the three traditional ordinances of baptism by immersion, annual communion, and foot washing. Women cannot serve in any association office. Duck River Baptists maintain conservative dress standards, although they are not the most conservative among all these groups.

Duck River Baptists have been concentrated in the same area of the middle and upper South throughout their history (see map 2). They are most concentrated in Alabama and Tennessee, which are home to more than 98 percent of Duck River and Kindred Baptists.

Duck River Baptists are concentrated in rural areas. More than nine in ten are outside metropolitan areas. Even those in rural areas tend to be away from towns. In correspondence with the author, Allan Gleason reports his own observation that these churches "favor the agriculturally poorer areas. They are noticeably weak or absent in the cities," with few even in "cities" such as Tullahoma, Shelbyville, Manchester, or McMinnville. This conforms with my general impressions of most of the Baptists I study, which county-level statistics can neither confirm nor deny.

A group of eighteen contiguous rural counties of Middle Tennessee and northeastern Alabama, home to 90 percent of all Duck River Baptists, forms the core of their territory (see map 3). All these counties have populations less than 100,000; nine have populations less than 25,000. Within these counties, one gets an impression of stable, proportional growth by Duck River and Kindred Baptists, an impression that is supported somewhat by the few statistics available.[17]

The core counties provide an impression of stable, working people (see table 2). Nearly all Duck River and Kindred Baptists live in slowly growing, predominantly white rural counties of the mid-South where manufacturing has largely supplanted agriculture in the local economy. Living standards are below those of the nation, but are roughly comparable to those of Alabama and Tennessee. Working mothers and two-income families are the norm for area households. Politically, this area is more Democratic than the nation,

Table 2
Duck River and Kindred Baptist Core Area Characteristics

	Duck River and Kindred Baptist Core Counties (%)	U.S. Totals (%)
Total Population (as % of 1990)		
1950	78	61
1960	77	72
1970	81	82
1980	98	91
1990	100	100
White	94	80
Under 18	25	26
Over 64	15	13
Males currently married[a]	65	57
Females currently married[a]	59	52
Did not graduate high school[b]	41	25
At least some college[b]	27	45
Civilian unemployed, 1990	6.6	6.3
Working mothers	69	68
Selected industry data		
Agriculture, forestry, fisheries	4	3
Manufacturing	33	18
Wholesale and retail trade	19	21
Other services	24	40
Selected occupational data		
Managerial or professional	17	26
Technical, sales, or support	24	32
Skilled craft, repair	15	11
Operator/assembler/inspector	18	7
Other labor	12	8
Voted Democratic for president[c]		
1980	57	42
1984	48	41
1988	47	46
1992	52	43
1996	50	50
Per capita income, 1989	$10,355	$14,420

NOTES: [a] 15 years of age and older.
[b] 25 years of age and older.
[c] of votes for major candidates for president.

Alabama, and Tennessee. A small number of Duck River Baptists live in more affluent areas of the metropolitan South, particularly in the Atlanta, Chattanooga, and Nashville areas. There they live in fast-growing, increasingly affluent counties, where per capita income is above both national and state levels, and housing costs are below national levels.

"Old" Missionary Baptists

Several sources make scattered mention of "Missionary Baptists" as a separate denomination, but none give a systematic review.[18] The Missionary Baptists I study are a group of mutually corresponding associations based in south-central Kentucky and north-central Tennessee who refer to themselves as "old-fashioned" or "old-time" Missionary Baptists. The "old-fashioned" label refers to the many customs typically found in more traditional rural churches. Despite being "Missionary" Baptists, they share many of the antimission attitudes of the others I study.

Some trace Missionary Baptists to Paul Palmer, a North Carolina General Baptist preacher of the eighteenth century who emphasized "free grace, free will, and free salvation."[19] Palmer's themes contrast with the Calvinist notions of predestination that more typically mark these groups' histories. The "free will" emphasis and a concern for Baptist tradition led many Missionary Baptists, including those I study, to adopt the New Hampshire Confession of Faith. This document originated among those seeking to calm disputes between Calvinistic and Free Will Baptists.[20] This moderately Calvinist creed continues to be popular with those striving to maintain a modern Baptist orthodoxy. Its use by "Old" Missionary Baptists indicates a group struggling to bridge a world of rural tradition and decentralized churches, on one side, and more cosmopolitan areas and their growing church establishments, on the other.

This creed has also been a standard for many in the Southern Baptist Convention (SBC). Old Missionary Baptists, however, are careful to add that there are "some [SBC] innovations in evangelism that we don't endorse." These innovations, they say, lead to conversions "from the head instead of the heart." Many Old Missionary Baptist churches at one time were in the SBC. They left because they felt themselves to be "far more traditional, or old-fashioned," than the SBC, or because they "wanted to be free of the control of the state convention," which they felt "was trying to usurp authority over the local churches." A small number of Old Missionary Baptist churches were once United Baptist.

Old Missionary Baptists do not view themselves as being as conservative as the more traditional sects, such as United Baptists, but they do view themselves as far more traditional and concerned with local authority than the SBC. Their ambivalent position between the more traditional sectarians and the more "liberal" SBC is evident in their attitudes toward missions, clergy, and conversions. They are not strictly antimission, but they do not give foreign missionaries any formal support. They do not prohibit a paid or formally trained clergy, but those paid or trained constitute a small portion of their clergy. They disdain massive conversion drives, but, unlike the more traditional sects, claim that conversions can happen when the new member is at "a very young age" (e.g., less than ten).

The Old Missionary Baptists in this study number 17,697 adherents in 84 counties in 23 counties of Colorado, Kentucky, Michigan, Ohio, Tennessee, and West Virginia.[21] More than 94 percent are in 14 contiguous counties of south-central Kentucky and north-central Tennessee (see map 4).[22] One in four (25 percent) are in Macon County, Tennessee, while more than one in seven (15 percent) are in Davidson County (Nashville), Tennessee, and more than one in six (18 percent) are in Sumner County, Tennessee, a northeastern suburban county of the Nashville area.

Old Missionary Baptists are a mostly rural sect. About three in five live in nonmetropolitan counties. Within the 14 contiguous counties that are home to nearly all the Old Missionary Baptists I study, there is a core of 9 contiguous counties that are home to a majority of adherents (see map 5). Eight of these counties have populations less than 16,000, and none has a population above 35,000.

Old Missionary Baptists of the core counties live in static, homogeneous, conservative rural communities of the upper South that rely heavily on manufacturing employment and have more "downscale" demographics than are evident nationwide (see table 3). Residents of the core counties are less educated and have lower incomes than the rest of the nation, although unemployment here in 1990 was comparable to national levels. Manufacturing is now the largest employer in the area, but a considerable number still work primarily in agriculture. Households in the core area are more likely to comprise traditional families than households nationwide. Politically, the core reflects the South very well.

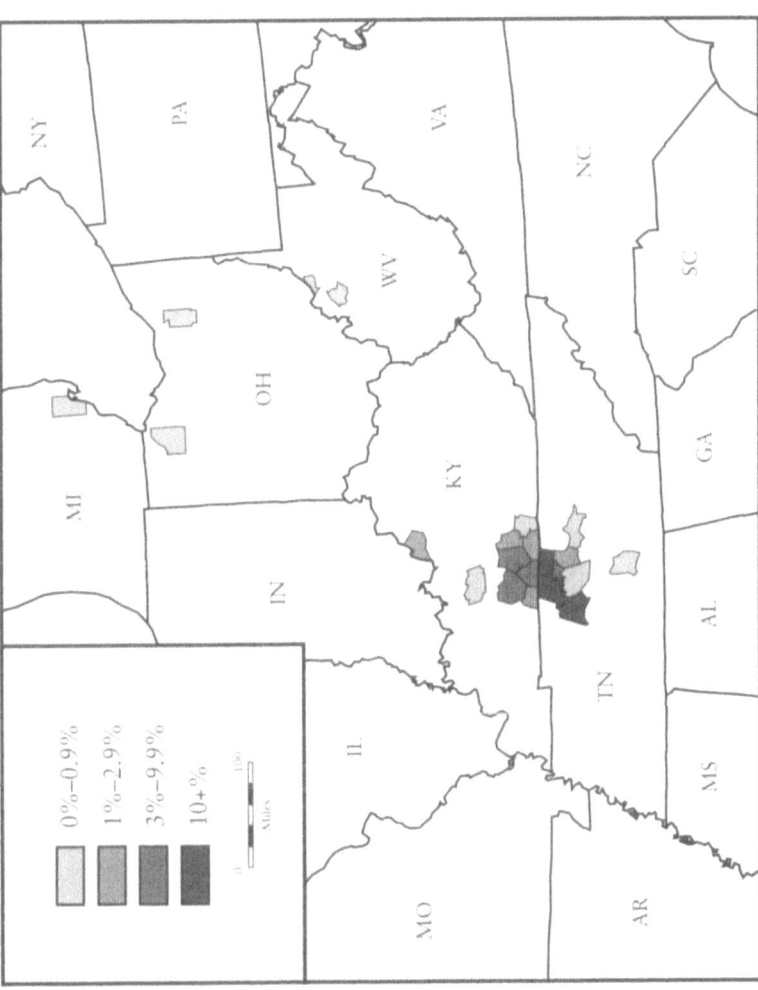

Map 4. "Old" Missionary Baptist Distribution by County, 1990.

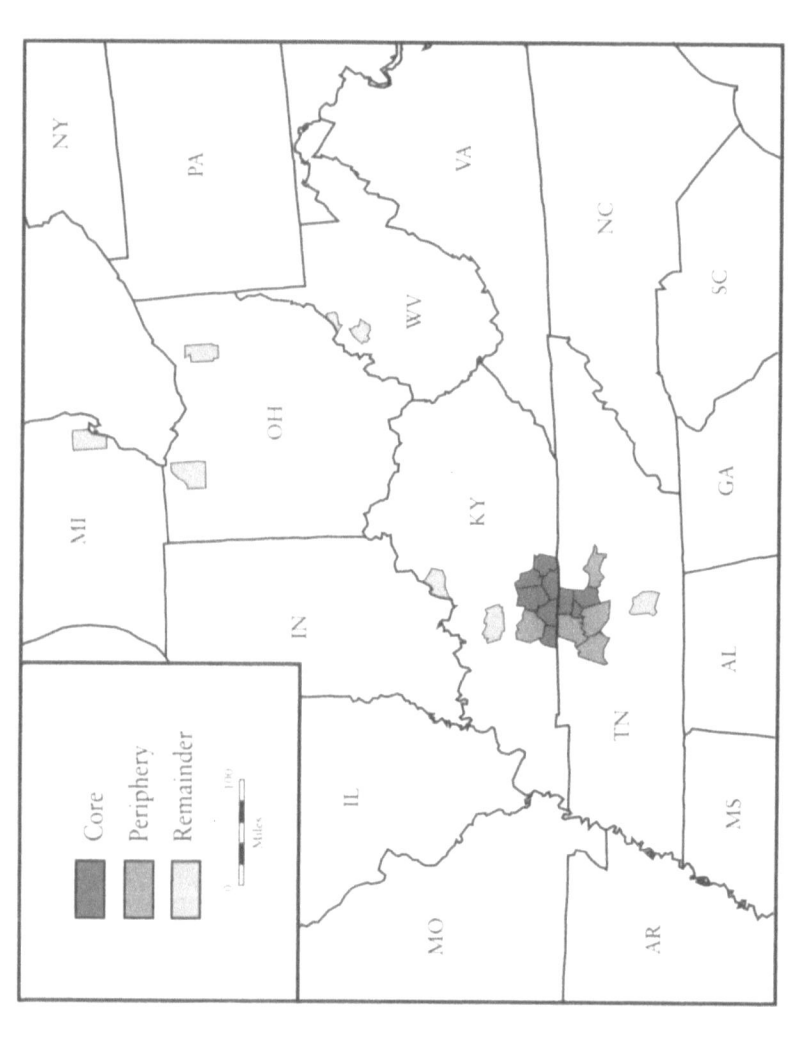

Map 5. "Old" Missionary Baptist Analysis Areas, 1990.

Table 3
"Old" Missionary Baptist Area Characteristics

	CORE AREA (%)	URBANIZING FRINGE (%)	U.S. TOTALS (%)
Total Population (as % of 1990)			
1950	95	56	61
1960	86	66	72
1970	87	78	82
1980	101	91	91
1990	100	100	100
White	95	82	80
Under 18	25	24	26
Over 64	16	11	13
Males currently married[a]	67	57	57
Females currently married[a]	60	50	52
Did not graduate high school[b]	49	26	25
At least some college[b]	18	45	45
Civilian unemployed, 1990	6.7	5.2	6.3
Working mothers	70	73	68
Selected industry data			
Agriculture, forestry, fisheries	9	5	3
Manufacturing	35	16	18
Wholesale and retail trade	18	23	21
Other services	23	41	40
Selected occupational data			
Managerial or professional	13	27	26
Technical, sales, or support	21	34	32
Skilled craft, repair	14	10	11
Operator/assembler/inspector	21	7	7
Other labor	12	8	8
Voted Democratic for president[c]			
1980	44	57	42
1984	37	45	41
1988	39	44	46
1992	47	50	43
1996	44	52	50
Per capita income, 1989	$8,251	$14,266	$14,420

NOTES: [a] 15 years of age and older.
[b] 25 years of age and older.
[c] of votes for major candidates for president.

In the past five presidential elections, it has voted Democratic only once, in 1992 (Al Gore's family home is near the core). Among Democratic presidential candidates, it prefers southerners over northerners.

For Old Missionary Baptists in the urbanizing fringe of this core, the demographic reality is quite different. These counties have growing, dynamic, heterogeneous, liberal, affluent, urbanizing communities. They are either in the Nashville metropolitan area or home to a university. This area is growing rapidly, nearly doubling in population in the past four decades. It is more "upscale" than the core, with higher educational levels and lower unemployment. It is more transient than the core. One in four (24 percent) of its residents lived elsewhere five years ago, compared with less than one in seven (13 percent) in the core. Politically, the fringe counties are more Democratic than both the South and the nation.

Nearly all Old Missionary Baptists are split between these two neighboring but differing areas. The small number who live elsewhere are in counties very much like one of these two extremes, albeit sometimes outside the South. Like the other Baptists I study, Old Missionary Baptists confront either poorer, static rural communities, or they face rapidly changing, more affluent, and cosmopolitan centers.

Old Regular Baptists

Nearly all Old Regular Baptists descend from the New Salem Association of Old Regular Baptist.[23] New Salem began by "arming off," or separating amicably, from the Burning Spring Association in 1825.[24] Associations "arm off" another when, among other reasons, the parent becomes too large or numerous or unwieldy to be identified as a single association. This might be thought of in the same terms as when any church body splits should members feel it has become too large, or when members believe a subgroup of distant communicants can now support their own body. These are not schisms, and an association that "arms off" another typically continues to correspond with its parent. With only two minor exceptions, New Salem, through "arming off" other associations, has become the ancestor of every other Old Regular Baptist association. Old Regular Baptist history thus overlaps greatly with New Salem association history.

Like Burning Spring, its mother, New Salem began as a United Baptist association.[25] New Salem's history in the late nineteenth century highlights several themes of my work. The debate then over whether Baptists could be involved with missions and nonchurch organizations deeply divided New Salem and its correspondents.[26] The story of this controversy highlights the establishment of "case law" dictating Old Regular Baptist attitudes towards religion, church establishments, and, to some extent, the world at large, as well as to what extent these groups can adapt their tradition to secular circumstances.

By 1870 New Salem styled itself as a more traditional "Regular" or "Old Regular" Baptist association.[27] It emphasized an increasingly sectarian faith until, in 1875, it declared "non-fellowship with all modern institutions called benevolent: such as missionary, Bible and tract societies, Sunday-school Unions and Masonry, and all societies set on foot by men, whether secret or open, religious or political, outside the Word of God."[28] New Salem's antimissionism presaged a revival of antimissionism across the South. David Harrell writes that in the 1880s, "Southern religion began to experience some serious strains," particularly as "Baptist and Methodist leadership attached itself firmly to the middle-class aspirations of the New South."[29] In reaction, the South saw a sectarian revival.

Not all of New Salem's daughter associations joined this reaction. When one objected to its command, New Salem, rather than seek reconciliation, reiterated its opposition to "all societies set on foot by men or devils, outside the Word of God."[30] After this, nine New Salem churches broke away. This only provoked the association to exhort its fellow Baptists a third time to "cleanse yourselves of secret organizations."[31]

The move against "benevolent" and "secret" orders pushed New Salem toward predestinarian beliefs. In 1891, New Salem stopped short on the path toward belief in absolute predestination, which was taken by some Primitive Baptists of the time, resolving it could "not endorse the sentiment teaching absolute predestination of all things."[32] Such a belief was objectionable since holding God to have predestined *all* things could also hold "God to be the author of sin, or that He influences men thereto."[33]

The reaction against absolute predestination marked a turning point in Old Regular Baptist doctrine. Since then, it has been vaguely between predestination and free will, holding that man is not "in total control of his own salvation, able on his own and at any time to work his way into redemption or will his way there . . . the initial call and ultimate salvation come from

God."³⁴ This theological settlement has held now for more than a century, although questions of worldly organization that raised the conflict remain an occasional source of agitation.

Labor unions have been one source of agitation. By the time of the massive labor mobilization in the 1930s, most Old Regular Baptist associations had dropped or ignored prohibitions against worldly societies. The Kyova Association was an exception. It decided in the 1940s that the United Mine Workers and other labor unions were in fact secret orders, and hence prohibited its communicants from belonging to them.³⁵ Kyova dropped correspondence with New Salem, which had accommodated unions. Kyova itself split over this rule, with the anti-union remnant becoming an isolated outcast. In fact, all available evidence—or, more precisely, lack of evidence—indicates that the anti-union rule appears to have killed Kyova. In 1960 Kyova had just 4 churches and 140 members.³⁶ In all the correspondence I have had about Old Regular Baptists, in nearly ten years I have not found any definitive evidence on the current size or existence of Kyova.³⁷

The New Salem Association moderator at the time of my interview with him was a retired banker and Democratic activist in Pike County, Kentucky. Pike is a heavily unionized and Democratic coal county. In 1995, Paul Patton, a former judge-executive (or chief executive) of Pike County, extended the Democrats' hold on the Kentucky governorship. The New Salem moderator opposes neither "secret orders" nor labor unions. Most Old Regular Baptists ignore the question of "secret orders." Some even endorse them, particularly when they are perceived as organizations run by and for the benefit of local residents.

Old Regular Baptists today are more worldly in their regard for secular organizations, but they remain highly traditional. They practice the ordinances of baptism by immersion, annual communion, and foot washing. They prohibit musical instruments in their churches. All strongly discourage divorce and remarriage. They permit women no voice in church governance.

Most emphasize Deuteronomic dress codes, and many command men to cut their hair and women not to do so. They cite I Corinthians 11:14–15, which states "Doth not even nature itself teach you that, if a man have long hair, it is a shame unto him? But if a woman have long hair, it is a glory to her: for *her* hair is given her for a covering." One association prohibits nearly all paintings of Jesus in its churches, for such portrayals typically show Christ with longer hair than would ever be worn by a male member in good standing. To make this point clear, the association moderator insists Jesus must have had short hair. There is actually some scholarly evidence that Jesus' hair was not as long as other Jewish males of the time,[38] but it appears that, judging by some photos of Old Regular Baptist men from the early twentieth century, either some Old Regular Baptists now place more emphasis on men's hair length, or their standards of what defines long hair for men have changed.[39]

Some questions about traditionalism divide Old Regular Baptists today. The more liberal ones are not as strict on all matters of dress or hair length. They do not, for example, expect a woman never to cut her hair, and they are more accepting of women wearing slacks outside church. The more liberal tend to be farther away from the geographic core of Old Regular Baptist membership, though many highly traditional members are also away from the core.

Old Regular Baptists number 19,257 adherents in 326 churches of 94 counties spread as far apart as Arizona, Florida, Maryland, and Washington state (see map 6).[40] Three in four (75 percent) are in a small band of eleven contiguous counties in Kentucky, Virginia, and West Virginia (see map 7). Like the population in these areas, Old Regular Baptists are overwhelmingly white. Nevertheless, a small number of Old Regular Baptists in the region are African Americans.[41]

The fortunes of this core area have fluctuated with those of the coal industry. It has many problems common to those dependent on extractive economies (see table 4). Despite massive out-migration in the 1950s and 1960s, the population of this area today is younger than that of the nation. Unemployment is chronic, which is perhaps one reason nearly two in three women here with children are not in the labor force. Per capita income is just over half the national level, and poverty is more than twice the national rate. Politically, this area is staunchly Democratic.

Many Old Regular Baptists have followed outward migrations from this area, particularly to northern industrial centers. By one estimate, of all those between the ages of eighteen and thirty-five in "central Appalachia" between 1950 and 1970, three in four left the region (included in this out-migration were the author's mother and four of her five brothers).[42] More than one in ten Old Regular Baptists are in Illinois, Indiana, Michigan, or Ohio. There they confront the opportunities and problems typical of those facing rural migrants to metropolitan centers, as well as those confronting industrial workers in deindustrializing economies.

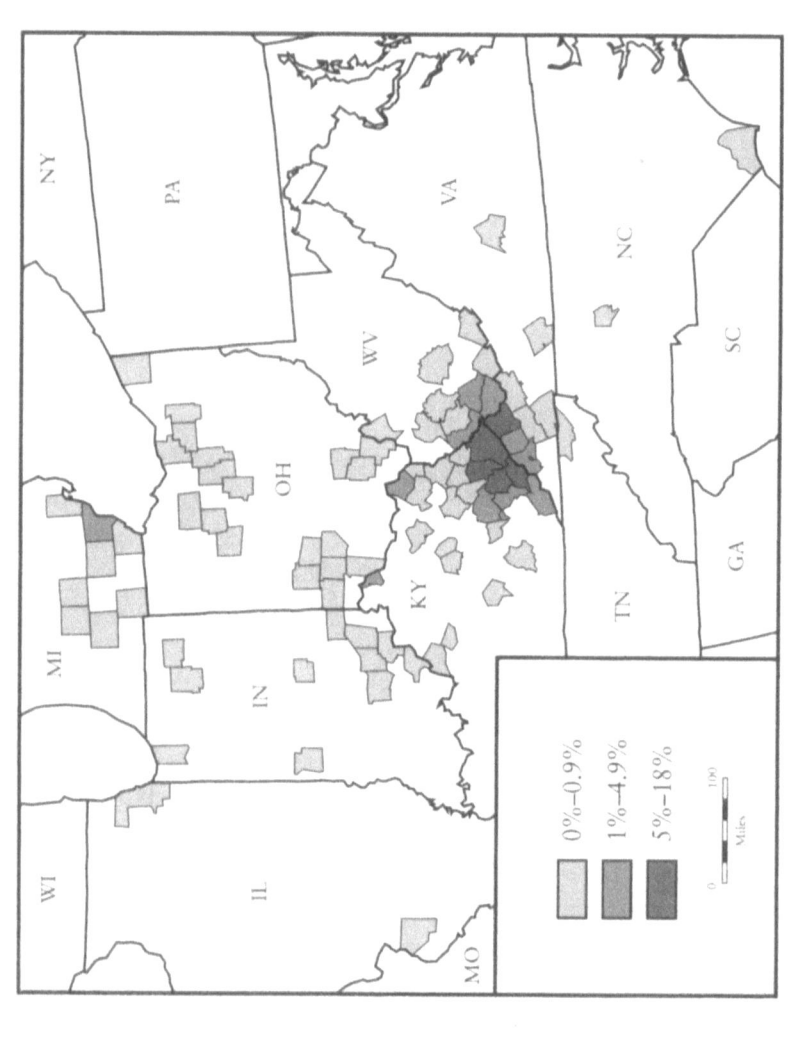

Map 6. Old Regular Baptist Distribution by County, 1990.

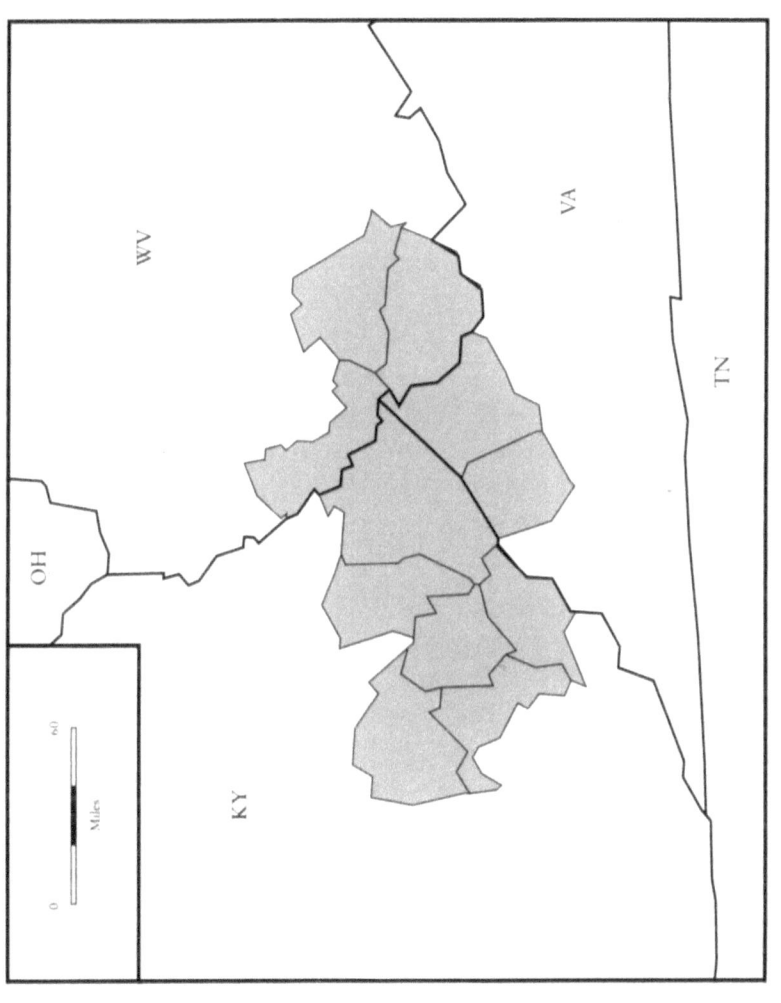

Map 7. Old Regular Baptist Core Counties.

Table 4
Old Regular Baptist Core Area Characteristics

	OLD REGULAR BAPTIST CORE COUNTIES (%)	U.S. TOTALS (%)
Total Population (as % of 1990)		
1950	142	61
1960	116	72
1970	95	82
1980	116	91
1990	100	100
White	98	80
Under 18	29	26
Over 64	11	13
Males currently married[a]	65	57
Females currently married[a]	59	52
Did not graduate high school[b]	52	25
At least some college[b]	19	45
Civilian unemployed, 1990	14.2	6.3
Working mothers	37	68
Selected industry data		
Agriculture, forestry, fisheries	1	3
Mining	25	1
Manufacturing	4	18
Wholesale and retail trade	20	21
Other services	32	40
Selected occupational data		
Managerial or professional	18	26
Technical, sales, or support	24	32
Skilled craft, repair	22	11
Operator/assembler/inspector	3	7
Other labor	19	8
Voted Democratic for president[c]		
1980	61	42
1984	60	41
1988	65	46
1992	65	43
1996	64	50
Per capita income, 1989	$8,056	$14,420

NOTES: [a] 15 years of age and older.
[b] 25 years of age and older.
[c] of votes for major candidates for president.

EASTERN DISTRICT PRIMITIVE BAPTIST ASSOCIATION

CCMUS 1990 lumped all Primitive Baptists together, but there are at least five separate traditions within this group.[43] One of these is the Eastern District Primitive Baptist Association. I classify Eastern District as a separate division because it does not correspond with any other Primitive Baptist body and because its size makes it unique among Primitive Baptist associations, nearly all of which have fewer than one thousand members each.[44] The Eastern District association is of particular interest to this work because it spawned another sect I study, Central Baptists. It is also useful for analyses because the tensions between tradition and modern life it has faced have been exacerbated by the departure of the Central Baptists, and because, as one scholar notes, "It is somewhat easier to distinguish among various Baptist groups when one has the Primitives as a basis for comparison."[45]

Primitive Baptists originated with antimission sentiment of the early nineteenth century. They represented a hard core of opposition to rising church establishments. They opposed "everything connected with church life that was not included in the clearly presented statement of New Testament writers."[46] They condemned all "'modern, money-based, so-called benevolent societies,' as contrary to the teaching and practice of Christ and His apostles, and, furthermore, announced that [they] could no longer fellowship with churches which [e]ndorsed such societies."[47] They later declared nonfellowship with all who "had 'departed from the simplicity of the doctrine and practice of the gospel of Christ ... uniting themselves with the world and what are falsely called benevolent societies founded upon a money world and ... upon a money basis,' and [that] preach ... a gospel 'differing from the gospel of Christ.'"[48]

Primitive Baptist disdain for "uplift" and "benevolence" easily blended with strong Calvinism. Calvinist beliefs can spur resistance to "uplift" and "benevolence," for if the world is predestined then such work is foolish and sentimental. Soon Primitive Baptists formalized such an attitude in their theology, expressing belief "that God elected or chose His people in Christ before the foundation of the world."[49] A recent narrative analysis of fundamentalism explicitly includes Primitive Baptists with other fundamentalist populations, although I am aware that many who are knowledgeable about Primitive Baptists will be skeptical about such links; I note this only to bring attention to links others have made between this population and fundamentalism.[50]

The Eastern District has its own 1848 origins in a similar reaction against "benevolence" and church establishments, originating following a split within a Mulberry Gap Association of United Baptists. Little historical documentation of this split exists, but those most knowledgeable of Eastern District history think the split came about because of Mulberry Gap support of a foreign mission board. There is today a Mulberry Gap Association in the same area that is affiliated with the Southern Baptist Convention. It is not clear whether this is the same association from which the Eastern District Association separated, although the evidence that exists seems to indicate that it is. Allan Gleason, in correspondence with the author, notes that this association has been extant since 1836 and that it is one of the most "old-fashioned" within the SBC. If it is the same association from which Eastern District split, then those attributing the split to support of foreign missions are most likely correct.

Continuing resistance by the Eastern District Association to church works and establishments led some churches to break away and form the Central Baptist Association. The break appears to have shaken many Eastern District Baptists. Despite maintaining an article of faith "in election according to the foreknowledge of God," their moderator says that, in practice, their beliefs in salvation are now closer to those of the SBC than to those of other Primitive Baptists. They believe the plan of salvation was foreordained, but individual salvation is not.

They maintain the three traditional ordinances of baptism, foot washing, and annual communion, but they have become less traditional in other ways. They now hold revivals and Sunday school. They leave the use of musical instruments to local church discretion. They do not support foreign missions, but do not prohibit individuals from doing so. They rely on a called, unpaid clergy, but they do not prohibit seminary or Bible school training. They have dropped opposition to nonchurch "benevolent" societies, such as fraternal organizations and labor unions.

They are now more permissive on women's roles. They do not have a dress code, and they permit women to vote for all association offices and to hold any office that nonclergy can hold (e.g., clerk, treasurer), although they prohibit women from commenting publicly on association operations and policy. They do not oppose any particular role for women outside the church, such as public office.

Their modernization has coincided with a demographic shift toward the Tri-Cities area. Before World War II, the association was centered in Lee County, Virginia, the southwesternmost county of the Old Dominion. But, as one preacher who moved told me, after World War II "industry picked up and the agricultural way of life wasn't so good any more, so the people scattered. Quite a few of them came to Kingsport."

In 1990 there were 7,259 adherents in 67 churches of the association distributed in 15 counties (see map 8). The demographics of the Eastern District stronghold reflect those of the Central Baptist core area, though the Eastern District remains more rural. Three in ten association members are in southwestern Virginia, with more than one in eight in Lee County. Hancock County, Tennessee, the southern neighbor of Lee and one of the most isolated counties in the Volunteer State, is also home to more than one in eight association adherents. More than one in three are in Hawkins and Sullivan Counties of Tennessee, which have seen great expansion since World War II. Some association members are in the Dayton, Ohio, area, as well as near the Ashland, Kentucky, area.

Eastern District Primitive Baptists are still most concentrated in four counties of southwestern Virginia and northeastern Tennessee. These are Lee and Scott Counties in Virginia (the original home of Central Baptists) and Hancock and Hawkins Counties in Tennessee. These are isolated, sparsely populated areas. Despite the growth in Hawkins County, its population remains fairly small (below 45,000 in 1990), with a population density not much above that for the nation and its vast rural areas as a whole. The other three counties all have population densities below that for the nation as a whole. The four counties are overwhelmingly white, and all four combined have not had much population growth in recent decades (see table 5). Their workforce is disproportionately concentrated in manufacturing, as well as in jobs of skilled and other labor. Education and income levels in this area trail those of the nation, but in other ways metropolitan standards are beginning to encroach. More than one in five area adults, for example, have some education beyond high school, and most women with children are in the workforce. Politically, this core area as a whole reflects the nation, with a slight preference for southern over northern Democrats.

From their rural origins, Eastern District Primitive Baptists have come to occupy three different types of areas. Their focus outside the core is on the

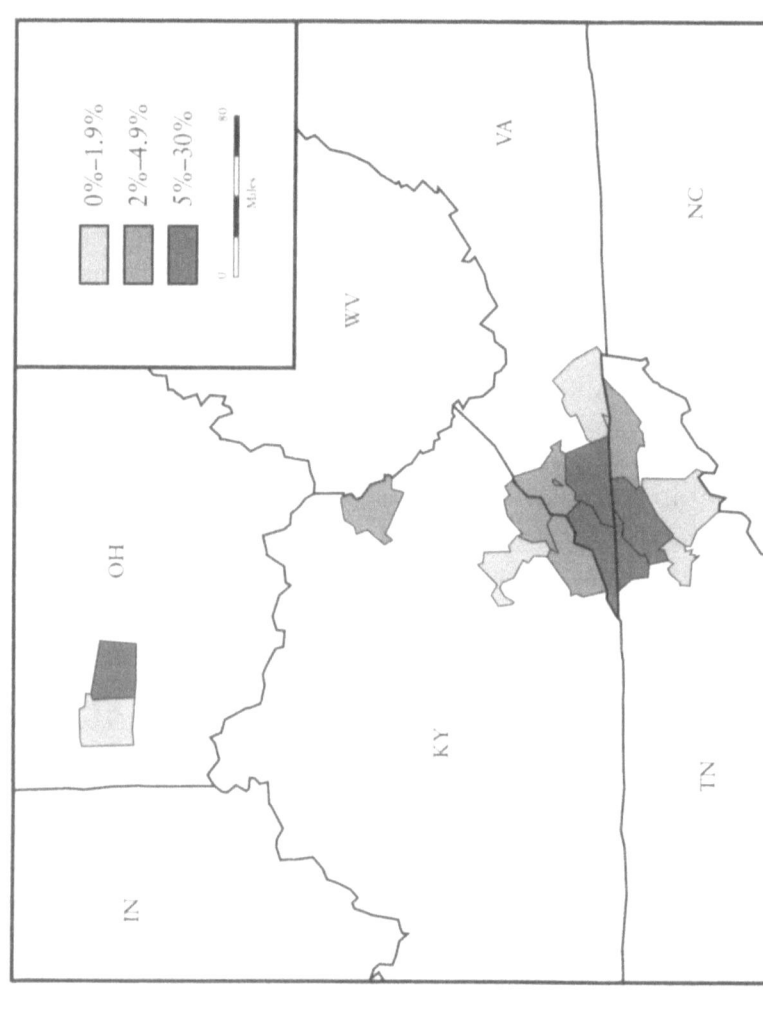

Map 8. Eastern District Primitive Baptist Association Distribution by County, 1990.

Table 5
Eastern District Primitive Baptist Core Area Characteristics

	EASTERN DISTRICT CORE COUNTIES (%)	U.S. TOTALS (%)
Total Population (as % of 1990)		
1950	104	61
1960	91	72
1970	86	82
1980	103	91
1990	100	100
White	99	80
Under 18	24	26
Over 64	15	13
Males currently married[a]	65	57
Females currently married[a]	60	52
Did not graduate high school[b]	47	25
At least some college[b]	21	45
Civilian unemployed, 1990	9.6	6.3
Working mothers	55	68
Selected industry data		
Agriculture, forestry, fisheries	5	3
Mining	3	1
Manufacturing	33	18
Wholesale and retail trade	17	21
Other services	26	40
Selected occupational data		
Managerial or professional	15	26
Technical, sales, or support	22	32
Skilled craft, repair	16	11
Operator/assembler/inspector	18	7
Other labor	13	8
Voted Democratic for president[c]		
1980	44	42
1984	39	41
1988	42	46
1992	44	43
1996	43	50
Per capita income, 1989	$9,161	$14,420

NOTES: [a]15 years of age and older.
[b]25 years of age and older.
[c]of votes for major candidates for president.

Tri-Cities, a typical small southern metropolitan area. They maintain a strong presence in rural counties surrounding this metropolitan community, in counties where the political and social outlook has been set either by mountain Republicanism dating to the Civil War or by early-twentieth-century coal mine labor mobilization. A small number of Eastern District Primitive Baptists are also in industrial areas to the north. This shift from rural to more metropolitan environs, as well as the encroachment of metropolitan standards upon rural communities, has been accompanied by the departure of some churches over continuing insistence on Primitive Baptist doctrine. But this rupture was followed by adaptation, which led away from some traditional standards.

United Baptists

United Baptists are the largest and most dispersed of the groups I study. They comprise 77,396 adherents in 476 churches of 120 counties (see map 9).[51] Nearly three in five (58 percent) are in Kentucky, but there are also United Baptists as far apart as Arizona, Idaho, Florida, and Wisconsin.

United Baptists have their origins in a movement for unity among Separate and Regular Baptists along the southern Appalachian frontier in the late eighteenth century. These churches sought a greater sense of community but without encroachments by outside authority. Separate Baptists in the movement agreed to emphasize less strongly their free will doctrines, while the more Calvinist Regular Baptists agreed to allow special customs such as foot washing wherever they were desired. United Baptists grew rapidly in the early nineteenth century, with each association exercising great autonomy.

United Baptists typically took one of two paths. Some found that with their gradual accommodations they were no longer distinct from other, larger Baptist bodies, such as the SBC, so they enrolled with them. Others, through their insistence upon an unpaid clergy without formal training and upon the traditional ordinances, including foot washing, continued to assert their independence.

United Baptists today have beliefs similar to those of Old Regular Baptists and Duck River and Kindred Baptists, holding that salvation is by grace alone, yet it is conditional upon performance of other Gospel requirements. United Baptist beliefs so strongly converged with those of Duck River and Kindred that there was some discussion about the two groups joining, but no formal

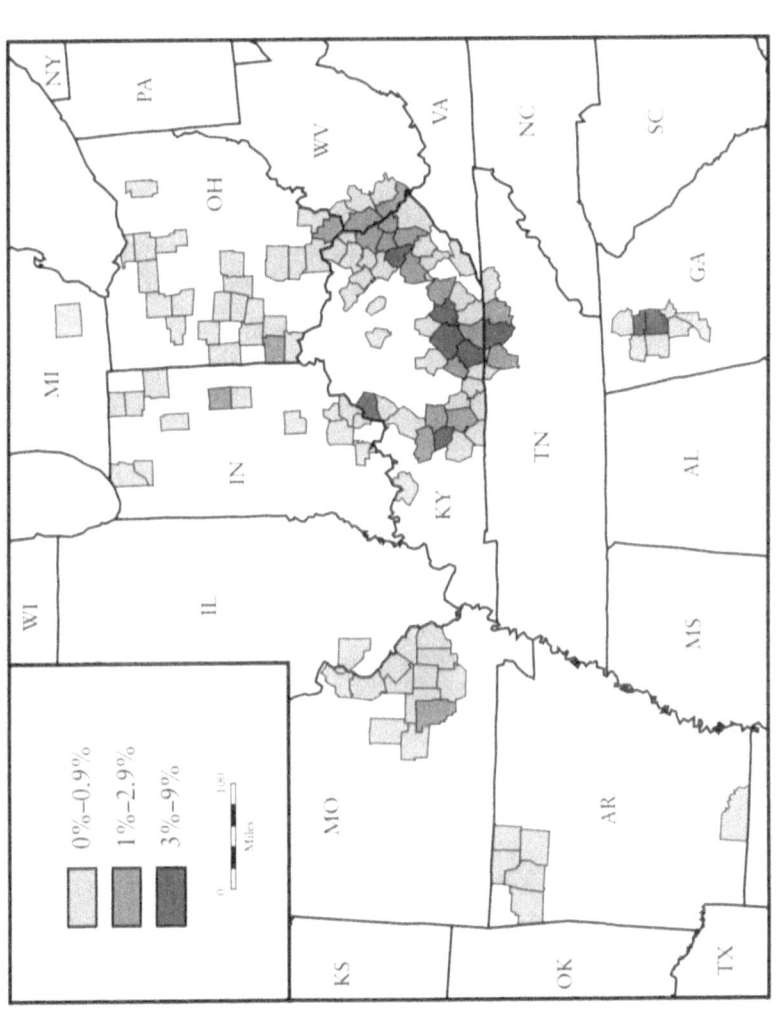

Map 9. United Baptist Distribution by County, 1990.

moves were made.[52] United Baptists hold that the Gospel is to be preached to all, but they will not support foreign missions. They refuse to support a formally trained, professional clergy. The only missionary commitment they will make is to have their ministers preach wherever their secular work might take them.

United Baptists are quite traditional in many other ways. Most will not allow women to hold church office or to vote for men who do. Nearly all still practice baptism by immersion, annual communion, and foot washing. Most do not allow musical instruments in church. Some insist on traditional dress codes, with the most conservative not allowing men to wear shorts. Those few groups that do allow women to hold church office or that permit musical instruments tend to be located away from their Kentucky stronghold. The most traditional typically are in eastern Kentucky.

Despite some metropolitan presence, United Baptists are overwhelmingly rural. Four pockets of rural counties are home to three in four (74 percent) United Baptists (see map 10).

The largest of these rural areas is a group of fifteen contiguous counties in northeastern Tennessee and southeastern and south-central Kentucky (Area A in map 10). More than one in three (34 percent) United Baptists reside here. Manufacturing has largely displaced farming as the chief source of employment (see table 6). The population of this area dipped sharply from 1950 to 1970, but it has grown since. The area shows many signs of economic stress, including low levels of education and income and high levels of unemployment and poverty. Politically, these counties are firmly Republican, a partisan preference largely dating back to their northern sympathies in the Civil War.

The area with the second-largest number of United Baptists is a group of twelve counties near the border between Kentucky and West Virginia (Area B in map 10). This area is typical of the central Appalachian coal belt, and its fortunes have waxed and waned with those of the coal industry. It is highly dependent on mining; one in five (20 percent) workers are miners. Its education and income levels are well below those for the nation. Its population has fluctuated with the coal industry. Like the first area, this region had northern sympathizers in the Civil War, but coal labor mobilization made it staunchly Democratic.

The third core region for United Baptists is seven contiguous western Kentucky counties (Area C in map 10). More than one in eight (13 percent) United

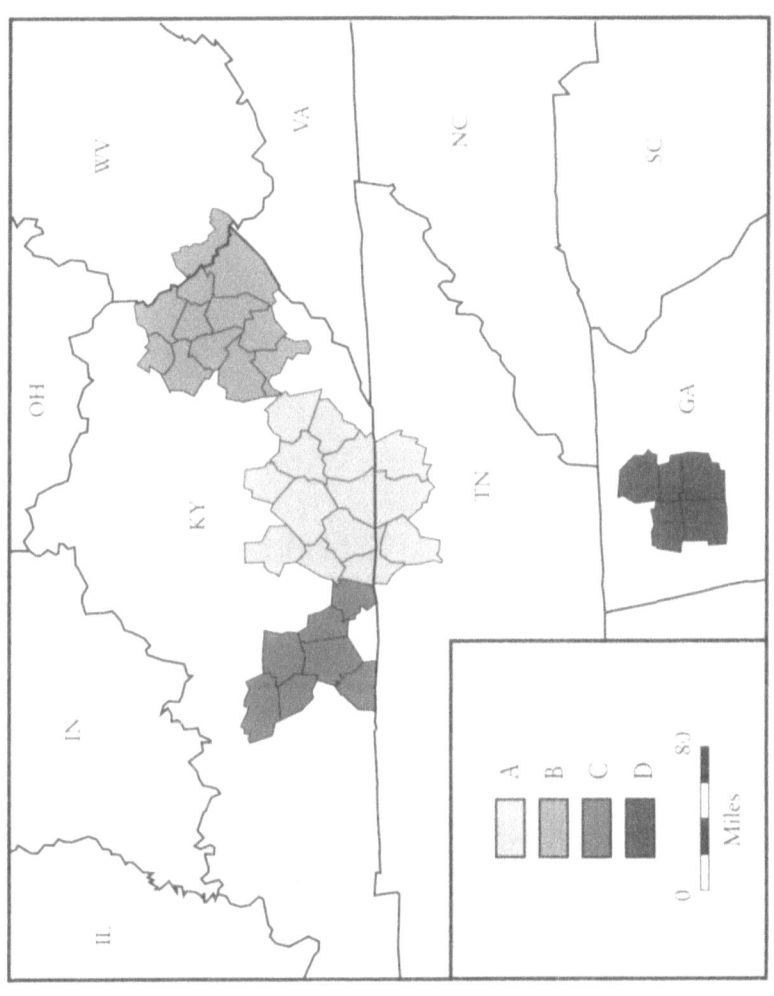

Map 10. United Baptist Analysis Areas.

Table 6
United Baptist Area Characteristics

	AREA A (%)	AREA B (%)	AREA C (%)	AREA D (%)	U.S. TOTALS (%)
Total Population (as % of 1990)					
1950	92	120	93	41	61
1960	79	98	86	42	72
1970	76	84	86	51	82
1980	98	109	100	70	91
1990	100	100	100	100	100
White	99	99	96	95	80
Under 18	27	29	26	27	26
Over 64	13	11	15	9	13
Males currently married[a]	65	65	67	67	57
Females currently married[a]	59	60	61	64	52
Did not graduate high school[b]	51	51	51	35	25
At least some college[b]	19	20	18	33	45
Civilian unemployed, 1990	10.4	13.8	8.9	5.2	6.3
Working mothers	56	39	64	71	68
Selected industry data					
Agriculture, forestry, fisheries	4	1	10	3	3
Mining	3	20	0	0	1
Manufacturing	24	5	29	27	18
Wholesale and retail trade	21	21	19	21	21
Other services	31	33	25	28	40
Selected occupational data					
Managerial or professional	16	19	13	20	26
Technical, sales, or support	24	25	21	30	32
Skilled craft, repair	15	19	14	16	11
Operator/assembler/inspector	14	4	18	12	7
Other labor	14	19	12	10	8
Voted Democratic for president[c]					
1980	34	61	40	59	42
1984	29	57	34	31	41
1988	31	61	38	29	46
1992	35	61	40	34	43
1996	36	61	39	34	50
Per capita income, 1989	$7,900	$7,941	$8,605	$12,906	$14,420

NOTES: [a] 15 years of age and older.
[b] 25 years of age and older.
[c] of votes for major candidates for president.

Baptists live here. Following population decline in the 1950s and 1960s, this area has experienced some growth since 1970. This area has a disproportionate number of agricultural workers. Area demographics are "downscale," with educational and income levels below national levels and unemployment slightly higher. Politically, the area reflects a long-running tide toward Republicanism among rural white southerners. Ron Lewis, a fundamentalist Baptist minister who ran successfully as a Republican to succeed the late Democratic Rep. William Natcher in the U.S. House, represents much of this area.

The fourth area of United Baptist concentration includes five rapidly changing counties of north Georgia. This area has seen much exurban movement from Atlanta. Its 1990 population was nearly three times that of its 1950 level. Social and economic indicators in this area lag somewhat behind those of the rest of the nation, but they are well ahead of those for the other United Baptist cores. Booming southern suburbia is rapidly invading or encroaching upon this area. Its unemployment rate is below that of the nation, and most women are in the workforce. Politically, this region has transformed rapidly from typically southern Democratic to typically southern Republican. Much of this area lies in former House Speaker Newt Gingrich's district.

COMMON CHARACTERISTICS

Many traits common to all these groups suggest themselves. Nearly all have predominantly rural, overwhelmingly white memberships. The few exceptions have roots in rural areas. Nearly all are in areas with modest economic circumstances, though some face harsher conditions than others, and some are in relatively affluent suburban and exurban areas. Despite their prevalence in rural areas, none live in a local economy that relies primarily on agriculture. Manufacturing and coal mining have forced even those in rural areas to come to terms with a modern industrial economy.

These sects also share many religious characteristics that make them far more alike than dissimilar. Below I explore these religious and social similarities. What becomes evident is that this religion is a religion of the common people, and that the common people shape it to meet secular needs. Some of the similarities these Baptists share highlight the characteristics they share with broader, similar groups, while others point to their distinctiveness. In all we can see both how much of their religion is adapted to their social and economic circumstances, and how they maintain their religion as a resource in confronting the many secular challenges of their lives.

Among the characteristics these groups share are:

Belief in the King James (i.e., Authorized) Bible as the Unerring Word of God.[53] This insistence on the King James version reflects a desire to follow the ancient origins of the "true" faith. An insistence on the King James translation maintains a popular standard to which all can refer. It is a translation commonly accepted and unsullied by experts presenting new translations that add unwanted ambiguity to biblical text or meaning. It is a popular standard that will likely never be discarded by these groups. Indeed, in recent years, many associations have adopted as an article of faith an explicit specification of the King James Bible as the rule for all elements of faith and practice.

In broader "fundamentalist" populations, those insisting on a King James translation do so out of fear of distancing themselves even further from the original meaning of the "autographs," or the exact message the Almighty supposedly dictated to the human scribes of the Bible.[54] As each word of the sacred text becomes subject to more and more exegeses, new translations face a skeptical or hostile audience accustomed to the old translation and the nuances discovered within it. Modern concerns over the grounds of interpretation join a concern for the ancient origins of the faith in generating skepticism or hostility to new biblical translations.

Allan Gleason adds a more nuanced interpretation of the popular use of the King James translation and suspicion, particularly among "evangelicals," over changing biblical translations.[55] Both in his own work and in further correspondence with me, Gleason notes that specification of the King James version is a modern concern. This simply would not have been an issue in the early twentieth century, both because of the dominance then of the King James translation among published Bibles, and because of wider familiarity with its particular version of biblical language.

A few of the Baptist preachers I interviewed say an acceptable alternative to the King James translation might someday be found, and some even occasionally use other versions for private reading. But none know of any alternative that their churches would accept. As one Old Missionary Baptist told me, these Baptists "think that the King James version was sufficient at the time it came out . . . other translations . . . have not brought anything new to . . . the King James Bible."

This insistence on the King James Bible does not lead to insistence on many unwavering, legalistic formulae for behavior. In fact, it appears to have led to an even greater ambiguity and flexibility for each church member to be able, as much as any other, to adapt the sacred text to local circumstances. What Deborah Vansau McCauley says about the use of the Bible in Appalachian religion applies to these Baptists both in and outside the highlands. She writes that "their preference in biblical literature differ[s] profoundly from a preponderance of evangelical fundamentalists in particular . . . [they] accept ambiguity—running deep and broad—as an indisputable fact of life. They do not feel driven to resolve it in their preaching with semantically fancy footwork that artificially overcomes ambiguity by forcing all the pieces to fit together in neatly packaged 'biblical solutions' or 'answers' to the pressing problems of daily living, from personal finances to moral dilemmas dividing the nation."[56]

Emphasis on Ancient Origins of Their "True" Faith. Some of these Baptists object to being called "Protestant," as they insist they are "protesting" nothing. Instead, they insist on a tradition they say runs back through "the valleys of Wales" and, from there, to Jesus Christ and John the Baptist, making their religion one that truly was founded by Christ.[57] Many of these groups' self-published histories contain translations of documents from the time of Christ that purportedly show their ancient origins as the true church.

These Baptists usually tell one of two general histories linking themselves to Christ. One claims that Paul was not martyred in Rome, but went toward or on to Wales, where churches were established that are the direct ancestors of latter-day Welsh Baptists. This line was continued to America by those who founded the Old Welsh Church near Wilmington, Delaware. The other version sees a continuous line through the Montanists, the Waldensians, and the Anabaptists, who in turn influenced early British Baptists, who brought the faith to America. Regardless of which version is told, the common theme of a direct lineage from Christ remains.

Though there is no known formal connection between the Landmark movement and the purported histories of these particular Baptists, there are clearly many parallels. The Landmark movement of the middle eighteenth century attracted those "who went to the extreme of denying the Christian legitimacy of all others than Baptists, even of many Baptists."[58] Some of the Baptist associations I study have their origins in similar disputes, particularly over the issue of "open communion," or the issue of which Baptists are qualified to partake of communion in a particular church or association. More commonly the Landmark movement was a grassroots movement among poorer adherents that marked "a growing resentment and insecurity among rural and lower-class Baptists" and that attacked organized mission work.[59] Landmark tendencies thus reinforced the class divisions that spawned the Baptists of this work.

Landmarkists believed that "the only true churches are local Baptist churches," a claim they based "in part on a constitutionalist view of the New Testament [w]here the perfect makeup of a church, qualified members and authorized office-holders, is plainly laid out. It also rests on the perpetuation of that primitive essence in pure churches across the intervening centuries. Everything but Baptist and quasi-Baptist churches has been an aberration and perversion, they contend. In the divine design, these true communities enjoyed an unbroken succession . . . until Baptists, by that identification, emerged in the early seventeenth century. But Baptists did not *emerge* [emphasis in original]; they had been present in history all along. Only the identification by that name was novel."[60]

Samuel S. Hill contends—rightfully in the eyes of this author lacking much theological training—that "this reasoning is more Roman Catholic than Baptist, indeed, is not Baptist theology at all."[61] But the few Baptists I study who recognize any connection to Catholicism or other Christian traditions in their history do so in a bit of religious one-upmanship. A small number, for example, grant Catholicism its supposed Petrine roots, even claiming that at one time Catholicism's initiation rituals were the same as theirs. But they also point out that Catholics (as well as Protestant churches that indisputably split from Catholicism) need this extra level of intercession, whereas they have followed a religion which dates not to Jesus' commands to Peter after His Resurrection,[62] or even at the conclusion of His Galilean ministry,[63] but all the way back to His baptism and the very beginning of His public ministry.

Many of these churches make incessant efforts to re-create the new Zion or the new Jerusalem through, among other things, their sermons, their exhortations, and their adaptation of biblical names for their churches or their associations. One analysis concludes of Old Regular Baptists:

> It is clear that they live in the time of the original creation—the time of Christ's creative, divine acts. [One elder], speaking of the need to bap-

tize in running water, explains that "Jordan is a mighty swift stream." A layman rejoices in the fact that still the songs ring through the mountains of Zion as they did in the days of the Lord Jesus Christ. It is clear that the present mountain landscape has been assimilated as the geography of the Bible, the geography of the new Creation in Christ. Time is suspended. The Old Regular and other "foot washing" Christians live with Christ. This is the Old Fashioned Way. Reality is found by living in the archetypes established by Christ.[64]

Among these Baptists, there is some lighthearted joshing about this ultimately serious effort. The interest of many of these preachers in biblical landscape, for example, combined with increases in their affluence and in the availability of jet travel, appears to have spurred an increase in travel to the Holy Land. The interest in travel is selective. One Duck River Baptist told me, "A lot of them ain't been to Kentucky, but they've been to Israel." More seriously, what typically appears here, as appears in the Page County, Virginia, congregation that Jeff Todd Titon studies, is a "tropology," or "the view that the events and persons of the Bible transcend their times and places to live today in the Christian's life, not just as symbols but as reality."[65]

An emphasis on ancient, true origins of the church, free of distortions that others make of the faith, is a classic sectarian attribute. The importance of these Baptists' historical claims lies not in their accuracy. Rather, it is that such claims enable them to assert that they are keepers of the original faith and, if necessary, to justify their local interpretations as those which Jesus might make. Their pronouncements are not without humility. Many of these preachers, in warming up to their sermons, often claim that "we won't have no preaching here today unless the Lord Jesus returns." They clearly and repeatedly recognize their own inadequacies in presenting the Christian message. But they also can and do clearly claim that their local religious interpretations are at least as good as those that any other mortal authority can make.

The emphasis on the ancient origins of their true faith is a myth—that is, a traditional story of ostensibly historical events that serves to unfold part of the worldview of a people or to explain a practice or belief—that allows these Baptists to take at least as much comfort in their teaching and interpretations as Catholics take from the myth of Petrine succession or other Protestants take in their myths of grace found only individually, and without any mediating structures, much less without any influence from the first fifteen (Catholic) centuries of the Christian era.

A Duck River Baptist preacher once offered in a sermon that I heard an example of how these Baptists can claim legitimacy that other churches cannot. Referring to a young new member of his congregation, he said her friends and parents asked her why she did not take her religion to "a real church." The more appropriate question, the preacher said, is "why doesn't she take it to Jesus?" Presumably he sees the way to Jesus as more open and easily traveled in his church than in more formal "real" churches.

Belief in Salvation between Predestination and Free Will. This belief holds that the plan of salvation is foreordained, but individual outcomes are not. Even in its nebulous form suspended between free will and predestination, this belief has caused discord among these groups.[66]

Many of these groups developed in a reaction against the growth of evangelism, missions, Sunday schools, revivals, and other forms of church outreach, which were directed by distant "experts" of the times.[67] In defense, they adopted Calvinist beliefs pointing to the foolishness of such practices. In the absence of external evangelism, their theology changed again. Old Regular Baptists, for example, rejected the doctrine of absolute predestination in 1891, though also rejecting the following year "the doctrine of Arminianism that claims the work of the creature to be essential to eternal salvation."[68]

There is variation among these Baptists on the proper balance between predestinarian and free will beliefs. The crucial point, however, is that much of this theology followed their ecclesiastical conflicts. Many churches on the Appalachian frontier resented money leaving the area for distant missions; they also resented home missions seeking to "convert" them. Such resentments easily led to a Calvinist theology opposing mission work.

Some shed Calvinist beliefs as the occasion demanded. The Eastern District Association of *Primitive* Baptists, for example, ought to be strictly Calvinist to justify its name. Yet after some of its churches broke away to engage in church works of charity, the association, while formally retaining an article of faith in "election according to the foreknowledge of God," began to permit Sunday schools and individual support of missionaries, works that can only be viewed as pure folly by more predestinarian logic.

Emphasis on Personal, Experiential Knowledge of Salvation. This can include, for example, a prolonged "conviction of sins" after reaching the "age of accountability" and before baptism. The "age of accountability" varies. One Old Missionary Baptist told me, "I don't think there's any certain age when a person reaches the age of accountability . . . [it is] when you realize you need to get right with God. One person might become accountable at eight or nine years old. Another person might be fifteen . . . then there are a lot of people who after they reach the years of accountability realize they need to get right with God but don't do it yet." The reason for delay between "accountability" and baptism, another told me, derives from emphasis on "an experiential knowledge of salvation." There can be a delay between reaching the years of accountability and the personal, emotional experience of the knowledge of salvation that leads to baptism and conversion.

The particulars of the age to join the church vary. Old Regular Baptists, for example, would not baptize many eight-year-olds. A common strain among all, however, is the pointed rejection of massive membership drives, such as large evangelization rallies. They feel that "conversions" at such rallies come more from the "head" and not the "heart." The emphasis on individual responsibility for and experience of salvation and the antipathy to "man-driven" conversion reinforce their reliance on local, rather than cosmopolitan, authority. Whether a given conversion is an actual experience of the divine or a contrivance of man is a question that has long vexed southern evangelical Protestants and affected the class conflicts within it.[69] Richard Niebuhr notes one difference between churches and sects is that one is born into the church but joins the sect. By emphasizing personal, "experiential knowledge of salvation," and often a testimony thereof, as requirements for baptism, these Baptists renew sectarian character with each generation.

Nonprofessional Clergy without Formal Religious Education. Many of these churches refuse to ordain those with formal theological training, such as seminary or Bible school, because they believe only God can properly train a minister. Even the small number of churches that have formally trained clergy have never required such training. They do not oppose higher education in general; some of their preachers hold graduate degrees in secular fields.

One full-time preacher estimates that only about 5 percent of the clergy in his association are full-time or have any formal training for the ministry. Even this small figure exceeds the portion of full-time or formally trained clergy that can be found in the other associations and is augmented by those who turn to the ministry only after having made enough money in another career to support their ministry. This opposition to a formally trained or professional clergy leads most of these Baptists to disregard the teaching of more prominent, and formally trained, fundamentalists. Should they happen to follow the teaching of a more prominent fundamentalist, it will be for local reasons.

Opposition to formally trained clergy is not limited to these Baptists. Often in the nation's religious history, religious institutions of higher learning have inadvertently spurred lay religious movements when scholars were "unable to resist attempting to clear up all logical ambiguities... rather than celebrate mysteries" of the faith.[70] The laity, less inclined to systematic theology, do not always appreciate such "pruning and revising and redefining." Their preference for mystery spurs sectarianism. This has been particularly true among poorer laity, who resent the pretensions of wealthier brethren, the growing church establishments they foster, and new theology that often accompanies the development of such ecclesiastical establishments.

The attitude of the Baptists of this work is that God alone can train preachers and can tell them what to say. It is much like the Appalachian preachers Deborah Vansau McCauley cites who "believe it is the Holy Spirit who should speak when preachers preach... [their] preaching is not about preselected topics addressed by carefully crafted exegeses of biblical texts... mountain preachers ... attest that the Holy Spirit needs to say the same things hundreds of different ways, many of which may seem blatantly contradictory (which is also how they understand apparently contradictory texts in the Bible), in order to accommodate the kaleidoscopic varieties of needs and personal histories of the legions of people the Holy Spirit addresses through such preachers."[71]

Opposition to Missions. These Baptists believe missions, like seminary training, inspire a "man-driven" call to be baptized or to preach, rather than the appropriate "God-driven" call. They are like those who split from southern evangelical Protestantism in the early nineteenth century and sought to remind more organized churches that they were "simply too optimistic about what their vaunted agencies and conventions could accomplish."[72] Many areas where these Baptists flourish have long been churched, but outsiders rarely document this. Many missionaries expecting to find and convert the "unsaved" have instead met animosity from these sects and their "saved" neighbors. One scholar writes, "Never have so many Christian missionaries been sent to save so many Christians."[73]

As for Jesus' command to "go ye into all the world and preach the gospel to every creature,"[74] a.k.a. the "Great Commission," these Baptists take a passive attitude. One told me, "The Lord is able to call somebody [in mission lands] to preach from their own people that they know." This preacher would preach elsewhere if his secular work took him there. He interprets Jesus' command as one to preach wherever life might lead him. He does not see it as his place to force the issue.

This stand parallels opposition to man-driven calls to salvation. Some of these Baptists support foreign churches, but these are led by indigenous, local leadership. Those who support foreign churches or Sunday schools tend to be removed from these sects' rural strongholds. The most traditional will not support Sunday schools for the same reason they will not support missions: they interfere with the preordained plan of salvation, by which the saved must personally experience salvation without any intermediary.[75] As one preacher told me, "You can't teach people to be saved."

Some who have left these sects' rural strongholds see Sunday school as a necessary adjustment to the world. One preacher born in eastern Kentucky who is now an industrial worker in northwest Indiana told me: "I'm a great believer in teaching our young people and bringing them to the House of the Lord. . . . People who have never been taught have a hard time finding salvation. . . . We need to get our teenagers in Sunday school so we can turn this nation around. Our young people are not getting the teachings they need in our [public] schools."

This preacher admits that many in his association in eastern Kentucky would not agree with him, but he sees a more formal Sunday school as a necessary adjustment to maintaining a stable church community in a more cosmopolitan area. Another preacher of his association, who has a church in an eastern Kentucky coal-mining community, has adopted Sunday schools for similar reasons. His church and community follow the cycles of the coal market; the membership of his church has fluctuated between 75 and 350 members, depending on the state of the market. As a result, many persons from outside the area temporarily move to the community before leaving as quickly as they came. With such transience, this preacher sees the Sunday school at his church—the only church in its immediate community—and Sunday school use of materials from a national publishing house, as helping bridge the gap between his traditional church and the religion those from outside the community may know better. As with many other modern innovations, if these Baptists see a need for instruments they once disdained, they are willing to adopt them.

Simple, Egalitarian Style of Worship. These sects' services usually consist of shouted, seemingly extemporaneous sermons, occasional extemporaneous prayers and other shouting, and singing or lining of traditional hymns, often with the prohibition of musical instruments.[76] The only other rituals these churches recognize are their ordinances of baptism, annual communion, and, in the more traditional churches, foot washing. Foot washing in particular has long served as an intimate binding of Baptist communities against the outside world.[77]

They view sermon preparation as they view trained clergy. They believe the devices of man, whether in sermon preparation or seminary education, interfere with the will of God to speak to His preachers through the Holy Spirit. Preachers who do not conform to the typical style of shouted, extemporaneous sermons are either younger or in areas where they are concerned with evangelizing younger members confronting different religious standards. But even these sermons will have an extemporaneous quality to them, if not such a distinct style.

The opposition to formal sermon preparation and the seemingly extemporaneous nature of these preachers' sermons does not mean they undertake no sermon preparation at all. They spend considerable time reading the Bible and are expected to do so. They give much thought to how particular passages are to be presented. Many times their sermons will contain gleanings from association meetings or other church gatherings. Theirs is a more generalized sermon preparation. This broader approach gives them more leeway to address their sermon to the local needs of the congregation.[78]

They preach a religion of common memory, which allows for changing interpretations as times change. As McCauley notes of Appalachian religion, such "preaching is spontaneous, 'unprepared,' with no index cards or notebooks or sermon guides. Oral memory is the norm, and behind it is the assumption of oral memory on the hearers. This . . . allows the greatest leeway for the tradition of seeking the Holy Spirit to guide" both sermons and listeners.[79]

Their rituals emphasize the democratic nature of the religion. Those prohibiting musical instruments within church tend to be the most traditional, but even those with instruments never have anything more extravagant than a piano or an organ (they would never have percussion or synthesized music in their services). Those with hymnals typically use shaped-note hymnals. The practice of "line singing" among some appears to have a democratizing effect on worship, enabling those who cannot read music or lyrics to sing with the rest. Those with lined singing also emphasize only what is essential to their services, and they note that any musical innovations can detract from the proper focus on the divine. One preacher advocating lined music reminded me that it was only when "the spirit of the Lord had left Saul" that he needed "musical instruments to comfort him. Before that, the Holy Spirit, the true comforter, was his comforter."[80]

The overall impression of this religion is that it is a democratic, vernacular one. It is a religion in which any male can aspire to lead, any female can aspire to extraordinary participation through shouting, and any member can interpret the sacred text and its commands for the local community as well as any other. I will discuss the roles of each sex in these churches, but a word here about women's participation in these Baptists' services might be helpful. Women clearly have secondary roles in these churches' services and rituals, yet there are times when they can, like any other member of the congregation, aspire to greater equality through greater participation. Women have made up a disproportionate number of shouters during services I observed in field visits. For some women, testimony in church offers an opportunity that is similar to the one male preachers have in addressing the congregation.[81]

Many "egalitarian" characteristics that William Clements noted in the "folk" church are evident among these Baptists as well. Clements writes that "while folk preachers may enjoy certain prestige, in most groups they do not have any closer relationship with the supernatural than does the laity. This doctrine of the 'priesthood of all believers,' an idea central to Protestantism, is taken quite literally in many folk religious groups, for preachers often have no more spiritual or administrative authority than their congregations."[82] The equality of all participants is emphasized, with no outside hierarchical interference.

Weak Central Authorities. Among these Baptists, those that have a central denominational authority would recoil at having a large full-time staff or anything more than the most functional headquarters. The only authority these Baptists usually recognize outside the local congregation is the annual association meeting of neighboring churches of like faith and order.[83] There are only two minor exceptions to this pattern among these Baptists. The Duck River Association and its kindred associations meet in a General Association, which has no more authority over its member associations than they have over their churches. The Central Baptist Association has more bureaucracy than is typical for these Baptists, but only as much as is needed to operate their orphanage and their summer youth camp. Most remarkably, while the orphanage and camp operation are responsible to the clergy and laity of the association, they are the only part of the association in which professional standards commonly recognized elsewhere prevail. In all cases among all these Baptists, outside authority is weaker than that available to the local church. The association serves more for fellowship than authority.

One preacher's ambivalent comments about the uses and effectiveness of exclusion underscore the individualism of these churches, and the extent to which they must rely on agreement among individual members in order to ensure church harmony. This preacher told me, "We don't exclude anymore. When you start doing that, when you start excluding people, then you start rocking families. You know, you get Granny back there, that's her great-grandson you're going to exclude, and you know, you start excluding, and everybody is not playing on the same spiritual field, and you really cause a lot of trouble." I asked him whether this was good or bad for preserving the church in the long run: "Well, I don't know. I guess I'd have to say it's a neutral thing. If I came in there now and tried to start excluding people it would just cause such a ruckus that we would have so much trouble. But if we had been practicing that all down through time, I think it would be better, because I think discipline is needed."

Regardless of the "discipline" he may feel is needed in his congregation—and our conversation referred to churchgoers' opinions and actions on public issues as well as more recognized forms of disreputable behavior—it is unlikely he could get the church to follow a strict denominational discipline. What McCauley says about Appalachian religion applies to these Baptists, both inside and outside the highlands. She writes, "Denominationalism or organized 'religion' simply makes no sense to them, and is seen as a major hindrance to worshipping God as the Holy Spirit directs and responding unencumbered to the work God would have you do."[84]

Many preachers cite more practical reasons for not being affiliated with larger national bodies. Some of these churches began independently, were later affiliated with a state or national body, and still later reasserted their independence when they thought the larger organization was trying to usurp local authority or was misappropriating local resources. One preacher, for example, told me his association affiliated with the Southern Baptist Convention only to disaffiliate after calculating that it was giving the SBC more money than the SBC would ever return.

Nearly all these Baptists oppose ecclesiastical institutions, and those who institutionalize do so only for their own church works, such as the Central Baptists, who accept professionalism to run their children's home. Werner Stark, however, raises a crucial point that can also apply to these churches. He writes, "It is not the *institutional* character of the church that arouses the misgivings and inspires the actions of the sectarian: it is its *established* character, the fact that it is one of the bastions built into the fortress surrounding and protecting the social order which the revolutionary condemns and would like to overthrow [emphases in original]."[85] The point has to be made most carefully about these Baptists. Many do indeed oppose religious institutionalism, but none would consider themselves revolutionaries because of their opposition to religious institutions or establishment.[86] It is the established character of more formally organized religion which has defined sharply this opposition for all.

These churches look not to any establishment or institution but to their laity for confirmation of authority. One preacher with a new pastorate told his church before starting a sermon: "It's your job to make sure I stay in the Word. If I get out, it's your job to get me back. I encourage you to study to keep me in the right way." Since their theology is usually summarized in a publicly developed statement of ten to twelve points that are published on a single page of the associational minutes each year, the laity easily find the standards by which to judge their clergy.

The laity become the "experts" who guide the church. The laity supply the clergy and the expertise to guide the religion. The laity enforce the claim that the Bible alone suffices for religious guidance. The laity do not want church historians or a systematic theology or any other trapping of religious establishment to constrain them. They ensure the continuing independent nature of these churches, and they insure that their churches will adapt, within broad cultural concerns, to current needs.

Traditional Sex Roles. Women never preach within these churches. Often they cannot hold any church office or vote for those who do. The most traditional of these Baptists segregate the sexes at worship, and adhere to biblical dress codes such as prescribing long hair and proscribing slacks for women, proscribing long hair for men, and proscribing shorts for either sex.[87]

On the surface, males appear to benefit from such customs. Nevertheless, there are less noticed benefits to females emanating from strictly enforced sex roles. These include ensuring that males become disciplined household providers. These Baptists are like early southern evangelical Protestants in seeking to control predatory male behavior through enforcing traditional sex roles.[88] American sectarian religion has long played a role in training males, especially those in more isolated areas, for family life.[89]

These sex roles take the form of a social exchange. Males conform to family discipline in exchange for official authority over the church and perhaps even actual authority within the household. Throughout the world there is little to attach low-income males to the discipline of family life. They may abandon economically distressed places such as those where these sects flourish. The task of disciplining males to provide for households becomes more difficult for a marginal people who live within sight of wealth, consumption, and apparent freedom from family discipline, areas like those where many in these sects have migrated. These churches make a virtue of abstinence from the temptations of nearby cosmopolitan areas and require disciplined behavior as a condition for male authority.

Many males implicitly recognize this exchange, particularly as it reflects repudiation of their formerly dissolute living. One man told me that just before he had been saved, he had been drunk and was shocked into realizing that unless he changed his ways quickly he would die damned. Another claims, "The day before I got saved, I experienced every ungodly sin I had experienced in my life." A third tells a more nuanced story of what he says was gradual recognition of the life God wanted him to live, a life of sobriety and responsibility. He says of his gradual conversion,

I thought I could resist . . . I got in trouble with the law and different things. I didn't steal or kill or anything like that, but I was just pretty wild. . . . I'd used drugs and alcohol and things like that. But it got to the point that I felt if I didn't turn to God and submit to His will, that He was going to take me out of this life . . . [then] God really blessed me, and He's put me in a life like this. He had to drag me kicking and screaming . . . until I went through thresholds of faith and learned what God can do. . . . I really submitted and broke down and said, "OK. Lord, I'll go out and do what You want me to do." After I did that it was like, man, all these things that others have been preaching are true. I'd been saved when I was nine years old, but I was twenty-something when I learned what God was about, how good He is. Then I was like, I've heard this stuff all my life, but now I'm like, hey, it's applicable.

There is a discernible pattern to such "conversion narratives." As Titon notes of the Page County, Virginia, congregation he studies, the stages of such narratives typically "proceed through sin, conviction, repentance, confession, salvation, and assurance. The prototype is Paul . . . particularly for the vileness of his sin and the simplicity and swiftness of his conversion."[90] However much narrators may simplify the story of their conversions, I would suggest that they still have a basic truth, holding that the narrators know they must curb their impulses in exchange for authority, and that they recognize other males seeking authority or greater stability in their lives must do the same.

These males recognize that this authority is not complete. If, for example, the third preacher I quote above expected his prolonged conversion to lead to unrestrained authority, he has since learned otherwise. He is the same preacher whom I quote earlier about the need to recognize "Granny's" feelings when one of her descendants may merit exclusion. Informal matriarchal authority can function many ways within formal patriarchal authority.

These Baptists will change, to the extent tradition permits, their enforcement of traditional sex codes when the benefits from enforcement change. In the most depressed sections of eastern Kentucky, where unemployment is very high and two-thirds of women with children are not in the workforce, enforcement of traditional roles for each sex cuts competition for scarce jobs, reinforces the need for males to take whatever work they can find, and ensures females a protected place within the community. Those in areas where working mothers are much more common abandon some traditional codes on dress and hair length and even some roles for women that inhibit their entry into work outside the home.

Nearly all recognize the need for the existence of some female authority, however informal, but there are limits to this recognition. The most conservative recoil at secular female leadership. Here the adaptability of the religion can falter. It can become unable to reconcile the traditional needs and demands for disciplined male behavior and accompanying authority with the changing standards and expectations of modern life. Typical are the comments one preacher made to me in discussing women in politics: "I think that's what's wrong with our country today. There has to be women that has a role in our society, like nurses and teachers and doctors, but I think for the running and ruling of our country and our nation, we've been taught down through the Bible that it's been done by men. God laid down specific roles for men, women, and children in the Bible. I believe women have left the roles that God has made for them, and I think that's one of the problems today, with our children and all this."

Despite his anti-feminist rhetoric, this preacher will accept women in jobs they have not traditionally held (e.g., doctors). He also has shown ingenuity in stretching traditional dress codes to cover more modern standards. A trivial but telling example of this is a story he related when I asked about dress codes for women. He told me:

> One of the old brothers a few years ago had a few of his people come by that were really troubled over the women wearing pants in church. They came to this old brother's house, and he was a fine old man. So he invited them in, heard their problems, and then he goes into his bedroom. He gets some of his slacks and some of his wife's slacks and he spreads them out on the floor back in the front room. Then he says, "I want you to pick out [my wife's] slacks," and they picked hers up. So he asked "Why, then, do you say they're men's apparel?" So he gets over a point that this is something we are looking upon as humans. But God doesn't look on the outward appearance. He looks on the inward person.

We may still argue that this preacher, and the other Baptists I study, have not achieved change in behavioral codes for each sex quickly enough for a modern world. Yet from the perspective of many of these Baptists, the issue of adapting roles for each sex in a modern world does not have as its central question how to bring about equal rights between men and women, but how to achieve change balanced between traditional expectations, increasing cosmopolitan influences, and local secular needs in ensuring a protected and honored place for all leading austere and disciplined lives in the family and community.

The theme of exchange between male discipline and male authority is also evident in analyses of broader "fundamentalist" populations. Nancy Ammerman writes that fundamentalist "rhetoric of patriarchy and submission serves primarily as a normative counterweight to the individualistic and hedonistic ways of the larger society . . . fundamentalist families negotiate an everyday routine that encompasses as much discussion and compromise as male dominance—and more male 'nurturance' than male aggression. While final decisions and primary economic responsibility may rest with husbands, wives know that their mates are supposed to place the needs of the family ahead of personal (male) desires. . . ."[91]

The rural origins of the Baptists of this work further reinforce traditional roles for the sexes, including disciplined behavior by males as household providers. Titon captures this in describing "husbandry," in both its agricultural and religious senses, among the Virginia congregation he studies. He writes:

> In the metaphor of husbandry—the word that means both a farmer's loving relationship to the crops and livestock, and a man's loving relationship to his wife—we can see the linking pattern between life in the material world of the farmstead and life in the human, social, familial world. Significantly, the same metaphor connects to the religious world as well. Husbandry is a frequent metaphor in the Judeo-Christian tradition; "husbandman" is regularly used in the King James Version of the Bible to translate what today we would call farmer, herder, or fruit-grower. Here the metaphor means that the farmer stands in relation to his land as a husband to his wife.[92]

Rural Origins and Membership. All these Baptists are rural or have clearly rural origins, yet they increasingly confront cosmopolitan standards. The overwhelming majority of these Baptists are in nonmetropolitan counties. In rural counties, these churches tend to be located in the countryside, away from the county seat, and away from any other significant center of social, political, or economic activity. Commenting on the physical isolation of "folk" church structures, Clements writes: "Main Street is reserved for the edifices of official religion, and the folk churches appropriate portions of communities in less proximity to the architectural symbols of the secular power structure."[93] This applies to the Baptists of this work as well. They are removed, both physically and, often, in the public mind, from the citadels of official religion. This gives them a separate identity from those religious interests which might not always represent their interests in public disputes, but, at the same time, can make their interests easier to overlook when formal authorities make decisions affecting them.

As much as these Baptists might like to avoid the influences of metropolitan society, they are increasingly unable to do so. Many have migrated to industrial areas and have sometimes found themselves in typical confrontations occurring when conservative Protestant migrants encounter the bewildering modernity of metropolitan life. In other cases modern standards or wider social conflicts have come to them, whether through coal mining and the labor strife that often plagues it, or through industrialization of much of the rural South. In a few of these Baptists' core areas, agriculture still employs as many as one in ten workers, but even here, manufacturing now dominates the local economy. With these economic changes have come many social and economic upheavals, creating tensions not easily resolved between economic concerns and cultural concerns.

Such confrontations are heightened when expanding industrialism encounters a population that still likes to view itself as comprising self-sufficient freeholders. Even those still farming face increasing industrialism and the expanding federal and state bureaucracy that accompanies it. Conversion to a wage economy often brings conflict with the values of a community that still likes to view itself as self-sufficient but faces pressures from an expanding industrial society, its bureaucracy, and a persisting agricultural ethos.

These Baptists often find themselves on the margins of both the society and the economy. There they are within reach of cosmopolitan authority, but they have no control over that authority. In such circumstances, the appeal of a church directed by the laity and for its interests is heightened.

Stable Growth at Home but Losses through Migration. Since CCMUS 1990 is the only county-level tabulation of these groups ever completed, growth patterns are difficult to discern. What limited indicators there are show that these groups have had stable, proportional growth within their areas. The reader will remember, however, that many of these areas have lost population or have had many fluctuations in population or have not kept up with national population growth.

Because of these trends in the total population and because of the loss of members to areas without communing churches, it is likely that these groups have not kept up with national population growth. But there is no evidence indicating any drastic loss of membership over the years. What one sees instead are churches that can maintain their presence in their home areas.[94] They can sometimes extend their influence to places where out-migration is most concentrated, although sometimes their influence also diminishes in the face of encroaching exurban development.

THEOLOGY AND LOCAL NEEDS

The individual Baptist congregations discussed in this work assume local religious authority to meet local challenges or conditions, particularly those caused by external sources. They had, for example, many secular grounds for developing an antimission theology. They could have done so because they did not want to see their scarce economic resources going elsewhere, at the beck and call of an external authority, when these resources were needed at home. They could have done so because they saw firsthand how such monies were misspent, particularly in misguided efforts to "convert" them. They could have done so because they resented outside religious authority wrapped up in outside economic and political power. All these concerns, in fact, seem to have played a role in the development of their antimission theology. The larger point is that they were able to use their religion to develop a religious authority to justify locally needed practice, that of keeping charitable monies under their control and within their communities.

We can view their emphasis on traditional roles for each sex in the same way. Such emphasis makes great sense in a frontier or a low-income rural society needing to discipline males to provide for households. The codes of behavior for each sex have changed somewhat as secular circumstances permitting new roles for both sexes have changed.

I do not mean to say that these Baptists' theology changes exactly as their social and economic circumstances do. I agree with Richard Niebuhr that a purely economic, political, or sociological interpretation of this theology would be wrong-headed. It would also be inaccurate. There have been some declining emphases on the most traditional elements of behavioral codes for each sex, but these have not changed as quickly as social standards or economic circumstances. Tension between tradition and changing circumstances limits the range of these groups' theological adaptability.

Yet, as Niebuhr also writes, we cannot ignore the economic, political, and sociological conditions of these Baptists. Their theology has changed more readily in response to changing local needs than any external, formal, systematic theology would have changed it. These Baptists have been able to use their religion as a means of justifying or sheltering practices that have aided transition to modern life. This local use of religion is not as readily available in more formal church bureaucracies.

In reviewing the specific issues that animate "Bible-based" Protestant politics, we have seen a recurring theme of biblical interpretation that helps meet familial and economic needs. Yet at some point these needs force a contradiction. The cultural tradition assisting the family in protecting itself from the outside world also serves to reduce these churches' political actions in the secular world. The contradiction becomes explicit in the politics these Baptists practice in secular organizations. When the secular organizations are most subject to local control of these Baptists, when such organizations help these Baptists bring about limited, specific goals that all unequivocally desire, and when they do not conflict with other, larger goals these Baptists most desire, then these Baptists can use such organizations to great effect. When, however, their concern for tradition contradicts the use of tradition to validate economic struggle, the limits and possibilities of their politics appear in more stark relief. The story of labor unions among them points to the strengths of using secular organizations in their politics, while the story of a movement seeking more diffuse goals of "reform" government shows the limits.

CHAPTER 3

The Strengths of Adaptation for Labor: Organized Labor and Traditional Protestantism

Nearly all analyses of "Bible-based" Protestant populations assume that they neither have nor desire social participation outside the church. Labor unions, however, appear to be a particularly popular and powerful means of secular political participation by the sectarians in this study. Unions direct their politics in unexpected ways.

To be sure, on many issues even the labor union members among these Baptists have profoundly conservative attitudes. Furthermore, secular organizations with conservative objectives influence them just as liberal labor unions have. I interviewed, for example, two preachers who both express great antagonism toward labor unions. This distaste stems not from any doctrinal opposition to labor unions in general but from their common experiences as industrial superintendents and their negotiations with unions, as well as from their experience as local civic leaders trying to attract business to the cheap labor in their regions.

Yet there are several reasons to focus on labor unions in examining the politics of secularism among this population. First, while there are few systematic analyses of labor union influences on "Bible-based" Protestants, there is evidence, dating back nearly two centuries and across different nations, of the influence of organized labor on such populations. Second, the apparent liberalizing influence of labor unions upon their members, in contrast to the conservatism assumed to be dominant among these groups, underscores the effects of a secular organization, rather than the church, as the social space for politics. Third, labor unions are a popular means of social participation by these Baptists, and these sects occupy some of the few areas where labor unions and biblically oriented Protestantism both flourish.

Nearly from the very origins of the industrial age, labor unions have had support among biblically oriented Protestants, particularly those who shape their religion to serve as a resource in acting for their own interests and against those of ecclesiastical establishments controlled by hostile economic powers. Edward Thompson documents the contribution of Methodism in England to the "chiliasm of despair," but he also writes of the development of working-class radicalism among many Methodist laborers, including lay preachers.[1] Although Thompson says Methodists were rarely initiators of working-class politics, they were present in many local parts of the labor movement.[2] Early Methodism made a twofold contribution to the trade union movement, providing it with examples of how to organize locally and nationally as well as how to make the labor movement self-supporting financially.[3] It taught some Methodist workers how "to unite in the face of exploitation or oppression [as] almost an instinctual response."[4] These workers soon learned how to interpret the Bible to support their cause, taking an oath based on Ezekiel's exhortations to "exalt him that is low, and abase him that is high," and justifying their rebellion against church leaders by charging "their vine is the vine of Sodom, and the fields of Gomorrah."[5] Biblical language had radical uses in the hands of English Methodists. This was because their religion "was not preached *at*, but *by*, the poor . . . the local preachers made the church their own . . . for this reason these sects contributed . . . directly to the later history of trade unionism [emphases in original]."[6]

William Jennings Bryan was among the first fundamentalists to support organized labor in the United States. This support continued to his last days. In the last issue of *The Commoner*, Bryan denounced a Supreme Court invalidation of a federal minimum wage law for women as "another Dred Scott decision."[7] Less than a year before his death, he told the convention of the Brotherhood of Locomotive Engineers that "something is fundamentally wrong when the most deserving people and those who work the hardest get the least and those who work the least get the most out of the system. . . . In my opinion, if it were not for organization among the laboring men, the wage earners of this country would be reduced to the position of serfs."[8]

J. Frank Norris, a Southern Baptist preacher of Fort Worth and one of the leading fundamentalist churchmen of the early twentieth century, also backed the cause of labor. He defended unions of the 1920s against charges that they were "anarchistic bomb-throwers," insisting that "the best security against anarchy would be precisely an organized labor force."[9] His labor advocacy was in support for those institutions most dear to fundamentalists. He believed the low wages of the years following World War I led to the destruction of families.[10] The work of labor unions to raise wages provided, in Norris's view, stability to the worker, his family, his church, and his nation.[11] Others of the time also linked fundamentalist establishments with the concerns of organized labor. One of the most influential Baptist preachers in Alabama, for example, identified poverty, child labor, and labor strife as among the most serious problems facing Christianity in the Heart of Dixie.[12]

The links between biblically oriented Protestantism and organized labor in the South, however, would become more tenuous. This was due in part to the increasing affluence of many adherents and the decline of the lay ministry. According to J. Wayne Flynt, southern institutional religion became a "hindrance to unionism" when

> Baptist, Methodist, and Presbyterian laymen entered the middle class [and] discarded the concerns that made many of them reformers. . . . Ministers became better educated, and fewer of them were bivocational, earning a living by farming, in mill or mine, while also pastoring a church. The deacons, stewards, and elders who governed congregations were drawn from the most successful parishioners and dampened the enthusiasm of the occasional minister whose social consciousness challenged the economic order. Within denominations, class differences persisted between poor congregations in mill-town and middle-class "uptown churches." Middle-class and affluent evangelicals were uncomfortable around their lint-head brethren. People in the mill churches felt equally uneasy in meetings with their coreligionists and sometimes resented middle-class dominance of associational and district affairs.[13]

The tension between upwardly mobile and lower class adherents of biblically oriented Protestantism over labor unions is most evident in Liston Pope's analysis of labor strife in Gastonia, North Carolina. The middling churches, or those with middle-class aspirations but lacking middle-class members, were co-opted by their benefactors and unable or unwilling to support those seeking to organize Gastonia mill workers. Pope suggests the "uptown churches" to which the mill owners belonged had more independence than the mill churches, supported by mill owners, to which workers belonged.[14] The diversity of the memberships and financial supporters of the affluent uptown churches gave those congregations a potential for independence in social politics that the mill churches never had. The mill churches, in their middle-class aspirations, were dependent upon the financial well-being of the mills. This dependence "largely circumscribe[d] all possibility for independent action by the [mill] church[es] or [their] minister[s]."[15] Their ministers could not take action for their members that would conflict with the interests of mill management, lest they threaten their own well-being.

There were Gastonia mill churches not circumscribed by middle-class aspirations. These were more sectarian and "fundamentalist" and, Pope claims, more ambiguous in their views on unionization and other volatile issues.[16] These churches were not the focus of Pope's work, but analyzing their characteristics helps present a complete picture of biblically oriented Protestantism and labor unions. Pope concedes that the sectarian preachers were "close to those most disadvantaged" in Gastonia and were "in better position to see the need for changes."[17] Yet he also says the sectarians were "otherworldly," leading them to acquiesce in the economic status quo.[18]

Pope's points reflect those of Friedrich Engels on the ambiguities and difficulties of using the Bible continually for economic reform. Engels writes: "Luther had put a powerful weapon into the hands of the plebeian movement by translating the Bible. . . . The peasants had made extensive use of this instrument against the princes, the nobility, and the clergy. Now Luther turned it against them, extracting from the Bible a real hymn to God-ordained authorities such as no bootlicker of absolute monarchy had ever been able to achieve. . . . Not the peasant revolt alone, but Luther's own mutiny against ecclesiastical and secular authority was thereby disavowed. . . ."[19]

Engels' point is one with which Pope would concur, if not as acidly. The Bible could have revolutionary implications in labor strife, particularly among those most emphasizing it in their faith. Those interpreting it locally can use it to combat external powers arrayed against them. As sectarian adherents become more successful in the world, however, religious leaders betray, either deliberately or inadvertently, the cause of poorer adherents. The Bible becomes corrupted and used for ends opposite to those for which it is first used in political and economic struggle. This assumes a sectarian spirit cannot persist for long, and that sectarian leaders inexorably become corrupted through attraction to growing ecclesiastical and secular authority.

Both sectarians in Gastonia and those I study provide a more complicated picture. They have continued to use the Bible in seeking religious authority because they have no other sources of power. They are unaffected by the attractions of ecclesiastical authority.

In Gastonia, the full influence of sectarianism that Pope documents appears more complicated than he always acknowledges. As the sectarians were otherworldly, they did not have middle-class aspirations. With no need for middle-class church accouterments, they had no need for the support of mill management. With no need for the support of mill management, they could foster attitudes that were more supportive of their congregations of mill workers than those fostered by mill churches of more middling status and middle-class aspirations. The fervor of the sectarian congregations led their members to tithe greater amounts than members of other mill churches, further strengthening their independence.[20] Pope claims that "on the whole" the sectarians were "normally against unionization," but he also observes that "they expressly stipulate[d] that members may join a union if necessity demands but must not take part in 'labor troubles.'"[21] Pope says that some sectarian congregations supported the union effort, that their "members and ministers . . . afforded a nucleus for labor organization," and that they "offered almost the only religious sanction accorded to strikers in Gastonia."[22]

Support for unions surfaces among more established "Bible-based" Protestant churches when they are given reason to recall humble economic origins. In the midst of the massive CIO organizing drives of the late 1930s, the Southern Baptist Convention reaffirmed support for organized labor by adopting a resolution favoring collective bargaining.[23] Such actions provide highly visible counterweights to other establishments of this broad tradition emphasizing that adherents should "be ye not unequally yoked together with unbelievers" through labor unions.[24]

No one offers a general approach to the relationship between labor unions and "Bible-based" Protestantism, but the contours of such a theory are evident.[25] This religion has often supported organized labor. This support has included local adaptations of theology to local needs as well as development of leadership and organizational skills and resources through the churches. The elites of this religion have also supported the labor movement, particularly when unions are seen as supporting institutions, such as the family and the church, which are dear to them. Their opposition to labor unions, however, has readily arisen when labor unions are seen as a threat to middle-class church aspirations.

Labor Politics and Baptist Sectarians of the Upper South

None of the sects in this study now oppose labor unions on doctrinal grounds. The question of labor unions and doctrine regarding them has split them in the past. Labor union members among these Baptists differ in how they will support their unions. These sects once debated labor unions along with "benevolent societies" and "secret orders" (e.g., Masonic orders). These debates were usually resolved in favor of the fraternal organizations, with labor unions gaining support shortly thereafter. Fraternal societies and labor unions won support when they were seen as self-help organizations.

Occasionally sectarians drag their churches along in support of labor unions. Some churches realized their members had all become labor union members or supporters and reversed their previous opposition to labor unions. Some Pentecostal churches of the central Appalachian coal belt, for example, completely reversed their anti-union teachings when most of their lay ministers became union members in the organization drives of the 1930s.[26] Within these churches, support for unions most often develops from the grassroots. The fact that government of such churches is often "simple, individualistic, and highly adaptable to the community" helps foster such support.[27]

An exception to accommodation of labor unions among the sects I study was the Kyova Association of (Old) Regular Baptists, which not only continually prohibited secret societies, but also forbade labor union membership. Kyova shunned all who accepted labor unions and saw its number of churches and members wither.[28] Today Old Regular Baptists cite other doctrinal disputes for differences with Kyova.[29] These differences appear real, but the decline of Kyova is persuasive testimony to the effects of working against the perceived economic interests of coal belt adherents.

Today these sects rarely question labor unions, benevolent societies, or "secret orders." One preacher described the change to me:

Years ago, this was something the brethren would split over. Secret orders was what it was, and unions was the same way. Then with all of the coal industry coming in here, the argument over unions soon faded out and it was all turned to the Masons. You never heard the union anymore other than when those that aren't a part of the union would say we're paying more attention to the Masons than we are to the unions, but that is the only time it is ever mentioned. But even on the Masons, well, one of the fellows stood up a few years ago at the association meeting and talked about withdrawing from anyone who belongs to the Masons. [His motion] died for lack of a second, but I guess it still is an issue with some.

There is a wide variety of opinions on labor unions held by those among these Baptists who are not labor union members. None dispute the right of their coreligionists to join unions, though they may disagree about the goals and good of organized labor. Their attitudes are often those of pragmatic church politics. Those who are in areas without a viable labor presence see no need to kick a phantom. Those in areas that are heavily unionized recognize the futility in opposing them. One preacher in the coal belt, discussing his neutrality on labor unions, told me that it would be futile for any preacher there to seek a sympathetic audience for an anti-union theology. Those who do not belong to unions simply do not see them as posing a religious question.

Those who belong to labor unions support them. None question the economic need or religious justification for labor unions. None appear forced along for a ride on organized labor because of union shop rules. They believe their union is necessary. There is variation in how much union membership affects other elements of their social and political life. It is this variation, and not a question of whether unions are too "worldly," or permitted by religion, that indicates the possibilities and limitations of a "Bible-based" Protestant politics of organized labor or secular organizations.

I consider labor union members among these Baptists in three groups. Those in the *first* group, while supporting their unions, are less likely to participate in militant union activity or to engage in broader union politics. Two examples are the Duck River Baptist preacher of northern Alabama mentioned in the introduction of this work and a United Baptist preacher and lifelong resident of an area now part of the exurban fringe of Atlanta.

The Duck River Baptist, an industrial mechanic in his late thirties, joined his local in a union shop. He finds labor unions to have both biblical and economic justifications. He explained to me, "I think unions are called for in the Bible when King Solomon joined the temple. Labor unions have done a lot of things I don't agree with, and the people I work with know I don't agree with those things and I won't take part in them. But the labor union is also the best thing to ever happen to a man who has to work on a job like mine and who has to provide for his family by working at a place like I do."

After reading the Old Testament accounts of the construction of the temple several times, the reader may wonder, as I do, exactly how Solomon's orders for temple construction called for labor unions. Such puzzlement misses the point. This preacher could have selected other biblical passages to justify labor unions.[30] The real point is that, free as he is to shape a Bible-based religion to meet local needs and circumstances, he is able to find on his own religious justification and authority for what he says is a needed organization for the economic well-being of his church members and himself.

His attitude toward the broader mission of his union reflects ambivalence over both its broader goals and his perceived need to be free from worldly conflicts and entanglements. This is evident in his statements about his union, its politics, and so-called right-to-work laws. When asked about what issues he doesn't agree with the union, he responds, "in politics, and in being mean to people, and in forcing them to belong to the union. I don't agree with that. But I think if you're going to work in a place and enjoy what the union has worked for, you should support what it's done. But as far as being mean to people and shooting through their houses and threatening their family, I don't buy any part of that."

His aversion to overt conflict stretches to both sides of the divide between labor and management. He says he "wouldn't take a union officer's job because I'm a man of God. I need to stay more or less neutral." He claims to have turned down a job as foreman which would have brought him across the divide. He explains:

> The man said, "We want you for a foreman." I said, "You don't need me." He asked why. I said, "If I got me a man working out here and it don't matter whether I like him or not, if you come to me and tell me I've got to drive him away from his job and fire him, I've got two choices. I've either

got to do that or leave myself, right?" He said, "Yeah, that's right." I said, "That's why you don't need me, because I couldn't do that. If that man's done a good job, I can't just fire him for no reason." He said, "Well, I can guarantee that hasn't happened since I've been a foreman." I said, "Can you guarantee it won't happen to me?" He said no, and I said, "That's why I don't want this foreman's job." As far as having a set of codes that says do this or don't do that, I can take a foreman's job as far as the church goes. And there's probably even some people who would say, "Well, you're moving up in the world, you're a foreman now," and such as that. But in my heart I wouldn't feel right about it.

Because his church does not have "a set of rules that says do this or don't do that" in the workplace, this preacher would encourage others of his congregation to take a foreman's job or a union officer's position. He says, "If I had a good, solid, sound, faithful church member that had an opportunity to take a union officer's job, I'd like to see him get it, because I feel like he'd convey what he's been taught in the church to the job. In other words, that he would take some of God's love to the union or the company or whatever he might do. But for myself, it would be wrong for me to do it because it would take the time that I should be devoting to God."

The United Baptist preacher in north Georgia is more clear, if still restrained, about his commitment to the union and how he would support it. A retired laborer from a local aircraft plant, he would take some material steps in support of the union, but he avoided overt conflict in which it might be engaged. He worked in an "open" shop, but says he joined the union "because I wanted to." He says, "There's a few preachers that would be opposed to it," but he finds no religious sanctions against unions. Rather, he finds secular justifications for them. He told me; "I feel like that they have done more to help the working man than about anything. They're not the best outfit, but they've done more to raise the wages of everybody . . . back in the thirties and the forties, if it hadn't been for the coal miners and John Lewis, we wouldn't have no decent wages yet. They raised the wages of everybody."

Still, as he says, "I never did take a big part in it," because the union could put him in too much overt conflict. He explains, "I wouldn't walk a picket line. I told them that down there. We were on strike three times. I went down there . . . when we were on strike, but I didn't feel it was the proper place for me, to be out on the street walking the picket lines, and I wouldn't. It just doesn't look like a place for a preacher. I just think if something comes up, and maybe you wouldn't have anything to do with it, but you could bring shame on the church. I don't feel like doing anything that could bring shame on the church." He would aid the strike materially. He cooked for those who walked the picket line and obtained from the local sheriff hogs to slaughter and feed the strikers.

Not surprisingly, given his reluctance to join in militant union activity, he does not take a great part in politics. He says, "I vote, and I believe a man ought to vote. . . . I think we ought to take part . . . but as far as getting out and politicking . . . that's getting out too far for somebody like me." Where he sees direct benefit coming to him from union participation, he justifies it. But where it would lead to open conflict, or a situation that would inhibit his ministry to all God's children—who, after all, can include managers and strike breakers—then he follows what he regards as his higher calling.

A *second* group of labor union members participates more actively in their unions, including serving as union officers. Those in this group, however, have many of the same attitudes as the two preachers quoted above, including a reluctance to carry liberal labor politics beyond the workplace.

An eastern Kentucky preacher shows to what extent asceticism can bend to support worldly activities. Of those I interviewed, he is among the most conservative and otherworldly in his religion. His association prohibits musical instruments and enforces a strict dress code for both women and men, prohibiting long hair and short pants for men. The severity with which his association follows these rules has caused it to break fellowship with all its previous correspondents, which it saw as too lenient in faith and practice. Despite his otherworldly religion, this preacher (now retired) was in a carpenters' union and a pipefitters' union. He served as an officer in both and says his interpretation of his faith does not restrict such work. He does not, however, tolerate much broader activity, and says members of his church should not pursue political office or partisan politics beyond voting.

An Indiana preacher, who is an eastern Kentucky native and is more aggressive in his faith, favoring evangelization efforts these churches typically shun, saw his union activity as an opportunity to evangelize in a new setting. Describing his stint as a shop steward, he told me:

I thought it was real refreshing. I looked at it like a pastorship. There's always been hotheads who think the company's always wrong or the union's always wrong. I remember these two hotheads in particular. The first procedure was to get the man and the foreman to settle their differences. These two didn't even want to do step one. The company said, "We can't ever get nowhere with your people." I said, "Wait a minute, I didn't take this step to be ornery or mean or contrary." We did step one, and when it had to go to the second step, once a man started to use profanity, I said, "Let's calm down and let's discuss this." The men quit bringing foolish grievances to me, and most of the time things were worked out with a few minutes of conversation. Both the company and the union said they appreciated me. They said they could see how things could work out. So why not a minister or a Christian in that office? I'm sure if it came to a point where I had to be contrary to being a minister or a Christian I wouldn't do it. But I had success with it. I had no problem with it and it worked real good. I actually enjoyed it. It was an opportunity to witness to my faith. We've got this opinion that unions and companies have to hate each other to be independent or effective, but I don't think that's what unions are, or what companies are.

An Ohio preacher and a Virginia preacher show how union membership and labor politics pull them one way and cultural concerns grounded in their religion pull them another. The Ohioan, a native of eastern Kentucky, moved north to work in an automobile assembly plant and was active in his United Auto Workers local throughout his career. To him, the need for labor unions is unquestioned. Without them, he said to me, all workers would be paid "slave wages." At the same time, he expresses many conservative values, particularly in opposition to abortion rights and gay rights. The tension between his cultural conservatism and liberal labor politics, combined with the current alignments of the major parties that fail to match his stands on both sets of issues, keeps him from broader political activity. He will not, however, discourage members of his congregation from pursuing broader politics, including partisan campaign work for either party.

The Virginian is a member of an electricians' union. He frets that the declining rate of union membership is one of the biggest economic challenges confronting the nation. He explained his opinions and those of his association on organized labor to me:

> As a young electrician, I became a member of the International Brotherhood of Electrical Workers, and I still have an active membership in that union today. So I don't have a problem with organized labor. As far as the issue of trying to dictate whether a person can belong to a union or not, our association has never had any restrictions or anything like that, because in this immediate area, and also in some of the other states, like up in Kentucky and Indiana, we've had a lot of members of the church who are members of the various unions. One in particular is the United Mine Workers, because we have a lot of members who are coal miners.... I was never forced into the union. I didn't have to join it. It was just a matter of personal preference and also because I feel like organized labor has made a great improvement in industry just like the church has made a big improvement in the world. I've always believed in checks and balances in government. The same thing is true in labor and management. You need some kind of organization to help the laborer. Otherwise you come down to where we're at now, about fourteen percent of the nation is organized, but we've never had as much turmoil in the labor industry since the turn of the century as we're having now. So that shows unions did a good job, even though everything has its corruption in it. I certainly endorse organized labor myself, and I know we have many people in our association that endorse organized labor.

His support of liberal labor politics does not go far beyond this endorsement. This is most clear when he discusses Clinton and his policies on gay rights: "Certainly I disagreed with some of his appointments and some of his views on homosexuality. The Bible has always, and it always has and always will, condemned homosexuality, and you cannot change it in my viewpoint. It has never promoted homosexuality to be something that God honors. He always dishonors it and always had judgment for it. And for people to try to open that up to the general public, they're just asking for the judgment of God, in my viewpoint."

This preacher is not totally committed to social or economic change in the political world. Discussing his ambitions for his children, for example, he joked, "It'd be nice to have a son that was a Congressman or even a President. But if God wanted him to preach, I'd rather he followed the leadership of God as to have one of those piddling little jobs." In the more immediate realm, he said members of his church would not picket abortion clinics or participate in any demonstrations that could bring reproach upon them. It is wrong to claim that organized labor is what keeps him from wanting his children or members of his church to be militant in the pursuit of culturally traditional politics, but it is also clear that his cultural conservatism will not extinguish the influences of organized labor on his economic politics.

A *third* group of labor union members largely ignores the cultural traditionalism of its religion in pursuing broader liberal politics. This group represents those for whom secular organizations most completely define social and political attitudes and participation.

The Old Regular Baptist preacher from southwestern Virginia whom I mention in the introduction of this work best represents this group. A retired railroad maintenance worker, he says that "in order to work and raise my family, I needed the protection of the A. F. of L. I'm still a member, and I still pay dues." He is not oblivious to his fellow Baptists' cultural concerns, but he feels as entitled as they are to interpret their common religion to individual circumstances. He says that he once received a letter "from an old preacher talking about unions and the mark of the beast and all that," but he disregarded it because it represented just "the opinion of one man, not the opinion of me."

He overlooks some cultural issues in order to preserve the harmony of his broadly liberal attitudes. He opposes school prayer because he does not "think we ought to allow the school system to determine the Baptist faith and order." Granted, this stance reflects traditional Baptist desires for separation of church and state, which have been drowned out in the cacophony of modern cultural politics. Yet the lengths this preacher will go to defend Democratic politicians, including those with whom he disagrees about abortion or gay rights, would surprise anyone who is familiar with these Baptists' services. At one service, he told me, he interrupted "an old preacher hollering about abortion, gays, and all this stuff" by saying, "Brother, I don't want to hear a thing. I don't want to hear it now. There's people here that voted for Bill Clinton.[31] Don't get that started. I don't want to hear it. There's no place for it in this church, about whether in politics it's right to do this and wrong to do that and so on and so forth."

This preacher does not seek directly to convert others to his Democratic political faith. He identifies many Republicans in his church who are his friends and appears to have their votes when he is annually re-elected association moderator. For him, the church is not the sphere for partisan politics. Rather, its members are free to pursue Democratic, Republican, or other politics outside its walls.

For some in this third group, the wall separating the church from politics is permeable, allowing complex social identities. Rather than believing they have one identity in church and another in the secular world, they blend these in a social identity with differing emphases, including emphases far different than those stressed by the modern religious right. For example, there is the eastern Kentucky preacher who "lectured the state police with fervor during the Brookside strike in Harlan County for mistreating the women on the picket lines."[32] Those of our first group of labor union supporters, much less economic conservatives on the religious right, would not seek such confrontation. It came easily for a man who could "state with a profound certitude, 'I'm three things: I'm a Christian, I'm a Baptist, and I'm a union man.'"[33]

The extent to which these sectarians feel certitude in being union men is the extent to which their secular politics overrides cultural concerns of their religion, or the extent to which they will adjust both their labor politics and their religious attitudes to accommodate each other. Such certitude or belief that union concerns form either a strictly separate or mutually reinforcing sphere with religious concerns varies among them. Not all union members feel that their labor politics can override their cultural concerns. It is clear, however, that labor politics greatly influence labor union members among these Baptists. There is no discernible theological antipathy toward labor unions. All leave union membership to individual conscience. It is also clear that labor unions, in particular, and secular organizations, in general, can affect the politics of such Baptists beyond how the church itself can affect them.

Church-Sect Polarity Reversed in a Local Union Movement

In an exceptional case, not only can these Baptists find and act on religious justification for labor unions, they do so in opposition to hierarchical churches that falter in supporting the labor movement. The story of a recent small East Tennessee organizing campaign illustrates this.[34]

The campaign to organize a mine of Colquest Energy, Inc., in Clairfield, Tennessee, did not attract attention similar to that given other, larger coal strikes of the time, such as the Pittston strike of 1989 or the national coal strike of 1993. What it lacked in national notoriety it made up for in local venom. The organization campaign began following the 1990 firing of a miner who had missed five months of work while recovering from a back injury suffered in a mine accident. After five months of recuperation, he returned to work, but was terminated for having missed more than thirty days of work, violating a rule of which he said he had been unaware.[35] The incident helped the United Mine Workers of America (UMW) mount a campaign for the right to represent workers at the mine, which it won by a thirty-nine to thirty vote.[36]

Colquest refused to recognize the UMW victory and, in a bid to rout the union, terminated nineteen union supporters.[37] The move backfired. The UMW struck the mine on 1 October 1990 and all miners walked off the job in support. Workers at neighboring facilities of Four Leaf Coal Company and Kopper-Glo Fuel, Inc., also walked off their jobs, halting all mining in the area.

The relationship between the three companies is complex and was a point of dispute not only between the UMW and Colquest but also between church leaders with differing perspectives on the strike.[38] Four Leaf and Colquest leased their lands from Kopper-Glo and sold their coal exclusively to Kopper-Glo. William Dippel of Morgantown, West Virginia, owned Kopper-Glo. Norval Dippel, William's brother, was president of Four Leaf. Kore Q. Chedester III, who ran Colquest, is the son of Kore Q. Chedester II, William Dippel's brother-in-law. In addition, Kore Q. Chedester II was listed in public records as a registered agent for Kopper-Glo.

Four Leaf and Kopper-Glo said the lease and sale contracts were "arm's length transactions" and that family ties were immaterial to whether the corporations were separate entities.[39] Four Leaf therefore sued the UMW for engaging in an illegal secondary boycott. Neither the National Labor Relations Board (NLRB) nor the federal court of appeals, however, would hear the Four Leaf complaint, instead recognizing the UMW strike as one against "allied companies" rather than as a strike coupled with an illegal secondary boycott.[40]

Despite other NLRB findings and lower court rulings against Colquest on charges by the UMW of unfair labor practices, the company steadfastly refused to bargain. One of the owners, in a conversation with a mainline church leader offering to mediate the dispute, said the coal market at the time was so weak it may have been just as well that the mines were shut. Even were the market robust, the owners insisted they could not "afford a union."[41]

While the owners pursued appeals to higher courts, the miners vowed to wait them out. One told a local newspaper, nearly eleven months into the strike, "They still think they can wait us out. They need to talk to some of the folks at Decker, where poplar trees grew up in the mine entry before the strike ended."[42] (Decker, Montana, was the site of a long strike in the 1970s where the UMW won the right to organize western mines.)

As the Colquest strike continued, the workers sought to shore up public support in several ways. They got their Congressional delegation, including both Tennessee senators and the representative for the area, to ask the Tennessee Valley Authority (TVA) to review its contract with Kopper-Glo in light of the strike.[43] The halt in mining operations placed Campbell and Claiborne Counties, two of the poorest in Tennessee, and their local governments under great economic stress.[44] In response, the miners organized repair crews for public school buildings in Campbell County, saving the county roughly $15,000.[45] Just how badly this money was needed was underscored in late October 1991, nearly thirteen months after the strike started, when Campbell County ran out of money to operate its school buses, which had brought 70 percent of students to class.[46]

Finally, the workers sought support from area churches. An organizer for the UMW told me that miners can always expect help from coal belt churches. He said:

> It was only natural for the ministers and deacons to support us, because they're simply supporting their parishioners. Without the union, those counties are very, very depressed. We're the only thing that can elevate the standings of the communities. Not just the workers know that, but the merchants, too. If they're making minimum wage in the mines, they can't buy anything elsewhere. You can't pass the collection plate around and expect the church to thrive if the parishioners aren't making any money. They've got to be economic realists like everybody else.

His reasoning may read like union boilerplate, but it resonates among those who have stepped forward to support the UMW. Deborah Vansau McCauley notes that "mountain churches played one of the central roles in organizing coal miners during the region's labor struggles throughout the labor century," providing labor leaders from among their preachers and meeting places in local church houses.[47]

For many preachers supporting the Colquest strike, the question was not one of supporting members of their church as much as continuing a struggle in which they had been involved. One United Baptist supporting the Colquest workers was a retired miner who told me he was "always for the union. There were a lot of people I knew in the strike, and I was for them, but I've always been for the union." His support was not based on any specific religious doctrine, but, he says, because "I was raised in the union. I've always supported the union. I believed in the union, because it can be good for all men. That's what it was set up for, to help all the members. There ain't nothing that beats the union if it's run right. If the coal company wants to be dirty, the union keeps them right."

While he preferred to work in union mines, he would work nonunion mines "when I couldn't get a union job." He is not unqualified in his support for the union, claiming that some workers with union protection "would just lay around and hurt the company. They would load two cars a day and get their travel time and call it a day, and that's not right. It would hurt the union and hurt the coal company. Your union is only as strong as you make it. Your union is just like a church. If you don't work to build the church or the union, you're not doing any good."

His broader politics are even more pointed than those of the preacher who defended women on the Brookside picket line. He says, "There's three things I've always been—a union man, a Democrat, and a Baptist. My step-dad said if you weren't all that, you weren't anything. The way I see it, the Democrat is for the working man, and the Republican is for the rich man."

Another United Baptist preacher with fewer ties to the UMW—while a miner, he never worked a UMW mine—still found personal reasons to support the strike. He had suffered the same experience as the fired Colquest miner, injuring his back on the job and then being fired upon his return to work. He won a $13,000 settlement, but he is still bitter over the incident. He told me the Colquest incident showed coal companies "have been bad for that, and they still are." The back injury ended his work in the mines. After a painful stint with a bridge construction firm, his primary source of income today is disability benefits.

Within his church he leaves to individuals decisions on union membership and support. He knows the difficulties of finding union work. He was able to find work only in nonunion mines or those represented by the Southern Labor Union, which is regarded as a company union started only to halt the advance of the UMW. Although his church, like most others, had little money, church members cooked food for the miners. Those that could gave money to help particularly destitute strikers. Other preachers held services for miners on the picket lines; some gave sermons in support of the local UMW struggle.

The strikers sought more visible support from the churches. They received it in a full-page advertisement in area newspapers, including the *Knoxville News-Sentinel,* the daily newspaper with the largest circulation in East Tennessee, and the third-highest circulation in the state.[48]

The ad, an open letter to the owners of Colquest, Four Leaf, and Kopper-Glo, signed by more than sixty area clergy, ran nearly thirteen months after the strike began. It was remarkable for three reasons. First, while both the Catholic and Episcopalian bishops of Knoxville signed it, most signatories were from Protestant churches outside the mainline of Anglicanism, Lutheranism, Methodism, and Presbyterianism.[49] In addition to several from the sects examined in this study, signatures typically came from pastors of such local churches as Free Will Baptist, Way of Holiness, and Church of God of the Mountain Assembly.

Second, the ad combined biblical and theological imperatives in asking the owners to recognize the union and open negotiations. Sectarian Protestants, the Protestant mainline, and the Catholic Church had joined in an alliance for labor of a type rarely seen or publicized. Claiming "God Calls on Us to Speak on Behalf of the Striking Miners," the ad read, in part:

> Our vocation demands that we be sensitive to the call of God as we hear it in the voices of the powerless and those in need. We are deeply concerned about the ongoing dispute between your companies and the United Mine Workers of America. In light of this, with the Bible as our common ground, and in accordance with our respective traditions, we feel compelled to cry out on behalf of the people most adversely affected

by this dispute. The summons by the Hebrew prophets to do justice haunts us, as do the words of Jesus: "As you have done it to the least of these you have done it to me." After considerable thought and prayer, we believe that God calls on us to speak on behalf of the striking miners of Colquest Energy, Four Leaf Coal Co., and Kopper-Glo Fuel. We are deeply concerned about the fact that the National Labor Relations Board has cited Colquest Energy for violating federal labor laws. We are further concerned that Colquest has chosen to ignore the NLRB's order to sit down with the union to negotiate a collective bargaining agreement and has instead sought to delay a resolution to the dispute. Efforts by your companies to take retribution against the coal miners—who, after all, work in very dangerous situations and have loyally made your companies profitable—for organizing a union are immoral, unlawful, and a violation of the Judeo-Christian ethic.

The third reason this open letter was remarkable, however, was the fragility of this alliance between sectarian, mainline Protestant, and Catholic clergy. Following publication of the ad, the UMW sought to publish a similar ad in the newspapers of the Morgantown, West Virginia, area, home to the owners of Kopper-Glo and Four Leaf. The union and some mainline clergy who signed the East Tennessee letter approached Catholic and mainline Protestant hierarchies in West Virginia about signing the Morgantown letter, but they met resistance.

"The Catholic bishop in Knoxville had been great," a UMW organizer who gathered signatures for both ads told me, but the "mainline bishops in West Virginia weren't great, including the Catholic bishop there. Kopper-Glo's owner was a member of the Reformed Church of the Latter Day Saints, and he was an active churchgoer in Morgantown. Some of the downtown churches in Morgantown didn't want to rock any boats, period, because he's tied into the business community and the chamber of commerce."

A mainline Protestant preacher who solicited signatures for both ads told me that the conflict over the Morgantown ad became one of "management churches versus worker churches." He gave credit to the son of the Kopper-Glo owner for the resistance of the West Virginia hierarchies, saying the Kopper-Glo owner "was pre-historic in terms of labor relations, but his son was smoother and went to work with good public relations on the ground.

So when we went in asking for help, they [church hierarchies] weren't going to give it."

The West Virginia hierarchies offered other reasons for refusing to sign the Morgantown ad.⁵⁰ They protested the tone of the Tennessee letter, but declined to draft a different one. Some protested they did not want to involve the clergy of their denominations in a labor dispute, a stand which left a mainline petitioner "theologically and morally bewildered."⁵¹ Others said the pressure on the Morgantown owner of Kopper-Glo was inappropriate, claiming the companies which the UMW struck were truly separate entities, despite the rulings of the NLRB, the federal courts, and the beliefs of Tennessee legislators intervening for the strikers. One mainline signatory of the Knoxville ad, claiming some Colquest lawyers said negotiations would never take place because of the intransigence of the Kopper-Glo owners, asked in exasperation, "Under which shell is the pea? In Knoxville, it is under the Morgantown shell. In Morgantown, they're convinced it is in Knoxville. It's not a very new game."⁵²

The Morgantown ad that was eventually published repeated verbatim the Tennessee letter. It had fewer than half the number of signatures the Knoxville ad had, and about half of these were from Catholic and mainline Protestant clergy.⁵³ None were from Catholic or Protestant hierarchies in West Virginia who had signed similar letters during more prominent UMW strikes, such as the 1989 Pittston strike. The only bishop to sign the Morgantown ad was an "Evangelical Christian" bishop of Fairmont, West Virginia. In the end, in symbolic church support for the UMW, the sectarians maintained support for the strikers where the more celebrated supporters of organized labor in Catholic and mainline Protestant hierarchies faltered.

The Colquest strike ultimately failed. The company terminated thirteen years of operations at the site rather than negotiate with the union.⁵⁴ The mines were sold to concerns outside the Dippel and Chedester families and later reopened with nonunion labor.

Yet on another level, as the Baptist preachers I interviewed pointed out, the strike had some success. It succeeded in organizing, maintaining, and solidifying the ties between these churches and their communities, as well as increasing the ability of these communities, with the help of their churches, to pursue their own interests in the face of hostile outside interests. The local was authorized by a thin margin, yet it never cracked under the pressure of the lengthening strike. Those supporting the strike maintained that it was needed as much for the dignity of the workers and their communities as for any immediate goals of the strike itself.

These sentiments were best summarized by one United Baptist preacher who told me that, without fighting for a union, "miners have no chance for anything." While he says Colquest "won the battle" of the strike by ultimately avoiding negotiations with the union, he is adamant that the workers needed to strike to keep their dignity in the economic war they often must wage. He argues that, without at least the threat of unionization, coal companies invariably and continually would "treat workers like dogs." He adds that from his perspective, the strike was not about wages, but about company callousness in firing a worker injured on the job. This echoes the claims of UMW negotiators, who also maintained that the strike was more about workers' dignity than about wages.[55] Indeed, the wage in the mine before the strike, while far below that of union scale prevalent at the time, did not draw any other comments from those I interviewed. All were more upset over personnel policies leading to the strike than they were over pay rates.

The Colquest workers did not win a union mine, but they did win the support of their communities and their churches. More specifically, they were able to command the support of local churches which, as laity, they controlled. These were "Bible-based" Protestant churches that, contrary to standing media images of sectarian "otherworldliness" or conservatism, went further in supporting a local labor movement than did more established churches more accustomed to being acclaimed as allies of the labor movement.

BROADER BOUNDARIES OF SECULAR ORGANIZATION POLITICS

Support from these Baptists for the local labor movement was due not only to the presence of miners in their congregations, but also among their clergy. These churches were miners' churches in every possible sense. Their sectarian characteristics included an ability to shape religion to aid local secular life and not have other, more distant authorities oppose them within church.

The sectarian nature of these groups is the key feature in their support for labor movements. Because they are sectarian, because they have few, if any, worldly aspirations for their churches, their members are free to shape their religion and its commands as they see fit. They are able to adapt their religion and its commands to local circumstances. Their religion, with its emphasis on local autonomy and authority to interpret the Bible, which they claim to be the sole guide for faith and practice, allows them to seek their own sources of religious authority when faced with those holding economic, political, or ecclesiastical power hostile to their interests.

In the mid-1990s, even in the midst of increasing speculation on the role of the religious right in fueling an ascendant conservative Republicanism, there is other evidence of liberal labor politics combining with sectarian religion that complements the evidence above. These churches are among the most prominent in southwestern Virginia, where Democrat Chuck Robb, with the backing of UMW president (and later AFL-CIO vice president) Rich Trumka, won large margins over Oliver North and his Christian Coalition supporters in Virginia's 1994 U.S. Senate election.[56] In the two southwestern Virginia counties of the Old Regular Baptist core, Buchanan and Dickenson, Robb won 56 percent of the vote, compared with the 46 percent he won statewide.

In Buchanan and Dickenson, those employed in mining make up 33 percent of all employed, and Old Regular Baptists make up 18 percent of enumerated church adherents, being outnumbered only by Southern Baptists. Analyzing individual voting behavior from raw aggregate voting statistics is, of course, treacherous, but at the least these statistics tell us that Old Regular Baptists, or any other similar biblically oriented church, did not spearhead a successful effort by the religious right to carry the area for North. Given the predominance of the Baptists I study and other similar churches in these two counties, as well as the large number of miners, it is likely safe to conclude that Robb carried a good number of "Bible-based" Protestant miners who voted for the economic interests advocated by Rich Trumka rather than for the cultural interests of Pat Robertson or Jerry Falwell.

A similar story of religion and labor politics appeared in Kentucky gubernatorial politics in recent years. These churches are among the most prominent in rural eastern Kentucky counties, where Democrat Paul Patton, with Trumka's backing, won large margins over Republican Larry Forgy in the Kentucky gubernatorial election of 1995, despite a Christian Coalition distribution of a half-million flyers for Forgy.[57] In the six eastern Kentucky counties of the Old Regular Baptist core, which include Patton's Pike County home, Patton won 73 percent of the vote, compared with the 51 percent he won statewide. He carried these counties by a margin of 24,606 votes, or more than two thousand votes above his statewide margin of 22,509. Of all workers in these counties, 23 percent comprise those who work in mining. Were it not for his support in these heavily unionized coal counties with large numbers of "Bible-based" Protestants, Patton would have lost the election. The story was nearly identical in the eleven eastern Kentucky counties of the United Baptist stronghold near the Big Sandy River valley, which the Old Regular Baptist core partially overlaps. In these counties, Patton won 69 percent of the vote, and those in mining account for 20 percent of all workers.

Again, it is treacherous to analyze individual voting behavior from aggregate election returns, but the least we can say is that biblically based churches in these regions, including those I study, did not spearhead a successful effort by the religious right to carry the region for Forgy. More likely, large numbers of "Bible-based" Protestant miners voted for the interests advocated by Rich Trumka rather than for the cultural interests of Forgy supporters on the religious right. This is all the more remarkable since Forgy's support of these churches' cultural interests went beyond the widely recognized cultural issues of the 1990s. In 1985, for example, he successfully represented clients seeking to overturn election results that had ended local prohibition in four counties, including counties in these sects' core areas.

What may be most remarkable is that when Patton's support declined in these areas, it was not because of his cultural politics, including involvement in an emotional, name-calling dispute over abortion rights, but because of his support for changes in workers' compensation laws that he pushed through early in his term over the objection of union coal miners. Subsequent Democratic primaries for county executives and state representatives saw several incumbents in these areas tied to the Patton initiatives suffering losses, with abortion politics drawing no mention in analyses of election returns from the area.[58]

The possibility for liberal politics based on labor unions or on some other cause varies tremendously among biblically oriented Protestants. It appears to vary particularly by the strength and configuration of sectarian characteristics and by the strength of cultural conservatism among them. Even among those Baptists presented here, social conservatism sometimes trumps economic liberalism at the ballot box, either through votes for socially and economically conservative candidates, or through a more general reluctance to engage in politics. Sectarian characteristics can work toward opposing political goals. "Otherworldliness," or cultural conservatism, assists the family in protecting itself against many undesirable characteristics of the modern world, but it can reduce direct action in the secular world, particularly for broader liberal politics espoused by labor unions. Even among some labor union members of these sects we see limits to the influence of liberal labor politics. This is particularly true for those who wish to avoid overt economic conflict or those who continue to emphasize cultural concerns in their politics.

A consideration in the next chapter of an environmental movement led by a female United Baptist that was transformed into a political reform movement in an eastern Kentucky county will show the limits to liberal politics of secular organizations among these Baptists more clearly. These limits are approached when the politics of secular organizations shift to vague collective goals and when the style of organizations contrasts more pointedly with sectarian traditionalism.

CHAPTER 4

The Limits of Adaptation for Reform: The Problem of Local Versus Public Goods

There are at least three reasons local Baptist churches were more willing than more distant church hierarchies to support the Colquest strike. First, these local churches were miners' churches in every possible sense. They acted in the interests of the workers and their union because the workers controlled them. Second, though modest, these churches were self-sufficient and hence independent of the financial pressure like that which the mine owners could bring upon the West Virginia hierarchies. UMW and mainline religious leaders who failed to gain signatures from mainline religious hierarchies for the Morgantown ad blamed the reluctance of these hierarchies to offend wealthy churchgoers or benefactors. The Baptists of this work, being quite modest and having few worldly aspirations for their churches, had no reason to fear such retribution. Furthermore, since they lack any outside hierarchy or control, it is less likely that, even if they had more worldly aspirations, those who could help them attain such goals—the wealthy among their own—would be as susceptible to financial pressure from out-of-state business titans as out-of-state hierarchies were.

A third reason for sectarian support of the miners may be in the limited, specific goal that they sought and the local incentive that local churches had in helping to seek it. The good of worker dignity that the Colquest workers sought is collective in nature, but enough workers and preachers had individual motives to make fighting for this good easier to organize.

The goods that the UMW provides to the community at large, including financial benefits to local businesses and the patronage of churches by workers with steady work and steady pay, are goods the community at large benefits from and from which it has an incentive to help provide. This was a local incentive that more distant hierarchies did not share. The West Virginia hierarchies, not wishing to irritate local financial supporters, had a disincentive to aid the Tennessee miners.

The effect that the specificity of a goal has on gaining sectarian support becomes more evident in a comparative analysis. The ease with which these Baptists were able to rally around the miners' goal of union representation becomes more evident when their story is compared with another secular organization in these sects' communities. This second organization, like the UMW, first sought a specific public good. As its goals become more general, its support among local Baptists dropped.

The story of a movement that originated to stop a proposed landfill in Magoffin County, Kentucky, shows several limits on these Baptists in any activity in which they might engage for a diffuse public good. These include limits these Baptists confront in undertaking public action as the number of those seeking the good increases; limits stemming from their attitudes toward church establishment and the fostering of local authority and community; and the more general difficulties they have in shifting from working toward a specific, easily identifiable good, e.g., stopping a landfill, to a more general good, e.g., reforming a historically venal county government, which initially had approved the landfill.

Mancur Olson's findings on public goods and collective action provide a useful, albeit imperfect, model for interpreting the differences between sectarian action in the Magoffin controversy and in support of the Colquest strike. One problem with using Olson's theory to interpret these two examples is his interpretation of labor unions as providing a collective good.[1] The UMW at Colquest was seeking to provide a series of collective goods to the miners and to the community at large. This, however, presents only a superficial problem to applying Olson's work here. His theory would predict the comparative ease with which these local Baptists were able to rally for the Colquest union, and against the Magoffin landfill, compared with the difficulty they had in rallying for the more general goal of reforming Magoffin government. Applying Olson's work to the Magoffin story would lead us to predict that organization is more easily accomplished for stopping the county landfill, an immediate goal of an intermediate group, i.e., a group whose members have both immediate and more general interests in its goal, than for changing county government, a more general goal by a latent group, i.e., a group whose members have only general interests in its goal.[2]

An additional difficulty these Baptists had in reforming county government is the challenge reform would present to the general good of local authority and community that the local Baptists seek to protect. The Colquest union fight, although a fight for a collective good, had the advantage of having an identifiable goal with many tangible benefits for all community members. The initial fight against the Magoffin landfill, while a fight for a collective good, had the advantage of having a fixed, definite goal that carried many individual benefits to county residents. The goal of county government reform does not have such tangible, easily identifiable benefits. When the grassroots movement against the landfill turned to reforming the county government that had approved the unpopular project, the good sought became too broad to draw its previous level of support.

The leading landfill opponents, drawn primarily from the immediate vicinity of the proposed project, had the incentive to provide the initial organization against the landfill. They were able to draw active support in this battle from other residents of the county, including many of the Baptists I study, who had great incentive to fight the landfill but less incentive to provide the initial organization. Very few of the initial leaders or their followers had the same incentive to push change in county government as they had to fight the landfill. When the battle shifted to the more broad goal of changing the county government, support for the movement withered.

There were many reasons for this. Reforming county government threatened the values of local authority, autonomy, and community these sects emphasize above all. Acquiescing to the professional female leadership of the movement threatened the broader good of traditionalism that these Baptists provide to adherents. Other reasons for the decline of the movement will become apparent in reviewing the specific story of the proposed landfill and local reaction to it, as will other strengths and limits of Olson's theory for interpreting sectarian political action. The sectarian congregations I study did not themselves participate in the fight against the landfill or in changing county government, but many of their individual members were involved. My analysis will show reasons for this individual participation and the lack of participation by the churches themselves, but first I present the story of the controversy.

Magoffin Politics and Churches

Magoffin is an eastern Kentucky county located approximately 145 miles (or a 175-mile drive) east by southeast of Louisville, the most populous city in Kentucky, and 80 miles (or a 95-mile drive) east by southeast of Lexington, the second-most populous city in Kentucky (see map 11). In some ways Magoffin is even farther away than these distances indicate from these cities and from Frankfort, the state capital, located between Louisville and Lexington. Local television viewers, for example, are more easily able to tune in stations from Huntington, West Virginia—whose news programs, of course, feature out-of-state news—than they are able to tune into stations closer to the capital. Although this situation has changed with the spread of cable television and satellite antennae, Lexington stations still run newspaper advertisements ("You Live in Kentucky. Why is Your TV in West Virginia?") in the area encouraging viewers to tune in for more Kentucky news.

Magoffin County was formed in 1860 and was named for the governor at the time, Beriah Magoffin.[3] Magoffin is not remembered for valiant public service. A Confederate sympathizer, he resigned from office after Unionists in the Kentucky legislature forced him to ease enforcement of commonwealth neutrality in the Civil War. Many public servants in the county have not even lived up to his standards. Vote fraud, for example, has been a recurring problem in the county since its creation.[4]

Politics and politicians are held in low esteem by some county residents. Preachers sometimes join them there. One area resident told me that some in the county trust neither politicians nor preachers, since whenever they leave a home they have visited, they are either "zipping up their pants or wiping off their mouth." The cynicism about religion and politics is directed toward these institutions in general, rather than anyone in particular. Ambivalent feelings about religion are often seen in local attitudes toward the most famous native of the county, pornographer Larry Flynt, who still owns land and maintains ties there. Some local residents applaud his success, some are indifferent to him, and some resent the notoriety he brings.[5]

Still, if any one ethos predominates in Magoffin civic life, it is a "Bible-based" Protestant ethos. United Baptists make up more than half (52 percent) of county church adherents enumerated in *CCMUS 1990*. In only two other counties in the nation do United Baptists form a larger share of church adherents, and in

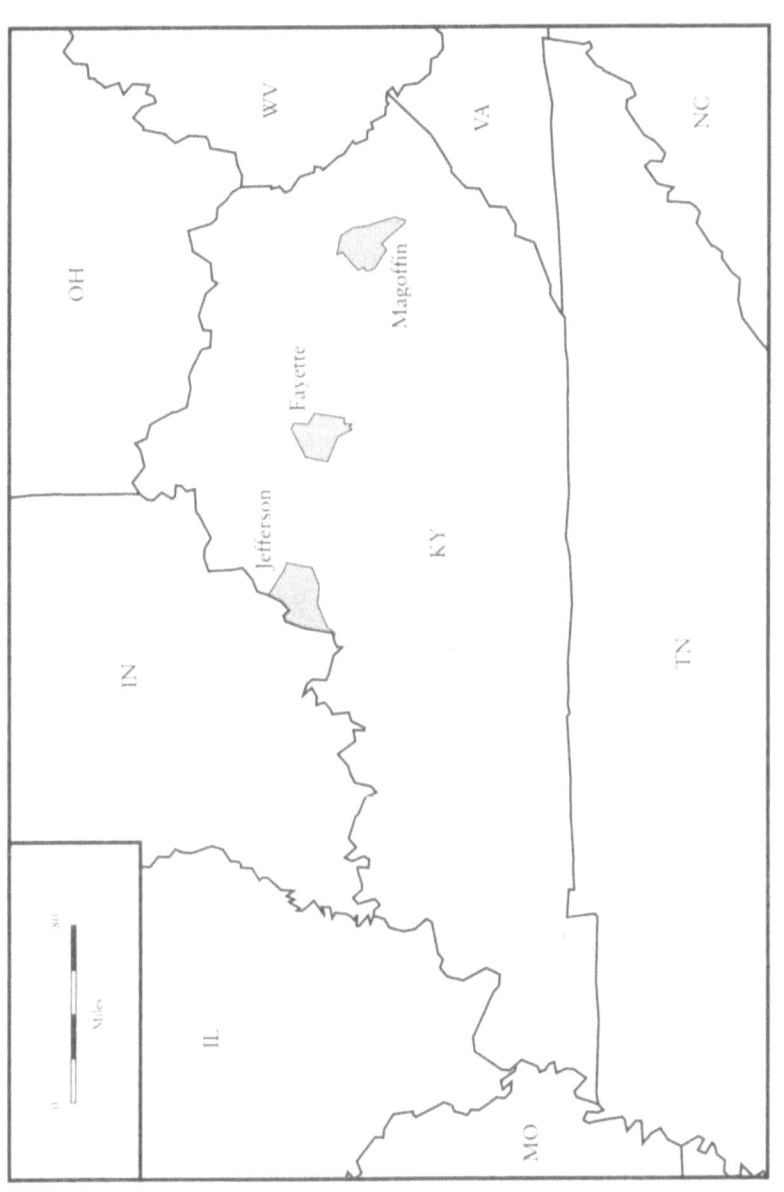

Map 11. Magoffin, Jefferson, and Fayette Counties, Kentucky.

only three other counties are they a larger share of the total population. Other similar Protestant churches with biblical orientations, including Southern, Free Will, Old Regular, and assorted Primitive Baptists, as well as various Pentecostal churches, account for most other Magoffin church adherents. *CCMUS 1990* likely underestimates biblically based Protestantism in the county. The local phone book lists many similar churches that were not included in *CCMUS 1990*, and in my fieldwork I have seen many more such churches (without telephones) also not included in the church membership study.[6]

These churches and their adherents are in a desperately poor county. The county is nestled between the bluegrass and the coal belt, and it has few of the economic advantages its neighboring regions sometimes possess. The county population is young, poor, badly educated, and economically disadvantaged (see table 7). Its population growth in recent decades has been static or erratic. More than three in five adults do not have a high school diploma, compared with one in four nationwide. Magoffin unemployment rates are consistently in the double digits, typically among the worst in the state and often four times the national level. More than one in three (35 percent) with jobs have to go outside their home county to work, compared with less than one in four (24 percent) nationwide.

Magoffin women are less likely to be in the workforce than women nationwide. Children there are more likely to be in a two-parent family. Two in five (40 percent) children live with two parents of whom the father only works, and an additional 14 percent live in a two-parent family where neither parent works; the respective national figures are 25 percent and 2 percent.

Per capita income in the county is less than half (44 percent) the national level and ranks twenty-fifth lowest among 3,141 counties (or equivalents) in the 1990 Census. Poverty is worse among Magoffin families than it is nationwide. Within Magoffin poverty is lower for families headed by married couples or those without children (see table 8). For those with children, stable marriages and disciplined male behavior cut poverty in Magoffin as they do nationwide.

Much of the housing stock in the county is below national standards. More than four in seven (58 percent) Magoffin households rely on private wells for water, compared with less than one in seven (15 percent) nationwide. Just over one in eight (14 percent) have public sewer access, compared with six in eight (75 percent) nationwide. These figures are changing as the water system in the county seat becomes more accessible to rural households, but

Table 7
Magoffin County Population Characteristics

	MAGOFFIN COUNTY (%)	U.S. TOTALS (%)
Total Population (as % of 1990)		
1950	106	61
1960	85	72
1970	80	82
1980	103	91
1990	100	100
White	99.8	80.3
Under 18	31	26
Over 64	10	13
Males currently married[a]	66	57
Females currently married[a]	64	52
Did not graduate high school[b]	62	25
At least some college[b]	15	45
Civilian unemployed, 1990	18.4	6.3
Working mothers	35	68
Selected industry data		
Agriculture, forestry, fisheries	2	3
Mining	13	1
Manufacturing	9	18
Wholesale and retail trade	18	21
Other services	37	40
Selected occupational data		
Managerial or professional	19	26
Technical, sales, or support	25	32
Skilled craft, repair	27	11
Operator/assembler/inspector	5	7
Other labor	28	8
Voted Democratic for president[c]		
1980	57	42
1984	56	41
1988	57	46
1992	57	43
1996	56	50
Per capita income, 1989	$6,289	$14,420

NOTES: [a] 15 years of age and older.
[b] 25 years of age and older.
[c] of votes for major candidates for president.

Table 8
Magoffin County Families and Poverty

	MAGOFFIN COUNTY (%)	U.S. TOTALS (%)
1989 Poverty by Family Type		
Married couple with children	41	7
Married couple without children	31	4
Other family with children	66	33
Other family without children	28	9

many will likely remain without access to city water for many years, if not decades, to come. Magoffin households are more likely to lack complete plumbing, telephones, and vehicles than households nationwide.

In addition to these dire demographics, Magoffin has faced a wide variety of other problems in recent years. These have included a nearly bankrupt county government, problems with a local landfill and trash disposal, and a public school board whose members commonwealth education officials forced from office. The county fiscal crisis is tied to the landfill controversy. The school board controversy is not tied directly to the landfill, but its repercussions have affected broader politics in the county.

Some incidents from the 1980s highlight some of the problems plaguing Magoffin politics. In 1982, the then sheriff of the county was charged with shooting a young girl riding in a car bearing the bumper sticker of a political opponent.[7] In 1986 and 1987, a commonwealth court ordered the Magoffin fiscal court (i.e., its county board) to produce a budget in order to end months of fiscal stalemate. During these stalemates, the courts and public offices in the county shut down, forcing the fiscal court to meet in another county, as trash gathered in courthouse halls, and prisoners in the county jail were transferred elsewhere.[8] When Kentucky's largest newspaper ran a series on vote fraud in the state, it cited Magoffin for many of the worst examples of election practices, particularly lavish vote buying.[9] Voter registration rolls in the county during the 1990s have consistently had a greater number of names than the number of persons of voting age.[10]

Local politics draws far more interest in Magoffin than do state or national campaigns. Approximately 5,800 ballots were cast in Magoffin for the 1992 presidential election, and less than 4,100 in 1996. By contrast, in the 1993 general election for county judge-executive (or chief executive of county government), nearly 6,200 votes were cast. Partisan primaries draw even more interest. In the 1993 primaries for county office, nearly 6,300 votes, approximately 4,500 Democratic and 1,800 Republican, were cast, while in the 1998 primary, nearly 5,600 ballots, approximately 4,100 Democratic and 1,400 Republican, were cast. Republican county primary turnout in 1998 may have been depressed by the lack of a contest for county judge-executive nomination and the lack of a candidate for county attorney.

Kentucky recently consolidated its elections, resulting in a special five-year transitional term for county officials who were elected in 1993, instead of the typical four-year term. Some observers of Magoffin politics believe the move will ultimately stimulate more interest in state and national contests. This may be true, but interest in such contests still trails that for local offices. In the 1998 primaries, the Democratic primary for Magoffin County judge-executive was the most popular contest on the Democratic primary ballot, drawing nearly 900 votes more than those cast in a hotly contested race for an open U.S. Senate seat, and over 1,200 votes more than those cast for an open state representative seat.

Magoffin politics is highly personal, stressing appeals based on friendship, personal qualities, or family ties. Some newspaper ads have featured candidates claiming to be "honest, sober, and dependable." In the 1998 campaign for fiscal court, one candidate touted his credentials in a county newspaper ad by claiming to be an "honest neighbor" and a "hardworking friend." Another stressed "his Christian ethics, sense of fairness, unselfishness and willingness to cooperate." The personal nature of county life goes beyond politics. A local bank official told me that in Magoffin "your family becomes your reputation. When I first arrived here, loan decisions were based on an applicant's family tree."

There has been some decline in the political (and banking) significance of family ties, but candidates can still find practical reasons to stress their genealogy. When I asked one recently successful Democratic candidate for county office about ads featuring his family lineage, he told me, "I tried not to run many of those. Maybe only one or two. But those can go a long way in a small county. Families can be really important in small towns or small counties. Those type of ads can also help me with a certain type of voter, particularly those over 40. I'm a young man [28 at the time of our interview], and maybe many of those over 40 haven't heard of me. They may not feel they know me personally. But it is likely that they would know my dad, or my grandfather, or my great-grandparents."

Broader influences are changing some local political attitudes. A recent candidate for county office failed to ride in on charges that the incumbent "is either pipefitting in Ashland, Kentucky, or playing poker in the local pool room" rather than being available continually for constituents. An observer of county politics told me, "That didn't work too well. He found out that there are more pipefitters than those who care about it, that there are more folks who have to work outside the county than those who care about it, and that there are more pool players than those who care about it."

Among factors bringing wider influences to bear upon the county have been increasing communication from outside the county (e.g., cable and satellite television), improved roads, and other more general contacts with broader powers. County residents often lack power over these changes. One of the largest influences in the county in recent decades was the construction, initiated by a governor from a neighboring county, of Mountain Parkway, a limited-access highway through the county linking it to Lexington, Frankfort, and Louisville. One business official told me that "when the parkway came in, a majority of the people here were against it. People here don't like change. They don't like anything that's going to bring change."

Another said that county residents "don't like to look at things like this, but Salyersville [the county seat] is smack dab in the middle of eastern Kentucky. The biggest problem we had for years was that we had no roads but now we've got roads everywhere. There's the parkway, and the new route [Kentucky Highway] 80, and the new route [U.S. Route] 23, and the new [U.S. Route] 460, and it's easy to get around."

Improved roads near and through the county have changed it in many ways. One of the most obvious is in the layout of the county seat. Most businesses have migrated toward the Mountain Parkway, leaving few in the old town center; many remaining there are law firms wanting close access to the county courthouse. The parkway helped lure a manufacturing plant to the area in 1971. The plant remains one of the largest county employers. The only controversy among area businesses regarding the parkway today is whether a proposal to widen it will force its rerouting farther away from the city limits of the county seat. Many residents have enjoyed the benefits of improved roads. Local workers can now more easily work jobs elsewhere while maintaining county residence.

In the midst of the changing influences on and controversies of Magoffin politics, the Baptists of this work have managed to maintain a reputation of stability and modesty. Others who sense their presence in politics do not resent it, particularly since, they say, such influence does not go far. One business leader told me, "They've got to be political in some ways. How can they not be political when there's 80-some churches like that in the county? They're everywhere, so they've got to be political. But their doctrine probably limits them a lot . . . if anything, they need to take more leadership, but they don't. They're afraid to take positions because [they fear] backlash in the community. They don't think that their opinion matters."

Another said that many individual local Baptists

> exercise influence, but they do it subtly. Everything about them is subtle. They could drive the flashiest Cadillac in the world, but they'd do it subtly. Take W.—he's got as much money as anybody in the county, but you'd never know it. He's real subtle about it. So if they get involved, their key role is behind the scenes. . . . They'll give their donations, but they won't run as candidates often, or be political about their religion. They're subtle about it. They're humble. That's something they pick up from their by-laws, and from their association rules. It explains a lot about how they act, and the effect the religion has on their politics. . . . How politics can affect them depends on the type of church they are. Now the Free Wills will split over anything, and a lot of times it will be politics in back of the doctrine causing the split. But the Old Regulars and the Uniteds aren't like that. They'll go into a community when there's enough of them for a church, and they'll start a church then. When you have a community church like that, then you're not going to get politics from within.

Magoffin Problems and a Proposed Solution

Several long-festering Magoffin problems culminated and dominated county politics in the 1990s. Foremost among these were perpetual fiscal problems that, combined with a waste-disposal crisis, helped launch a massive landfill proposal in 1991. How these issues played out in county politics, with local reaction first rallying against the landfill but ultimately faltering in support of broader reform, shows in sharp relief how far the Baptists of this work can go in local political action.

Kentucky law required each county to submit a solid-waste plan to the state by 1 October 1991 or risk losing intergovernmental funding. Magoffin was under further pressure because its old landfill could not meet state regulations and was scheduled to close in July 1992. Many small, illegal roadside dumps plagued the county. Faced with these problems, the county judge-executive of the time agreed to a request by a Salyersville businessman to submit a plan drafted by a Lexington environmental consultant. This, the judge-executive said, saved the county eight thousand dollars and helped meet state deadlines.[11]

The eight-thousand-dollar savings carried a multimillion-dollar hitch, in the form of a massive new landfill. The solid waste plan was pushed by a new company, Eastern Kentucky Resources (EKR), which had registered with the state only a few months earlier and was headed by a Republican ex-House member from northern Virginia. The tenuous local connections of EKR marked an inauspicious start. The only local connection the company had was the Salyersville businessman, who retired to Palm Beach, Florida, and a small, usually closed office on the Mountain Parkway near Salyersville. Phone calls to this office were forwarded to the home of a public relations representative in Louisville.

The plan, its size and location, and its lack of prior public discussion stunned county residents. The EKR landfill was to take in between 4,000 and 10,000 tons of waste per day; all of Kentucky produces about 7,000 tons per day.[12] The landfill was to be located near the headwaters of the Licking River. The river flows from the southern end of the county, through its length, then meanders through eleven other counties before joining the Ohio River opposite Cincinnati. EKR said it would use state-of-the-art liners, but Kentucky newspapers quoted federal environmental officials as saying all liners eventually leak.[13] This was an especially sensitive issue in a county where most households have well water, and nearly all the rest rely on a waterworks drawing from the river. Flooding in the county has prompted its inclusion several times in national disaster areas. Residents worried that the dump would contaminate local waters when they rose.

Fiscal court magistrates immediately voiced opposition to the plan. Some said a referendum on the proposal should be conducted. The judge-executive conceded that the fiscal court, which also comprises the solid waste governing body of the county, had not voted on the proposal, and it became clear that such a vote was needed for approval.

As word of the proposal circulated among county residents, more than five hundred signed a petition opposing the project.[14] Within a week after the proposal and details of its approval by the judge-executive became widely known, more than one thousand county residents attended a community rally against the project, at which three of the fiscal court magistrates reiterated their opposition.[15] Residents kept up pressure through subsequent fiscal court hearings: hundreds attended them and often sang traditional religious songs during their demonstrations.[16]

Violence soon racked the dispute. A landfill opponent shot the judge-executive's grandson in an argument over the proposal.[17] The transmitter of the county radio station, which featured extensive coverage of the proposal and reaction to it, was sabotaged.[18] The home of the ex-wife of a prominent landfill opponent was burned to the ground, an incident many speculated was linked to the dispute.[19] Landfill supporters attacked opponents at a fiscal court meeting, prompting the sheriff to suspect an orchestrated attack, although he never filed charges.[20]

EKR offered its own resistance to the anti-landfill movement. It purchased weekly several pages of advertising touting the project in the only county newspaper. It tried to foster a grassroots group in support of it. It filed a multimillion-dollar lawsuit against Magoffin Countians for a Better Environment, the organization that had sprung up to fight the landfill. EKR claimed its suit was to recoup revenues that MCBE was costing it. Courts refused to hear the suit, however, and said it was a strategic lawsuit against public participation. This kind of lawsuit is such a widely known—and, in Kentucky, illegal—tactic used against citizens' groups that it is commonly known by its acronym SLAPP.[21] EKR pursued this particular harassment of MCBE for more than three years, giving up only when a commonwealth court of appeals concurred with a lower court that the suit was indeed a SLAPP.[22]

EKR had more success in the Magoffin fiscal court. By December 1991, three magistrates who had opposed the landfill, including one who had pronounced it "dead," reversed themselves and approved it.[23] Opponents insinuated that the reversing magistrates had been bribed. In a full-page ad in the only county newspaper, MCBE ran an ad on "a few, simple facts," claiming that in the weeks before the vote "representatives of Eastern Kentucky Resources have met many times with county magistrates often in private, and possibly illegally" and advising readers to "draw your own conclusions."[24]

The remaining magistrate opposed to the dump said, "I don't really know why they changed [their opposition]. I didn't know until they got it up here on the desk. They had a reason."[25] State police investigated allegations of corruption, but did not file charges. Further infuriating landfill opponents was an EKR admission that the dump would take in long-haul waste from as far away as New York and New Jersey.[26]

There were legitimate economic reasons to support the landfill. The county was subsidizing its old landfill, which had to be closed, for $50,000 annually.[27] EKR was to pay the county a per-ton royalty on the waste.[28] The landfill was expected to create fifty jobs, which would have made it one of the largest employers in the county. The royalties the county was to receive for the dump would have been enough to provide free trash pickup throughout the county, as well as to finance most of the two-million-dollar annual county government budget. One of the magistrates who switched to support the landfill said, "With those royalties we could pave roads and put in sewer lines and bring businesses in for the future of this county. Those against it are just hooting and hollering and don't want to hear that this landfill would be safe. And the free trash pickup would help the old widow women who now can't pay their bills."[29]

A local business leader who initially favored the landfill also cited economic reasons for his support. He blamed emotional fear of the unknown for opposition to the project. He told me:

> In my ignorance, I favored the landfill. It's hard to figure opinion here sometimes, and I thought this could work out. I thought, economically, that it could be good for the county. We don't have much else going on here . . . after I said I was for it, I showed up for work, and there must have been thirty-five people waiting to see me. They wanted to see my board, most likely to get me fired, so I take a few of them to our next meeting. They get up and say their piece, and then I said, "How many of you have ever seen a landfill?" None of them. I said, "I can take you to see a landfill that operates cleanly out in western Kentucky. You can't even tell it's there from the outside. How many of you want to go see it?" None of them. "We don't want to see it," they said. . . . So there's a real fear of the unknown here. It's comical sometimes. The river is still

one of the most polluted around. Its fecal bacteria count is very high, from all the outhouses folks put near the branches and the creeks. Every time there's a flood around here, you can see disposable diapers hanging from the [tree] branches. But nobody wants to talk about that.

Landfill opponents cited their own economic and emotional reasons for the county to reject the dump. Rather than attracting new business, a local Baptist preacher argued that "no industry would want to move into The County with the Big Dump."[30] Another area resident cited concern for local drinking water, saying, "If this goes in, it'll be like one of those western movies where you see the sign with the skull on top of it: 'Don't drink the water, it's poisoned.'"[31] The lawyer for MCBE compared the proposal to environmental racism, saying, "First landfill operators wanted to dump trash on the Indian reservations, but they fought it. Then they tried to dump on the black communities, but they fought it. And now they're coming to Appalachia, where they consider us white trash anyway."[32] Charles Hardin, a prominent member of the group, was more succinct, saying, "I don't want Magoffin County to be the solution for America's garbage woes. I think rural Appalachia has paid its share."[33]

Despite its setback in fiscal court, MCBE carried its fight to several other fronts. After county approval of the landfill, an area state legislator promised to file legislation allowing voters to overturn fiscal court decisions.[34] In part because of MCBE pressure, the commonwealth refused to give the county extra time to iron out final project details.[35] When a fiscal court magistrate who favored the landfill resigned for health reasons, Brereton Jones, Kentucky governor from 1991 through 1995, appointed a friend of Charles Hardin, one of the most prominent members of MCBE, to fill the slot.[36] Hardin was a prominent figure in the county since he was one of its few physicians. His prestige was aided, in Jones's eyes, by his service as the governor's campaign manager in the county in 1991. The appointment deadlocked fiscal court opinion on the project.

By May 1992, the Kentucky legislature approved a measure to allow a vote on the landfill, and MCBE gathered roughly seven thousand signatures for a referendum.[37] EKR expressed bravado that it would defeat the referendum, but sued to stop it. A landfill opponent claimed the suit "just proves our point—that Eastern Kentucky Resources just wants to shove their landfill down our throats."[38] Magoffin never voted on the landfill, as the state law permitting the referendum was overturned as illegal special legislation.[39]

As the landfill controversy continued, the county government fiscal condition worsened. By September 1992, or three months into the new fiscal year, the county had spent 83 percent of what it had budgeted for road gravel for the year, almost twice what it had budgeted for pipe, and its contractor suspended trash-removal service for lack of payment.[40] The troubles prompted suspicion that landfill supporters in county government were engineering a crisis to reverse public opinion on the landfill and its royalties.[41] Just when the county government seemed on the verge of total breakdown, the judge-executive died after a long bout with cancer.[42]

The governor appointed another landfill opponent, also another friend of Hardin, as the new judge-executive.[43] This gave landfill opponents in general, and MCBE supporters in particular, control of county government. EKR implicitly recognized its weakening position, saying it would press to have its original contract honored and not bring the issue before the changed fiscal court.[44] The dispute still caused violent flare-ups; a county employee who supported the landfill once physically attacked the new judge-executive.[45] Yet Magoffin public opinion was running as strongly as ever against the landfill, and the tide had clearly shifted within county government.

The battle over the landfill shifted to several state and federal suits filed over it. Ultimately, the landfill would be stymied, though not permanently barred, from local commonwealth courts through the U.S. Supreme Court.

With the issue settled in the court of Magoffin public opinion and removed to the arcane arena of the judicial courts, MCBE leaders ventured elsewhere in county politics. One of the first issues they addressed was the precarious fiscal position of county government, which they recognized as part of the reason the landfill, and its subsidies, was first proposed.[46] One MCBE member said that the takeover of the fiscal court by MCBE allies meant the burden of balancing the county budget had shifted to those who opposed the landfill.[47]

Hardin, who remained one of the most prominent members of MCBE, sought and won the chairmanship of the county Democratic party. This is arguably the most powerful political position in a county where Democrats vastly outnumber Republicans on voter registration rolls and usually at the polls. Having gained, with his allies, the largest share of influence within the county Democratic party, he trained his sights on winning the county judge-executive office in 1993. He won the primary for that office by a thin, twenty-four-vote margin (or about 0.5 percent of the votes) and the general election by a more comfortable margin.

When MCBE and its allies turned their attention to broader issues and away from immediate, grassroots concerns, their appeal and power within the community became less certain. There were several reasons for this, including the challenges their "reform" politics presented to other values instilled in the community by local Baptist churches, the complexity of other issues confronting the community and entangling its leaders and their factions, and the explicit challenge MCBE leaders presented to "old guard"[48] county politicians who survived the landfill controversy.

The chief rival to Hardin for power in the county was Paul Hudson Salyer. Salyer, an "old guard" politician, though not in office at the time, had also opposed the landfill. Salyer is one of the most venerable politicians in county history. His family has long been involved in county affairs, and the county seat bears his family's name. In the 1980s, Salyer accomplished what no other Magoffin politician had ever done, winning re-election to succeed himself as county judge-executive. He is a second cousin of Paul Patton, who was elected Kentucky governor in 1995. Patton succeeded Hardin's friend, Brereton Jones, as Kentucky governor (prior to Patton, Kentucky governors were ineligible to succeed themselves). Salyer's wife is Patton's liaison to eighteen eastern Kentucky counties, including Magoffin. Relations between Jones and Patton, which have been strained over speculation that Jones wants to unseat Patton, have reinforced divisions between Hardin and Salyer.

Beyond intraparty divisions, as Hardin advanced in Magoffin politics, he had to overcome more personal aspersions cast at him, including some based on community standards and expectations. Hardin is a divorcée who is not a Magoffin native and is known more for attending his girlfriend's church rather than any identified as his. Some who supported Salyer in the 1993 primary for county judge-executive did so because he was identified as "a county boy . . . and a good Christian boy," though also a "boy" several years older than Hardin.[49] Salyer's home is in the southern end of the county, where the proposed landfill was to be built.

Although he opposed the landfill, Salyer received the help of landfill supporters, including other "old guard" politicians, in his battles against Hardin. This in turn allowed Hardin and his MCBE supporters to campaign against

Salyer as the candidate of landfill supporters, a tactic Salyer acknowledged hurt his 1993 candidacy.[50] The most striking evidence of this was Hardin's eighteen-vote margin (three-fourths of his very slim total margin) over Salyer in the area comprising the southernmost magisterial (county board) district. This area has typically been Salyer's core area of strength in county elections. The landfill surpassed as a campaign issue Salyer's stewardship of the 1980s, a period in which county government shut down over financial instability.

At the height of its influence stemming from opposition to the proposed landfill, MCBE support was not a sure predictor of electoral success. The group's female president, who had been elected in a special 1992 election to fill out a magistrate's term, lost her primary bid in 1993 to unseat the county clerk. The clerk, like Salyer, received support from "old guard" politicians supporting the landfill, although he repeatedly voiced opposition to the project during the campaign.[51]

At their height, reform politics in the county were within sight of their limits. As MCBE and its leaders tried to shift attention to the more general goals of reforming county government, their success became more spotty. For a time, MCBE members won control of county government, but not all MCBE members were part of this success. As the landfill battle receded further away from the consciousness of county voters, support for politicians most closely tied to MCBE would also diminish.

The churches of this study themselves were not part of Magoffin political struggles, but their members were. The actions and reactions of these local Baptists and the inaction of their churches during these conflicts help demonstrate the limits of a locally oriented, "Bible-based" Protestant politics as political issues become more general and less immediate. In Magoffin, these limits stemmed from the challenges local reform politics posed to local tradition and the more general conflict these local Baptists face when their demand for tradition encounters adjustments, including to the female leadership of MCBE, needed to overcome economic challenges, including the threat of an unwanted landfill industry.

LOCAL BAPTISTS AND LOCAL REFORM POLITICS

The View of Landfill Opponents

Such a large portion of the population comprises United Baptists in the county that, in any significant local dispute, they are, as individuals, bound to be in the forefront. Both the most prominent landfill opponent and the most prominent local landfill supporter were United Baptists.

The MCBE president is a native of the area who said she attended United Baptist services regularly until the landfill controversy erupted. She became disenchanted with the reaction of her church to her political participation, a reaction she says was based in traditional codes of the roles for men and women, codes that cannot accept political leadership by women. She has since stopped attending services at her church.

The MCBE president is a professional in her thirties who started her own business after losing her job as a secretary with Magoffin public schools, the single largest employer in the county. She sued the school board over her firing, charging that her opposition to the landfill was the cause; the school board eventually settled her suit for seventy-five thousand dollars.[52]

She told me that the landfill controversy was primarily responsible for leading her to political activism. She said:

> I'd done volunteer work in the past, but I'd never done anything much. But when this first came out in the newspaper, it upset me like nothing else had. There are so many children in this county, and I worried about them. A lot of this county has well water, and getting that landfill would affect the water and cause mental retardation in the kids. People would ask me how come I'd get so mad over this. I'd say if this doesn't make you mad, go back and read about it again until it does. A project like this destroys your economic future. So at our first meeting, after this comes out in the papers, I'm thinking there will be five or six people there. But the place was packed. I guess I got to be in charge there because I've got the biggest mouth and I'm the least bashful.

Female leadership of MCBE has involved more than those with loud voices or little bashfulness. As the goals of MCBE leaders have become more diffuse, the leadership has become more feminine. MCBE leaders offer two explanations for this. One is the time that area women have to devote to the organization and other politics. The other is the political sophistication Magoffin women professionals have, sophistication stemming from their comparatively high levels of education, which area men do not share.

The MCBE attorney, a male in his early forties, offers the time explanation. Discussing female leadership of the group, he told me, "The females have led the fight on this. Doc [Hardin] has done the political work, and I've done the legal work, but otherwise it's the women who have been out in front. I don't know how we would have gotten it done without them. They've done just about anything for us, from holding bake sales to raising funds for us, to getting us on the radio, to writing newspaper articles and letters to the editor about the landfill." When asked why the leadership has been disproportionately female, he responded: "A lot of their leadership has come because they have more time to work on it. A lot of the women are housewives who don't work outside the home. A lot of the men work a lot outside the home, and a lot of men work away from the county. So it's harder for the men to find time to work on things like this." Census statistics support this interpretation. Magoffin women are less likely to be in the workforce than either Magoffin men or all women nationwide. A large number of Magoffin men must travel outside the county for work, further restricting their time for politics.

Women who have made their way into the county workforce may possess more leadership skills than county men. The MCBE president told me:

> When I was growing up, there was some resistance to a woman getting much education. You didn't need much to raise children. But a lot of us have had to work outside the home. And because of this, a lot of females are actually more qualified for leadership than males. Most jobs for males around here don't require much education. You don't need as much education to work in a local plant or in a mine or in an oil field,[53] and the males can go after and get those jobs without much education. But if you're a female here and looking for work, you've got to have an education. The jobs open to females here usually require more education. . . . We've got an overabundance of good, quality teachers around here, and it's because of females who are trying for good jobs through education.

Census statistics support this interpretation, too. Among those in the Magoffin workforce, women are better educated than men. Among employed men in the county, for example, 48 percent have graduated from high school, only 18 percent have any education beyond high school, and just 4 percent have earned a bachelor's degree or higher. Among employed women in the county, 69 percent have graduated from high school, 36 percent have at least some education beyond high school, and 15 percent have a bachelor's degree or higher.[54]

Regardless of the secular reasons for women's leadership in the fight against the landfill, many local Baptist churches and their adherents did not accept it. The MCBE president is bitter over opposition to her political activity that she perceived from her church, as well as over the lack of support from her church for her during her financial troubles, including her firing from her job with the school board stemming from the landfill crisis. She told me:

> Hardly anybody from my church would come to the meetings. Some from up near the landfill would fight it, and would come to the meetings, but hardly anybody else would. . . . My church just wishes I'd shut up. They just don't want anything to do with me. They'll usually do what they can to help out when somebody's in trouble, but they wouldn't do anything to help me when I got fired from my job over this. They never would come up and say, "do you need help?" I was disappointed. I got no support from them. So I haven't been back to see them. . . . I didn't think my church should do anything political for me, but when I was getting in trouble over this, I thought they should have helped me.

The controversy apparently still affects her church and its members, including those who agreed with her on this issue. While other local Baptists in the county, including United Baptists, would discuss with me the landfill issue in particular and churches and politics and general, a notable landfill opponent from the MCBE president's former church was among the few interview refusals I had for this project.

The landfill proposal did not mark the first time MCBE's chief had disagreed with her church over secular political activity and its direction. Her comments on local prohibition indicate how women's interests in a more stable community can go against the traditional concerns of these churches. She told me, "The only thing most of the churches around here would get involved in is the wet/dry vote. And in the election here on that, I voted wet, and I'm glad I did. Since we've gone wet [in 1986], it's not as bad as it was before. Before, with all the bootleggers, anybody of any age could get liquor anywhere, but that's not true now. We don't have near as many liquor places as we did before we voted wet." Others shared her support for ending prohibition while being personally opposed to the use of alcohol. The access to wet areas that the construction of new highways gave to Magoffin appears to have changed some minds on the efficacy of local prohibition. One local politician told me voters had a sense of "relief" that "when we went wet, the bootleggers were gone . . . before it was almost like we had drive-throughs [liquor stores] around here."

The problems MCBE's president had with traditional sex roles rooted in the "Bible-based" ethos in the county extended beyond her church. They affected both her chances of success and her style in campaigning for elective office. She told me:

> When I first ran for magistrate, those churches looked askance at me. When I was first elected, I had to campaign extra hard, because I was a woman. The man I ran against thought he didn't even have to campaign. When I would go talk to the voters, I would have to make sure to talk to the man at home. I'd start to talk to the woman, but, as soon as I started talking politics, she would tell me to talk to her man. A lot of times I'd visit a house and the man would assume I wanted to talk to a woman, until I got it out that I wanted to talk politics, that I was running for magistrate. Then the man would talk to me. But I had to get the man to talk to me, or I wouldn't get the vote.

Local Baptist notions of traditional roles for the sexes do not work against all political participation by Magoffin women. MCBE's president says the deference and respect with which local Baptist men must treat women in certain situations sometimes helps her. She adds that some are uncomfortable with a woman in political office, but they will support her for a position such as the MCBE presidency. She said, "It sometimes helps to be a woman at fiscal court meetings. I get up and say my piece, and they can't yell me down, they can't cuss me out, and they can't beat me up. They've got to sit there and listen to me. I also think there's a tendency not to vote for females in political office, but they would support females for office in an organization like this because of that. So there is a difference that sometimes favors females."

Politically astute, she knew she could not ignore county churches in MCBE activities. Among other religiously oriented activities of the group, for example, have been its sponsorship of community gospel sings, which United Baptist preachers have attended. In local parades, MCBE typically uses a theme such as "victory through prayer" for its floats. MCBE meetings open with prayer. The president was also the one to lead landfill protestors outside the fiscal courtroom to sing religious songs when the landfill debates became too heated during meetings. She told me, "With all those television news cameras there, and with the sheriff having a tough time keeping things and tempers under control, there wasn't much else to do. It was better to do that and to remind ourselves to keep cool and non-violent than to stay there and have violence break out."

The lawyer for MCBE, a United Methodist, provides a more detached perspective on sectarian religion and reform politics in the county. He identifies these sectarians' reluctance to support any church establishment as part of the reason for their reluctance to engage in politics. He told me, "There hasn't been much church involvement per se. A lot of our people who are involved are church members, but the churches themselves don't get involved. My own pastor would speak out on this, but that was about it. My wife is a United Baptist, so I know those churches just won't get involved in anything like this. They don't support foreign missions or anything like that, so they aren't going to support an establishment like this. That's just something they don't do."

The View of Local Preachers

The attitudes of Magoffin churches toward involving themselves in politics largely parallels their stance toward evangelization and missions. Those most supportive of church establishments are most likely to support involvement of the church in politics, and those least supportive of church establishments are most resistant to church activity in politics.

There are three discernible groups of churches in Magoffin, as defined by attitudes toward church establishments and church involvement in politics. The smallest of these comprise churches such as the county's United Methodist congregation and its very small Catholic congregation. They are most supportive of church establishments. The United Methodist minister quoted above is identified by all involved in the landfill fight as the most outspoken preacher allied with the MCBE.

The second group comprises "Bible-based" Protestant churches that are more aggressive than those I study in evangelization efforts. These include the Free Will Baptist and various Pentecostal congregations. A small number of preachers in these churches are active in politics. One of the recent fiscal court magistrates is a Pentecostal minister. More typically, these preachers may be involved in short-term political activity, such as the original organization against the landfill, but withdraw once it is apparent that the organization can run without their help. None, regardless of their level of political activity, say they are interested in pursuing a systematic county (much less national) politics based on their religious beliefs.

The third, and largest, group comprises churches like those in this study, and is dominated by the United Baptists. These are most distrustful of church establishments and have historical reasons for shunning nearly all evangelization efforts. Their preachers are most likely to avoid any political activity. This avoidance has its roots in their distrust of centralized authority, in their desire to keep away from worldly entanglements of all types, and in their recognition of a wide variety of political viewpoints in their churches, the most broad-based in the county.

The United Methodist minister in the county, in the first group of churches noted above, cites two reasons why he was more involved than his fellow Magoffin clergy in the campaign against the landfill. First, he explained that, as a full-time minister, he had extra time to devote to it. Second, he accredited the broader worldview fostered by his denomination. He told me,

> Most of the clergy here work secular jobs, and they do not have time to get involved in politics and church and work. Handling both the church and another job is quite a lot, so they would not have the time I sometimes have for this. . . . They also may not have a worldview of Christian stewardship as both spiritual and material. They may think more of the soul and the spirit than of how it is in the world. . . . As for the landfill, some saw it as strictly a political issue, but I saw it as a moral issue, because of the environment. It was a moral issue, and one which I addressed biblically, spiritually, and as a Christian.

This minister is helped in his political involvement by a congregation that accepts and supports his political activity. Part of the reason for this support may lie in the small number of United Methodists in the county. *CCMUS 1990* shows the United Methodist population in the county to be one-eighth the size of the United Baptist population. A smaller population may have less diversity of viewpoints, or may give the minister fewer souls to placate over his politics.

One local politician told me, "The Methodists do seem to stick together more. That may be because there's fewer of them, or because they're more likely to agree with each other and their pastor, which lets him be more outspoken."

The politics of the Methodist minister draw disapproving comments from outside his church, but apparently no significant objections from within. He said, "I hear a few comments on my involvement, but I don't hear a whole lot. I haven't noticed any significant reaction. I really don't have that big a problem with people in my congregation over my involvement. I hear very little about that. Something occasionally, but not often."

More typical of preachers involved in the fight against the landfill is example of a Free Will Baptist of the second group described above. This preacher lives near the site proposed for the landfill. He said concerns for his community were the reason for his initial involvement in the fight against the project. He told me:

> I usually don't get too involved in politics. But I got involved against the landfill because it would have been right near my home. It was the right thing for the community, to keep that landfill out. . . . One of the biggest, best clearwater springs in the county is in the head of the hollow where they wanted to put that landfill. And it just makes sense with the floods we get around here not to do it. With the rain we sometimes get, even the rain we're getting tonight,[55] there's no way they could stop that from getting out of hand. We've seen the results of what's happened around here with floods, and nobody can convince me that the rains and floods we get around here wouldn't affect that landfill, that things wouldn't get out of hand with it because of the floods and the rain. And it just wouldn't be our community that's affected. There's eleven counties between here and Cincinnati that get their water from the river. So by stopping the dump here, we're helping them out, too. Not everybody agrees with me. One of my church members thinks the stupidest thing the county ever did was to stop that landfill. But I still feel right about it. It wasn't a church thing or a political thing with me. It was a community thing. Fighting that landfill was the best thing for the community.

While he felt that fighting the landfill was the best thing for the community, he also looked for the first opportunity to step away from the fray. This was not because he had any objections to the broader goals of some MCBE members. He supported, for example, his brother's successful bid to become a Democratic precinct committeeman. His brother ran at the request of Hardin, who was conducting a successful bid to retain the county party chairmanship against a challenge from Salyer. Instead, this preacher cites concerns for maintaining harmony in his congregation as the reason for his reluctance to continue his political engagement. He said:

> I saw the fight was going our way, so they didn't need me anymore. The politics of it all were going our way, so I didn't need to stay in any longer. ... If it could get along without me, then it could get along better without me, and it was time to step aside. I shouldn't get involved in things like this unless I have to, and at first on the landfill I had to, but later I didn't. ... That's usually what's best for harmony in the church. We got a lot of voters in church who, well, if I had put up a sign for [Governor Paul] Patton, I might make somebody mad. So I think it's just best if I stay away from signs and bumper stickers and things like that.

Another political issue on which this preacher got involved was a proposal that would have allowed Sunday liquor sales in the county seat. He said that "a big turnout of pastors" quickly rallied against it, but that more sectarian preachers would not get involved. He told me, "The Old Regulars didn't show, and the Uniteds didn't show. ... They don't have Sunday school, they don't have missions, and they just don't get involved in much of anything at all."

A bivocational Pentecostal minister who won election to the fiscal court as a landfill opponent provides a different perspective from ministers in this second group. His church itself was not involved in the landfill issue. Still, he wants to bring more "Christian people" into politics, while recognizing the difficulty of doing this. He told me of his troubles in trying to bring his fellow clergy into benign forms of politics:

> We've had some bad fighting in the fiscal court, that's been bad for the county. We fell into this situation on some problems in particular, like when we deadlocked on a budget vote. And the clerk and the judge[-executive] were into it. It got so that I got down on my knees and I prayed. And I sort of gave them a lecture by doing this. I was the one there, but I also had God with me, as the minister there. I felt like I had an advantage be-

cause God was with me. So I recommended we have prayer before the fiscal court meetings, and the whole courtroom was pleased with that. So I'd say a prayer, and then we would sit down for the meeting. Well last year, I felt like I was getting into too much of a routine, and I decided I would use different pastors for the prayer. I thought this would let them have some influence on the county, and also give them some insight into the governing of the county. But the first time I called on somebody else to say the prayer, I called seven pastors before I could get someone. With all the preachers we have in this county, I've only been able to get five to come, and one of them has been there twice.

What also may be at issue here is the overwhelmingly rural character of the county and its churches, particularly the churches of this study. Allan Gleason, who served as a United Church of Christ minister in the region, told me in personal correspondence that "I think I would have had a bit of difficulty if the County Board in Carroll [County, Virginia,] had asked me to open their meeting with prayer. I would have felt that they were willing to use a mountain preacher but not to concern themselves too much with the ordinary people. The people in my community felt a great gap between themselves and the Hillsville elite. I tried to stay on the mountain side."

It is hard in some ways to see a gap between the Salyersville "elite" and the rest of the county. Salyersville is small, with fewer than two thousand residents, far fewer than the rest of the county. Election results from the two Salyersville precincts typically are similar to those from the eleven rural precincts. Nevertheless, there is some evidence of differences. The Pentecostal magistrate's impromptu prayer drew a few snickers from some Salyersville leaders I interviewed. Political conflict between Salyersville and the rest of the county arises occasionally, as demonstrated by the decision of the Salyersville businessman to sell his rural land for the proposed dump. Most recently, conflict arose when a city income tax was levied on everyone working within city limits, including predominantly rural workers at an industrial plant that, with approximately two hundred employees, is one of the largest employers in the county. If conflict, or even the perception of conflict, were to arise in the county between a county seat elite and the rest of the county, the local Baptist churches I study, being most concentrated outside the county seat, would most likely be on the side of rural residents.

Still, these churches, which make up the third and largest group of county churches as defined by attitudes toward ecclesiastical establishments and political participation, are not likely to get involved in politics. Their preachers typically offer both traditional and community reasons for shunning politics. A United Baptist minister told me that not only did his church not get involved in the anti-landfill campaign, but it also did not get involved in the local prohibition votes that racked county politics in the mid-1980s. About local prohibition, he said, "I did not mention it in church, and I did not mention it outside church. The members on their own right might have talked about it, or they might have gotten involved in it on their own, but not in the churches. We really don't get involved in things like that. It's just kind of something we have not done down through the years. We just don't do it. It's the same with other issues . . . you very seldom hear the abortion issue mentioned in our churches. It's very rare to hear it mentioned."

Concern for preserving harmony in his congregation is one reason this preacher will not get involved in politics. He recognizes a diversity of viewpoints in his church both on local and on national issues. He said:

> You're liable to get all types to church. If you got people who are anti-Clinton in church, then I'm just as sure you got people who are pro-Clinton there, too. I figure you can't do too much in the world with what a small church like ours can do, so there isn't much reason to get involved in politics. . . . [O]n the landfill, one of our members was a magistrate at the time it was proposed, so he got involved, he was right in the middle of it. He was for the landfill, but we probably had a lot of folks in church who went to the meetings of Magoffin Countians for a Better Environment, and were involved on the other side as individuals. But I would tell everybody that my ministry comes before politics. The ministry is more important for me. I need to be an effective minister more than I need to get involved in politics.

Given the dominance of United Baptists among Magoffin church adherents, it is not surprising that both landfill opponents and landfill supporters would be among them, and even in the same congregation. With such a diversity of opinion in the county, and so many adherents belonging to the same denomination, maintaining community harmony is a real concern for these preachers. One local politician told me, "This is a close-knit community, but there's a good chance, if you were to bring politics into the church, you'd offend half the congregation on the other side of the issue. It wouldn't make good sense to raise politics in the church around here. So around here, the preaching in the church is about the Bible, not who's running." He could have added that even if these churches wanted to take part in local politics, their decentralization and lack of authoritative structures, while helping draw adherents when coupled with appeals to the sufficiency of local authority, also inhibit them from being resources for those who would use Christianity and its mandates for politics.

The tradition of these churches, which shun religious establishments and emphasize local authority, works to limit their involvement in worldly affairs. This is particularly true when church membership is divided on an issue. While we looked over a copy of the minutes of his association, one United Baptist explained to me:

> Look at our elements of faith, [pointing] here's the key one, that "we believe in the Scriptures of the Old and New Testament, as recorded in the Authorized King James Version of the Bible, to be the infallible Word of God, take it for our only true rule of faith and practice, and nothing is to be added or taken from it." What does that tell us? That all our rules have to come from the King James [Bible].... If we get a young preacher and he's citing something that's way out there, then we can stop him right away, but if we have some differences based on the King James Bible, then we can both use common sense to see whose interpretation is right.... The second thing I would point to in our churches is here, in our constitution, that the association "shall have no power to lord it over God's heritage nor shall they have any clerical power over the churches, nor shall they infringe on the internal rights of any church in the union." I would take that to mean... that we aren't to rule over God's people. We have no power as individuals to rule over other individuals. I'm under the jurisdiction of the church, and not of the association, or not of anybody else. And we can be concerned only about what is disrupting our church, what is best for fellowship in our church, and not over anything else.[56]

There is a final, poignant reason these churches may wish to avoid political activity. The violence that often plagues Magoffin politics gives these local Baptists an added concern that they might bring reproach upon the church, which is more poignant for them than it is for those I study elsewhere. Being involved in a political dispute where fisticuffs or even gunplay breaks out, both of which have happened in Magoffin politics, can, like few other things, bring reproach upon a preacher, his ministry, and his church.

Viewed in this way, association traditions and suspicion of ecclesiastical establishment and political entanglement do not prohibit political involvement by these churches as much as they foster attitudes that make such activity unlikely in some circumstances. In a tradition where adherents are suspicious of ecclesiastical establishments and where the emphasis is on local church authority and what is needed to maintain harmony within the local congregation, the clergy have good reason to avoid outside entanglements in areas most riven by excessive factionalism. Even when all members of a congregation agree on a political issue, its tradition may still cause it to look askance at clergy involvement on that issue.

On some issues, "agreement" within a congregation may not always be what it seems. There are, for example, many shades of opposition to abortion, even among these Baptists and their preachers. To cite another example, the reasons MCBE's president and others had for opposing prohibition show how community and family concerns can support a policy against these churches' concerns with public morality and maybe even can add to the hesitation these preachers have about political involvement.

The View of Landfill Supporters

When I asked the most prominent landfill supporter in the county, a United Baptist and a former fiscal court magistrate, whether there was any United Baptist church involvement in the controversy over the project, he said:

> None whatsoever.... I've never in my life seen the church here involved in politics. I just don't think, and most people here don't think, that's a place for a church to be, in politics. We've got such a diversity of all the churches here, I don't think they could withstand involvement in politics, or that the people would stand for it. You've got both Democrats and Republicans in all these churches, and this faction or that faction. I

don't think we'd stand for it, what with all types of people in all the churches. We're too hard-headed up here to let stuff go on like that in the church. That just wouldn't sit well.... Only one pastor got involved, and he's not a local person. That's the Methodist pastor.[57] How he's stayed here this long is amazing to me. He needs to be run out of the county, because as far as I can tell he's doing everything but ministering to his congregation. He wants to do everything but that.... I've never seen anybody but him from a church out there on this or anything else. As far as I can tell, the churches never get involved in anything like that. And if they ever do, it's usually because of somebody that isn't a native of the county, like that Methodist preacher.

His views on the women who have been involved in protests against the landfill, particularly his suspicion of their competence in public affairs, have some basis in these Baptists' traditional attitudes on roles for the two sexes. His comments confirm many suspicions MCBE's president has about these sectarians' opposition to women in public life. His comments are not quite as nasty as those of some local residents, who refer to MCBE leaders as "housewives from hell," but they are not much kinder. He said, "It's hard to deal with women in a radical situation like that. And it's worse when it becomes strictly political, and this has become strictly political. Hardin doesn't give a damn about that camp or anybody in it. He'd like to control the whole county, the school system, the whole works.... Those women have just been manipulated. I've lived here all my life, and I've never seen as manipulated a group in my life. Why, I think they'd murder for him."

He views the anti-landfill movement as an effort orchestrated by nonlocal interests, particularly Kentuckians for the Commonwealth, a statewide environmental group. Discussing his retirement from politics, he told me: "In every county around here you get a radical group of people getting involved in something like this. That is their only job, it seems. I feel it's their only obligation. The only thing they've got to do is to cause trouble." If he had wished to cite further "radical" influences on MCBE, he could have mentioned one of its attorneys, a resident of a neighboring county who ran a strongly liberal campaign for Congress in 1992, or another of the MCBE leaders, a pacifist Catholic whose farm was sold over his refusal to pay taxes, a refusal he made because of his views on defense issues. The larger point is not the veracity of the "radicalism" charge against MCBE, but that both sides within the county view their opponents as a nonlocal threat.

The EKR public relations representative offers a different perspective on churches and their influence in Magoffin politics, a perspective greatly affected by cultural insularity in the county. She found Magoffin ecclesiastical establishments to be so weak, or so buffeted by public opinion, that she did not think it would be worthwhile, even if possible, to enlist them in her cause. She suspects the religious and cultural homogeneity in the county have not helped her, either. She told me:

> I haven't spoken to many of the churches there. The one church I have spoken to is the Catholic church, where I have gone to Mass. Frankly, they were much more amenable to me. We didn't approach the churches like we approached the schools. We prepared an environmental program which had a part on recycling for the schools, and we presented it to some of them. But we had the door slammed in our face by the churches. There was so much hostility towards the landfill that it was hard to penetrate any institution there. There are people in the county that we have been able to persuade on the landfill, but they're afraid to say anything because of all the hostility towards it....

When I asked whether many persons in the county knew she was Catholic, she responded: "They'd probably shoot me if they did. I'm also Lebanese, and I'm also from Louisville, so those things don't help either. But I've made some friends down there, and I've gotten to know the people better. That goes for both sides."

Further complicating the EKR project, she says, was the overly ambitious nature of the first proposal. "There were some weird characters involved in this at first," she said. "We never could have built a landfill of the size they were talking about, handling ten thousand tons per day." The project proposal was eventually scaled back, with a proposed maximum intake of four thousand tons per day.

She says the way the project was first proposed may have been what damaged irreparably its chances of acceptance, since it "wreaked havoc on the county." But she also recognizes the political odds against acceptance of any large dump in eastern Kentucky. An aide to a former Kentucky governor, she also knows Gov. Paul Patton. And she says that Patton told her, "We will never get that landfill into Magoffin for psychological reasons alone. He said, 'regardless of the reasons for or against it, you won't get that landfill in, because I don't want to see eastern Kentucky become the dumping ground for the nation.'"

LOCAL CONCERNS AND THE DECLINE OF REFORM

The Effect of Education Politics

Landfill supporters were unable to win over public opinion on the issue. Instead, prominent MCBE members were able to ride the issue into county government. The prolonged court fights over the landfill, which anti-landfill forces ultimately won, kept the issue in the forefront of county politics and helped MCBE leaders maintain political power in the county. MCBE leaders were not, however, successful in using the support they won over the landfill issue on many other issues in county politics. As they ventured toward other, more general issues, or as the landfill issue slipped from the forefront of county politics, broader political support for MCBE and its allies receded. As the threat that had united county residents diminished, and as MCBE allies moved away from individual concerns—to which local Baptists often pay the most attention—and toward broader concerns, MCBE allies in county government lost political support.

A 1993 conflict over Magoffin public schools, though not directly related to the landfill issue, first showed the limits of reform politics in the county. After an investigation of irregularities in local school policies and finances, the commonwealth removed the superintendent of Magoffin schools and the entire board of education. Charges against the superintendent, a political ally of local landfill backers, included vote buying and misappropriation of more than $100,000 in public funds.[58] The school board had managed to approve $18 million in annual payroll expenditures, even though its total budget was $15 million.[59]

Both sides of the landfill controversy squabbled for advantage in the controversy. Landfill supporters, including the EKR public relations representative, suggested that the new school board appointed by the commonwealth was hand-picked by the interim judge-executive, who was a friend of Hardin.[60] MCBE leaders denied the charge, but in turn argued that "the installation of new, independent school board members means the corrupt elements in the county no longer . . . control votes."[61] They also took the opportunity to charge that, despite opposition to the landfill by every notable candidate in upcoming elections, "EKR and its supporters are backing candidates who have not taken a strong stance against the mega-dump."[62]

The landfill issue itself appeared to have little do with the routing of the commonwealth-appointed school board in 1994 elections.[63] Other issues of local control, including the maintenance of local control in the face of commonwealth-imposed standards, appear to have played a larger part. MCBE's president claimed that at least one of the newly elected board members may have run in a personal grudge against the interim judge-executive whose appointment gave landfill opponents control of county government. The outgoing members claimed that their challengers had ties to the ousted school superintendent, which the challengers denied.[64] Nevertheless, the new school board did try to fire the incumbent superintendent before public pressure forced them to ask for commonwealth approval, which the commonwealth declined to give.[65]

The fiscal court magistrate who supported the landfill saw the ouster of the school board as a repudiation of Hardin, although he viewed it in general rather than specific terms. He believed that the appointed board was strictly a tool of Hardin and Brereton Jones. The appointed board, he said, "Made a lot of radical changes that people didn't like, and that didn't go down too well." Beyond that, he said, it is difficult to interpret the meaning of school board elections, which are nonpartisan.

The commonwealth gradually eased its control of county schools, until the school board finally voted in 1998 to fire the school superintendent whom they had inherited.[66] The outgoing superintendent, who left his family outside the county while working in Magoffin, blamed the previous election results for his ouster, while the school board chairman said, "We just didn't see eye-to-eye."[67] The board's choice for the new superintendent drew media attention across Kentucky. He is a former official who worked under the discredited superintendent and who allegedly altered attendance records of politically connected students, an action for which commonwealth officials recommended a reprimand that the school board never issued.[68]

Some of the background issues in local education politics illustrate better the difficulties for those who would reform Magoffin politics. Kentucky launched a massive overhaul of its schools in the 1990s under legislation passed as the Kentucky Education Reform Act (KERA). KERA instituted statewide standards, testing, and benchmarks for each school in the state, including performance-based rewards and sanctions. Eastern Kentucky schools, including those in Magoffin, had been intended as a beneficiary of reform, but the gap between their performance and others widened after KERA passage.[69] Further complicating matters was the inability of the county school board to trim its budget to within state guidelines without political "cover" from the commonwealth on politically sensitive decisions such as school closings or personnel cuts.[70]

It is probably correct to note, as one commentator did, that "no school reform will ... overcome the socio-economic advantages that are enjoyed by children" in more affluent districts.[71] Yet, in such a context, even when local control is suspected to be corrupt, local resistance to broader standards and control becomes more understandable. A well-meaning reform has, in the short-run, put Magoffin students even further behind other Kentucky students. The general issue of broader standards and controls would eventually affect county leaders backed by MCBE more directly.

The Effect of Political Maneuvering

What hurt MCBE after its allies took power was a perception that the organization was too concerned with broader politics. Some of its initial decline in popularity appears attributable to the dissolution of support any organization faces. The Pentecostal minister who was also a fiscal court magistrate said of MCBE, "It's not as strong now as it was on the landfill issues. It's like most churches, where it can be strong at first, but after a while you get a lot of inactive supporters."

Some decline in political backing for MCBE members in county government appears to have arisen from an inability to keep all MCBE members under one political banner, or a more general inability, common to many other organizations, to subordinate all political aspirations to those of a few. One of the more prominent members of the organization ran an unsuccessful bid for state representative in 1996 that was backed by neither the county judge-executive nor the president of MCBE.

Other reasons for the decline in political support for MCBE allies appear to stem from a perception that the group is preoccupied too much with politics. When I mentioned to some opponents or former supporters and now skeptics of the group that I was interested in Magoffin Countians for a Better Environment, many would immediately retort with something like "the environment group? Oh, you mean the politics group."

Both MCBE's lawyer and its president recognize that the perception of their preoccupation with "politics" has cost them support. Both accepted this as a cost of political effectiveness. The lawyer told me that the perception of the group's preoccupation with politics "has cost us some members. This is a small county, and the factions run real deep here. So it's difficult to avoid the political divisions. The political divisions run real deep here, and with certain factions the division is deeper than that between Democrats and Republicans. But everybody here is against the landfill now. We've tried to overcome that perception by showing a lot of folks that this was a political problem, that it was a legal and political problem. Overall, we feel like we've addressed the politics of this as well as we could."

MCBE's president sees both political processes and broader politics as something her group had to address in fighting the landfill. She believes MCBE and its allies had to gain influence on Democratic Party machinery in order to control long-running Magoffin problems with vote fraud. She told me:

> I told everybody the first thing we had to do was to take over the Democratic Party. They asked why, and I said because I know how politics works around here. I'd seen votes bought here. So I knew we had to take over the local party, because without taking it over we'd have no influence on the election boards. And without influence on the election boards, we couldn't stop the vote buying in the Democratic primaries, where it really matters. So everybody asked me why we had to take over the party, why we would have to get involved like that. And I'd say unless we did, we'd lose everything, that we couldn't accomplish anything. That's why absentee ballots got so bad around here. Everybody would buy their votes beforehand because everybody was watching on election day. So they'd start buying absentee ballots because that way they could make sure votes stayed bought. But if we had the party, and we had influence on the election boards that comes with having the party, then we could stop some of it. Not all of it, but some of it. When we had the boards, they couldn't go in and vote the absentees like they had. They could still have the cash, but if we had the boards they couldn't go in and vote them.

Her concern with the county election board and absentee ballots is not apocryphal. Throughout its history Magoffin County has had troubles with vote fraud. Absentee ballots are widely suspected as the means of buying votes in many Kentucky counties, particularly those such as Magoffin, where absentees occasionally have accounted for nearly one-fifth of all ballots.[72] Vote fraud through absentee ballots may have occurred against MCBE allies in the 1993 election. In winning the general election for county judge-executive, Hardin won the vote cast on election day itself by well over one thousand votes, but lost the absentee tally by a 502 to 319 margin.[73] The county sheriff, another outspoken landfill opponent, easily won re-election on votes cast on election day, but lost the absentee tally by a 517 to 271 margin.[74] The county clerk, an "old-guard" politician opposed to MCBE's allies, who was indicted (but not convicted) for vote fraud, was the biggest beneficiary of the huge Magoffin absentee turnout, receiving nearly 700 absentee votes.[75]

While eschewing the more noxious campaign tactics traditionally used in the county, MCBE did not spurn them all. One observer of county politics told me:

> A lot of politics around here revolves around the personalities involved. That did happen with the dump . . . the group against the landfill got politicized real quickly. At first they did a good job, but two or three of them turned it into a political forum. . . . Hardin and the rest of MCBE froze out Salyer's wife over this, and tried to claim that the Salyers were in favor of the landfill, which wasn't fair, since everybody should have known they weren't . . . [the Salyersville businessman who owned the land for which the landfill site was proposed] had been around a long time, and he didn't have many friends. So right away [MCBE] made sure that everybody knew [the EKR chief executive] was tied to [the Salyersville businessman]. They didn't know [the EKR official] from dirt, but they knew they could get after him by tying [the Salyersville businessman] to him. . . .

The continued reappearance of the proposed landfill, through periodic reporting of cases involving it and their progress through various courts, helped Hardin and his MCBE allies. MCBE filed a suit in local courts charging that the original approval of the landfill was illegal and engineered in illegal, secret meetings.[76] MCBE won on every level, but EKR appeals to the commonwealth supreme court helped drag the case out for nearly five years. In ultimately ruling in favor of MCBE, the court said that the EKR contract with the Magoffin fiscal court was illegal because of Kentucky constitutional requirements that local governments advertise contracts and take competitive bids on them.[77]

EKR had filed a federal suit arguing that Kentucky regulations on waste management, spurred by the Magoffin controversy, constituted an unconstitutional restriction on interstate commerce.[78] EKR lost on every level from the circuit court up, and the U.S. Supreme Court declined to hear its appeal in April 1998.[79] Every time EKR appealed one of these cases, the landfill controversy was stirred anew. EKR also served as a convenient political foil for Hardin and his MCBE backers when the company demanded repayment of its initial payment on the landfill contract while the court cases were pending without promising to drop the project.[80] Hardin and his MCBE allies were able to maintain control of county government for as long as EKR kept the case alive in the courts. Some observers charged that MCBE members wanted "to keep the landfill issue alive for their politics."

Legal Victory, Political Defeat

While Hardin and his MCBE allies were able to draw political support from EKR maneuvering that kept the landfill issue in the forefront, rivals continued to pressure him in Magoffin. Following the election of his second cousin to the governorship, Salyer sought Hardin's ouster as county party chairman, saying he was too cool in his support of the Democratic nominee's campaign.[81] What ultimately helped undermine Hardin, however, was a zoning proposal that had some of the same political themes that so stirred voters' wrath in the landfill controversy.

In early 1997 the county planning commission completed two years of deliberation on a basic zoning ordinance for the area. The county government had never before systematically regulated use of land within the county. MCBE said it pushed the ordinance "as part of our overall strategy to stop the Eastern Kentucky Resources dump . . . support[ing] a lenient zoning ordinance after we learned that citizens in Lawrence County had stopped [a] proposed . . . hazardous waste incinerator with a similar ordinance."[82] The planning commission passed the zoning ordinance unanimously, as did the fiscal court on first reading the same night as the planning commission vote.[83]

As word of passage of the zoning ordinance spread, opposition to it among county residents quickly arose. MCBE supporters of the proposal tried to assuage concern over land use restrictions. One said county residents "are a group of less than 20,000 people and we are not united. This is a way of giving us more political power by uniting us."[84] A county attorney tried to soothe fears that the ordinance would restrict where to "build churches, station mobile homes and open country stores and businesses" on private property.[85] Still, opponents "condemned the 'briefcase toting bureaucrats that come and tell me I can't build.'"[86]

In the face of popular resistance to the proposal, the fiscal court reversed course and killed the ordinance on its second reading. Backers of the ordinance saved their wrath for those who thought the ordinance was being considered hastily. Hardin said that those voting to kill the ordinance "will tell you they did not know or did not have the time [to consider the ordinance before approval on first reading]. If anyone sitting up here says they did not know what they were doing when they cast their vote, then I wouldn't elect them for stupidity."[87]

A more detached observer of county politics blamed the demise of the zoning proposal on a combination of emotionalism and lack of widespread public discussion of it before the fiscal court consideration of it. A county journalist told me:

> The zoning issue looked too much like the way the landfill was passed, the way that it was getting rammed through. It was real quiet when it was proposed, but once word got out, everybody got upset about it. The support for it on the court changed between the readings, after some of the magistrates heard from their constituents. Then Doc [Hardin] didn't handle some things about it well. He called them all stupid, and that didn't go over well. I reported it in the paper, and Doc got all mad about it, but I said I had to report it, because he did say it. He later put out an apology, and said he didn't mean to call them stupid, but the damage was done.[88]

The damage would continue through the campaigns for county office in 1998. Candidates regularly touted their opposition to the failed zoning ordinance. One of the most detailed political broadsides against the failed ordinance came from a candidate for county attorney, who ran an ad stating:

What would zoning mean to Magoffin County citizens? The people of the County would have to petition a local zoning board, obtain a permit, and pay a fee just to ask permission to use <u>your</u> own land in a manner that you choose. Some examples of some basic land rights that would be REGULATED and RESTRICTED include: where family cemeteries can be located; where trailers/mobile homes can be placed; whether home improvements can be done, such as building decks, tree houses, play houses, garages, carports, sheds, barns, dog houses, etc.; where family farm animals and pets can be located, such as hunting dogs, game chickens, goats, horses, cattle, etc.; where families can put ponds, swimming pools or even grow gardens. I believe in our Constitution and the freedoms that it provides to all of us, such as the freedom to use our own land without local government regulation. <u>It's your land Magoffin County!</u> Most of us either paid for our land or have inherited it from our families as it has passed down through generations. Magoffin County is a rural, peaceful, farm community and is not Lexington or Louisville. **WE DO NOT NEED ZONING! DO WE TRUST THOSE WHO WOULD BE REGULATING OUR LAND USAGE? ASK YOURSELF, DO YOU WANT MORE GOVERNMENT REGULATING AND RESTRICTING YOUR LIFE?** [underlining, capitalization, and boldface in original].[89]

Although MCBE tried to explain the zoning ordinance as part of a comprehensive effort to help the county control future landfill proposals, the campaign debate over zoning was otherwise remarkably free of what had led MCBE to suggest zoning in the first place, the EKR proposal. What was most remarkable was that nobody recognized explicitly that, ultimately, county government maneuvering to keep the landfill project out, no matter how widely supported by the people, constituted "government regulating and restricting" what the Salyersville businessman who owned the landfill site could do with *his* own land.

When I asked the candidate who ran the antizoning ad why the county government should be able to restrict land use for the EKR dump but not be able to zone land, he said:

> I admit that is a fine line. My thinking on it was that the federal courts had the dump case, and there was nothing we could do at that point.[90]

We would have been zoning after-the-fact, and that would have had no effect on the federal case. Prior to the landfill it would have been OK, but not after-the-fact. People here want no restrictions on their land and what they do with it. The main way we can make sure nothing like the landfill proposal ever happens again is to keep electing judges and magistrates that a landfill company can't touch. It's up to the voters to elect good people, to keep it honest so that we can keep out any threats. But the way the zoning was proposed was like a back-door effort, like the landfill, and that didn't go over well.

A more impartial observer of county politics explicitly recognized the contradiction between public desires to keep out both the dump and zoning. He said traditional attitudes had much influence in shaping intractable attitudes on zoning. When I asked him why so few made a connection between zoning and the dump proposal, he told me:

I don't know. I was for zoning, because there's nothing that could keep a dump out as much as zoning could. You put zoning in, and you're not going to get a dump. People got all upset over it, saying they didn't want anybody to tell them what to do with their land. But it never occurred to them that then their neighbors couldn't do anything they might not like on their land. It was an emotional issue, which nobody really took time to connect with the intellectual parts of it. A lot of politics is like that around here. For example, I'm a Democrat because I've been raised that way. But I never stopped to think about it. . . . I'm a very conservative Democrat. Maybe if I'd thought things through more all along, I'd be a Republican today. But I've never stopped to think about it. If folks don't stop to think about something like that, they're not going to stop to think through things like zoning.

MCBE did attempt to explain its side of the zoning proposal in the 1998 primary campaign, as well as to stress its continued vigilance against the EKR proposal. The MCBE attorney sent a letter to all county residents noting that "we won the lawsuit against EKR in the Supreme Court _only_ because the prior fiscal court _did not advertise_ the contract. . . . Therefore, if we elect corrupt officials, who approve an out-of-state garbage contract . . . and the contract for bid is advertised . . . *I am here to tell you that the people of Magoffin County will be unable to stop the dump!* [italics and underlining in original]."

The effect of MCBE appeals to the landfill issue, however, were becoming limited. One reason for this was that in 1998, as in 1993, all candidates stressed their opposition to the EKR project. Another was that, with the U.S. Supreme Court rejection in April 1998 of the last EKR appeal on cases involving the landfill, the landfill company no longer posed as great a threat to the county as it once had. The landfill issue was already becoming ancient political history for newcomers to county politics. One young candidate who ran against an MCBE ally in the 1998 Democratic primary with the support of some "old guard" politicians told me: "I was taken aback by what Magoffin Countians for a Better Environment said about me in this campaign. I've never done anything to harm anybody in that organization. As for the landfill, when it first came up, I was away in school. I've always said I'm against the landfill and that there's no reason I would want a landfill in this county. I'm from here, all my family is from here, and I want to stay here. So why would I want a dump here? I think Magoffin Countians for a Better Environment were out for a good cause, but they just got too caught up in county politics."

What may have most hurt Hardin and his allies, particularly William Grover Arnett, the county attorney elected with him in 1993, was their neglect of the most local concerns, particularly maintenance of individual ties and a focus on individuals, their families, and their small communities, ties that are stressed and cherished by local Baptists and others in the county seeking local community and autonomy. Hardin's administration of the government came to be seen as increasingly distant from the day-to-day concerns of county residents. One reason for this perceived distance was the restriction he placed on his schedule to accommodate both his medical practice and his duties as judge-executive.

Referring to the "part-time issue," one county observer told me that "Doc was able to sell that the last time out, but folks here like to see their officials. They like the personal contact. And Paul Hudson was able to use that against him this time." Salyer ran a campaign ad saying that the "Rx" the county needed was to "remember the good old days when the county judge maintained an open door policy," promising voters that, in contrast to Hardin, they "can have a personal relationship" with him.[91] Even the discredited former school superintendent was able to launch a campaign based on more open access to county government, saying he would seek support as the Republican candidate for county judge-executive from "the whole community—no political base, just the grassroots people."[92]

The county newspaper editor told me that Hardin and Arnett

> had other issues they could have run on, but they didn't. . . . They ran a simple, brilliant campaign in 1993. But the second time around, when running for re-election, folks get lazy. I've got a saying, how everybody thinks they're a publisher now with their personal computer. That was Grover's problem. He ran his campaign from that computer. He designed all his posters and signs and brochures from that computer, and relied on the signs and the billboards and the newspapers and the television and radio spots. Last time out, it was brilliant. He just ran ads saying I'm Grover Arnett, and I want to be your county attorney. He visited every voter in the county. He took Doc into office with him, going around to every home in the county. But he didn't do that this time. And folks like to see their officials. They want to press the flesh with you and talk to you about their lives.

Instead of visiting voters again, Arnett ran perhaps the most lavish campaign in county history, including television, newspaper, and radio advertisements and laminated campaign posters. Commenting on the money Arnett spent, a local political operative said,

> He could have spent $30,000, which was far less than what he did spend, and have hired [a local political consultancy] to run his campaign for him. They could have told him, OK, Grover, now emphasize these issues, and don't emphasize these issues. They could have helped him spend his money a lot more effectively. If he'd done that, or just about anything but what he did, then he could have won 2 to 1. Folks around here get suspicious when they see you spending so much money for an office, when they see you putting up laminated signs or more than one sign for every vote than you could possibly get. They start to wonder what you're spending that much money for. The voters started to get overwhelmed with all the ads . . . they just got tired of it.

Magoffin County voters registered their weariness of Hardin and Arnett in the 1998 Democratic primary. Hardin lost to Salyer by nearly 350 votes, winning less than 40 percent of the vote. Arnett ran ahead of Hardin, but lost his race by just over 100 votes. As there had been five years earlier, there was a strong correlation between support for Hardin and support for Arnett in 1998, with each candidate running strongest in the same precincts and weakest in the same areas. The key to the campaign, however, appears to have been in Salyer's greatly improved performance in the southernmost magisterial district, his home district. After losing the area by an 18-vote margin in the 1993 primary, he won it by 317 votes in the 1998 primary. Salyer also may have been helped by his connection to the governor, particularly a local belief that he "has a pipeline straight to the governor," though some local businessmen scoffed at how little would flow through the pipeline. The only comfort MCBE allies could take from the election was that it appears to have been run cleanly. The clean primary, however, resulted in an "old guard" politician vying with the discredited former school superintendent, the Republican nominee for judge-executive, for control of a government from which MCBE and its reform-minded allies were shut out.

READINESS FOR REFORM

Magoffin County voters are hardly the first rural population to accept tentatively reform politics, only to reject it decisively later. The classic historical case of a rural population faltering in pursuit of the diffuse goals of reform politics occurred in the shift from Populism to Progressivism at the end of the nineteenth century. Both Richard Hofstadter and Robert Wiebe, while advancing opposing interpretations of Progressivism, identify common difficulties rural Protestants had in adapting from supporting the somewhat specific goals of Populism to supporting the more general reforms of Progressivism. As the Populist movement progressed, Wiebe writes, "That confident feeling of a whole countryside marching in unison was soon lost."[93] Hofstadter writes that as Populism gave way to Progressivism, reform politics passed from an overwhelmingly rural and provincial base to one that was urban, middle-class, and nationwide.[94]

In both the works of Wiebe and Hofstadter, particularly in the latter's discussion of paranoid politics in the rural base of Populism, we can find many of the same political themes that are evident in the resistance of Magoffin County and its local Baptists to the more diffuse demands of reform politics. In the immediate face of the landfill threat, Hardin and his MCBE allies, more urbane and middle-class than most county residents, were able both to rally county opinion against the crisis and use the controversy to advance their own politics. As the controversy receded, and as Hardin and the new county government sought to pursue other goals—particularly those that might limit local community and control—the political power of MCBE allies receded. Their appeal in the community was further diminished by their adoption of a sophisticated campaign better suited for "wholesale" selling of candidates in large urban areas, rather than the more intimate "retail" appeal Magoffin Countians most appreciate. Aloof from all this were the local Baptist churches of the county. Many individual local Baptists likewise either stayed away from these political conflicts or opposed anything, no matter what its ultimate purpose, that could threaten local autonomy and community.

To an outsider, the general distaste Magoffin residents had for MCBE "politics," particularly when MCBE allies confronted complex issues, may still seem strange. The landfill was a political problem, and it was a legal problem, and there appears to have been no way to address it but politically and legally, including through vigilance at the polls and some minimal zoning regulations that are comprehensive and fair to all. While the landfill project appears to have no current political viability, the MCBE attorney is correct that the proposal is not legally dead and that the county government could theoretically reverse itself yet again and approve the EKR project or something similar. The county had elected the school board that had hired the superintendent that the commonwealth had to force from office, so the schools are a political problem. The county employees attacking citizens at a fiscal court meeting were related to those who held office, so fisticuffs at fiscal court meetings are a political problem that can require remedies beyond a sheriff's investigation. The buying of votes and the inability of local election boards to control the practice is a political problem by definition, which MCBE allies clearly had both altruistic and self-interested concerns in addressing. The budgetary deadlocks the fiscal court has suffered over bitter factionalism are a political problem. An elected sheriff who is charged with shooting a young supporter of an opponent is a political and legal problem.

All these problems are related to many others and perhaps require more sophisticated and long-term vigilance than Magoffin voters are used to providing, even though they desire to have personal contacts with local officials who will pay the most attention to individual problems. On the surface, to expect MCBE, or any other group addressing a significant problem within the county, not to address broader politics in a county that has often been rife with corruption or debilitating factionalism, or to avoid addressing such problems so as to draw the greatest possible coalition against the most immediate problem, would appear to be naive in the extreme, if not plainly irrational.

From a more informed perspective, such resistance to political activity is less strange. Like rural populists who could not adapt to the more general demands of Progressive politics, Magoffin and its local Baptists are not without basis in fearing a more sophisticated politics and its practice. They have rational reasons to limit their political commitment and to keep their support of political reform in check. These reasons relate to the organizational demands of politics, to the threat they present to whatever sense of community local Baptist churches in the county are able to build, to the fact that the landfill threat comes from sophisticated politics, being led by a former Republican member of the U.S. House. Their resistance is related to other issues as well; for example, the supposedly better statewide educational standards, whose implementation was supposed to improve local schools, have, in fact, so far made things worse for local students. The abandonment of grassroots campaigning by MCBE allied candidates in favor of a lavish media campaign among voters who value personal contact with their officials only compounded the structural problems any politician seeking support for a broad reform agenda would have in Magoffin County.

Much of Mancur Olson's theory on groups and public goods paints resistance to broader "politics" not as naive but as rational behavior. Olson's theory easily explains the initial organization against the landfill. Those living close to it had a strong interest in keeping it out, hence MCBE leaders and local Baptist preachers from the area provided initial organization and support against the proposal. The rest of the county may not have had enough incentive to provide the initial organization against the proposal, but they had incentive in perceived threats to the county's water and its economic vitality to join quickly in the fight against it.

This initial political support for MCBE dissipated as the organization's goals began to include a broader program of county government reforms.

Many landfill opponents had poignant reasons for resisting general reform. State and local government jobs are a comparatively large source of employment for Magoffin workers. Nearly one in five county workers (19 percent) are employed by state or local government, compared with about one in eight workers (12 percent) across the nation. These workers and their families may have objected to the landfill and may have been willing to organize against it, but they also had incentives not to upset the local political structure.

More generally among the poor and badly educated population in the county, the landfill provided enough incentive for a short-term political commitment, but the more diffuse and distant goals of reform politics provided little incentive for continued commitment. Viewed in this context, local residents' distaste for MCBE's "politics" may not signal resistance to worldly activities as much as it signals reluctance to struggle for vague, distant goals that may never be reached. This is much like the reluctance Olson describes of large, latent groups to organize effectively for inclusive public goods.

We cannot overlook the conflict in Magoffin between two sets of collective goods. These are county political reform and the sense of community local Baptist churches seek to build in the face of difficult circumstances. We might agree that the broader goals of MCBE allies are a needed collective good for the county. But organizing and struggling for this set of collective goods would conflict with a collective good that these churches have already provided for the county, the good of local church authority and community. The neglect by MCBE allies of more intimate, individual-level politics made even more difficult the bridging of the gap between its broad goals and the more immediate demands of local community.

To be sure, local Baptist emphases on local authority and traditionalism are outmoded in some ways, particularly for women, who have compelling reasons for objecting to traditional sex roles of the church and to some of its implied policy preferences, such as local prohibition. Yet the local Baptist emphases on local authority and traditionalism and community can still serve many roles in a county as desperately poor as Magoffin, particularly to the extent that they encourage stable and healthy family life on modest incomes in the midst of so much poverty and so little opportunity.

The local Baptist ethos that serves these local needs is one that limits the broader perspectives of adherents. This ethos can serve a basic need of building stable communities in low-income areas. But the same attitudes it must adopt to foster local authority and community, attitudes disdaining centralized authority in any one person or shunning anything that can affect the harmony of the community and the autonomy of its individual members—attitudes stressing local contact with officials most concerned with individual problems—are those that can make adherents suspicious of broad political engagement addressing larger problems. The tension between traditional needs in a local community and broader threats, such as those presented by the landfill proposal, are exacerbated in Magoffin for local Baptists by their dominant position in the county and the accompanying need to accommodate all viewpoints within the church community.

Whether or how long Magoffin sectarians can cope with this tension remains to be seen. The local needs that call for an institution that can help families remain stable and subsist on modest incomes will continue. These needs, however, are increasingly joined by more cosmopolitan influences that may not require as much the establishment of patriarchal male families as a condition of male discipline. As the MCBE president told me, "By the time my mother was thirty, she had her seventh and last child, me. Now all of us are past thirty, and some of us don't have children and we may not have any. So I don't know how traditional this county is going to stay, or how that's going to affect our families and our future."

Her comments point to another consideration on the prospects of reform politics in the county. If reform politics ever succeed in Magoffin, it will be because Magoffin has become ready for reform and because those within Magoffin have made it ready for reform. It will be made ready for reform by those who are able to show great sensitivity to local Baptist traditions and their uses, are able to find the proper way to balance the changes demanded by cosmopolitan influences and the adaptations available to "Bible-based" Protestantism, and who can, above all, bridge the gap between local needs and cosmopolitan demands, combining a handshake for everybody in the county with an ability to explain the need for attention to more diffuse issues.

Whether such a candidate exists or all this can be done is not clear. Some members of MCBE, including its president, did make an effort to bridge the gap between local needs and cosmopolitan demands, continuing to emphasize part of this area's religious tradition and its uses in the community. Yet one of the ultimate failings of MCBE allies in county politics was their abandonment of a more intimate political style for a more sophisticated style more appropriate to larger communities. Perhaps abandonment of such a style is ultimately needed to make smaller communities, like larger communities, less susceptible to any single threat. Regardless, the more cosmopolitan members of MCBE failed in some ways to maintain consistently the adaptations needed to campaign in a small, locally oriented, rural community.

At the same time, it is not clear that the religion of these local Baptists, which has been malleable in the past, will ever prove malleable enough to support more sophisticated politics, even if more county residents were to become less convinced of their self-sufficiency and more convinced of the need to adhere to broader standards of modern society. "Bible-based" Protestantism in Magoffin is not, in the end, readily adaptable to every secular need. Regardless of whatever secular conditions may have been behind the first development of the religion in the county, it is clear that, while continuing to fulfill some secular needs, it can no longer respond to all secular problems confronting the county. The religion does provide a standard of community and family life that is invaluable in such an impoverished area. Providing this standard in the face of the dire conditions in the county may require an overbearing emphasis on tradition. The longer adherents insist on the traditional commands of the religion, the more difficult it becomes for them to adapt the religion to changing secular conditions.

The irony is obvious. Religious traditions that in their origins were partly a response to the challenge of secular conditions can become too rigid to adapt to changing secular conditions. The irony is heightened in Magoffin by the dominance of biblically oriented Protestantism. To the extent that social and economic disorder in Magoffin requires an overbearing emphasis on tradition is the extent to which it encounters further obstacles in adapting to modern circumstances.

It is also the extent to which sectarianism, particularly as described by Werner Stark, cannot continually meet changing secular needs. Stark's observation on the direction of the revolt of the poor—religious if political power is not feasible, political if it is—may have been accurate when "Bible-based" Protestantism first developed in Magoffin County. But because Magoffin sectarians—who, as a bloc, are now by far the largest group of county voters—have not sought to take political power, even when confronting a wide variety of threats to the county, we have further evidence that there is an inflexible core to their religion that cannot be changed easily. It is a core that especially poses difficulties when its pronounced emphasis on traditionalism encounters conditions requiring modern political techniques.

"Bible-based" Protestantism may help some Magoffin Countians on the first steps to political "reform," just as it helps county residents build communities no other institutions can sustain there. But as cosmopolitan threats become more diffuse and broadly based, such religion becomes less helpful. Much of the religion can remain malleable, but the traditional core, while serving some secular needs, cannot serve all in the modern world. It is not just the malleability of many sacred commands that marks this religion, but the increasing tension between the traditional core and more general modern challenges. This tension has had some unhappy consequences for Magoffin residents seeking to confront broader challenges, but this tension persists for others of this religion in less dire circumstances, too.

CHAPTER 5

A Theme and Its Variations: Sectarianism and Politics Revisited

Analyzing sectarianism as a political resource leaves one open to the danger of seeing it as only a resource to use in meeting material needs. Part of this danger lies in seeing sects always as small and short-lived, and thereby most adaptable to the social and political needs of adherents in their short life. Yet, as Max Weber notes, "A sect in the sociological sense of the word" does not have to be small or short-lived.[1] Troeltsch, Niebuhr, Werner Stark, and others offer many theoretical insights on the sects of this study when they point to why some sectarians are otherworldly and why others become more driven by secular concerns. Weber's analysis of sectarianism's sociological essence may best capture how the sects of this study have persisted for nearly two centuries, and what future religious, social, and political adaptation are available to them.

He writes, "The sect is a group whose very nature and purpose precludes universality and requires the free consensus of its members.... The sect does not want to be an institution dispensing grace, like a church, which includes the righteous and the unrighteous and is especially concerned with subjecting the sinner to Divine law.... The typical sect rejects institutionalized salvation and office charisma."[2] Some of these local Baptists may move to churches with greater establishments. Some may wish for greater establishments within these sects. Some may wish that these sects would ally strongly with the religious right. These sects, however, are unlikely to do any of these things without losing their character and appeal.

The nature of the sect is such that it can both promote democratic political activity and limit its influence. A "pure sect," as Weber describes it, insists on direct democratic administration and on treating clergy as servants of the congregation. These characteristics underlie the relationship it has with political power. He writes:

> The sect is a specifically antipolitical or at least apolitical group. Since it must not raise universal demands and endeavors to exist as a voluntary association of qualified believers, it cannot enter into an alliance with the political power. If it concludes such an alliance . . . the result is an aristocratic rule by the ecclesiastically qualified; lead[ing] to compromise and the loss of . . . character. . . . The pure sect must advocate "tolerance" and "separation of church and state" . . . because it is in fact *not* [emphasis in original] a universalist redemptory institution for the repression of sin and can bear political as little as hierocratic reglementation [*sic*]; because no official power can dispense grace to unqualified persons and, hence, all use of political force in religious matters must appear senseless or outright diabolical; because the sect is simply not concerned with outsiders; because, taking all this together, the sect just cannot be anything but an absolutely voluntary association if it wants to retain its true religious identify and effectiveness.[3]

The spirit of the sect is such that it must insist upon democratic administration, while at the same time treating its clergy in a manner that will keep them, and hence the sect itself, from exercising broader authority of the type the sect would not tolerate being exercised by an external authority over itself. Sectarian religion can assist democratic participation, but its practice can lead to local concerns that ultimately curb broader political influence.

Here we again see the characteristics that distinguish the Baptists I study from more politically aggressive strains of biblically oriented religion. Because these sects have historical, political, economic, and sociological reasons for emphasizing the local authority of the individual church, they cannot tolerate any religious sanctioning of external political authority. They likewise cannot support their own exercise of ecclesiastical authority over bodies external to it.

In concluding this analysis, some other models are also helpful in drawing lessons from those I study to broader populations and circumstances. These models include Samuel Hill's study of popular southern religion, Ted Jelen's and Mark Shibley's analyses of religiosity and political mobilization, and, most generally, Weber's concept of the routinization of charisma. A review of these models helps show the possibilities, limits, and lessons for broader application from a religion featuring local adaptation weighted by a traditional core practiced by those on the "margins" of society who often have many reasons to fear broader contact with more sophisticated elites.

Hill's passionate plea for the reform of popular southern religion is one that may echo among those I study, particularly those struggling to maintain their traditionalism in the face of modern encroachments. He writes of "popular Southern religion" that

> the old-time religion persists—in a new time. Barely adequate for the old time—a mixture of good and bad qualities—it is ludicrously out of step with the new.... Southern religion's rigidity is paradoxical, since historically it derived some of its shape, much of its relevance, and most of its success from the factor of adaptability in the formative period, 1740–1830. Today, faced with the eruption of a new social order, it tragically refuses to forsake apparatus given to it by a culture which is presently dying.... Having been by-passed by much of "early modern religion," completely out of touch with "modern religion," it languishes in a patently obsolete medievalism, calling it "timeless" ... three courses of action are open to th[e] new generation. First, they can attempt to conform to the diverging values of both the church and the contemporary world. Second, they can violate intellectual honesty and live in the world of the church. Third, they can practice integrity and reject the church. It is encouraging, however, that should the church become more responsive, a fourth path will lie before them, one which recognizes compatibility between the internalized values and outlooks of their ethos and the framework within which the church affirms its message and lays its claim upon their lives.[4]

Among many of these local Baptists, there is a growing divergence between the values of their church and those of the contemporary world. This is most clear where the emphasis they place on traditionalism comes into conflict with the adaptability they have practiced when confronting secular, particularly economic, threats. This religion lacks any ecclesiastical structure that might help adherents in confronting nonlocal challenges. Yet it is not clear that its traditionalism or its remaining adaptability has become completely irrelevant for modern settings. In the Colquest strike, this religion, featuring control of, by, and for adherents and their local needs, ultimately proved more helpful to adherents engaged in economic struggle than more structured religion would have, including those that often claim to exercise a preferential option for the poor.

A religion can prove most useful to the needs of individual adherents—can even be suited to face nearly all modern challenges—while ultimately failing as a political (much less spiritual) resource, particularly one that can affect a broader public agenda. There is a contradiction in what gives modern American religion its appeal, and the qualities needed for coalition politics. Ted Jelen captures the implications of this contradiction among churches in general, and the work of Mark Shibley adds some implications for a more specific population closer to that which I study.

Jelen draws a general lesson for churches and politics from analogies holding churches to be competitors in a religious marketplace seeking to differentiate themselves from one another in an effort to satisfy the needs of "customers" in particular market niches. He writes that it follows from such a model "that churches may engage in 'product differentiation' and emphasize the differences between themselves and other denominations. Indeed, it seems likely that churches in competitive religious markets will seek to distinguish themselves from their theologically adjacent competitors. An emphasis on such 'intramural' differences may render political cooperation somewhat difficult. The logic of lay recruitment may encourage fragmentation, whereas the logic of political mobilization may suggest the need for aggregation."[5] The "product differentiation" in which local Baptists engage, and the hindrances this puts on political aggregation, is manifest in two ways.

First, these Baptists largely distrust broader religious elites. Their "product" is one differentiated by its emphasis on completely local authority, and that emphasis can appeal to adherents with interests contradicting those of broader religious elites. The Duck River Baptist preacher of West Tennessee who wishes his church would become more closely allied with the religious right faces contradictory "market" demands in "selling" his "product" to his community. The "product" supposedly sold by the religious right, that of giving supporters broader influence over national values, is one of little value to those "buying" a religion best suited to those most interested in local needs and circumstances.

Second, the religious "product" local Baptists sell, while the same in its doctrine, theology, practice, rural orientation, emphasis on traditional roles for the sexes, and distrust of religious and secular elites, is one that cannot be used the same way in all circumstances. This religion cannot be taken from one place to another and yield the same views on or links between religion and society, even if the core of the religion remains unchanged. Within this religion, local views on or links between religion and politics and society change as local circumstances change. We cannot expect such views to remain the same in the agricultural, the industrial, the coal mining, or the metropolitan South. Local Baptists in coal-mining areas, or in industrializing areas, or in metropolitan areas, or Baptists who are upwardly mobile, have different needs and expectations in their lives and of their faith. A religion whose "marketability" rests on local adaptability will serve in different ways adherents in different communities encountering different circumstances.

Shibley, in examining the effects of "evangelicalism" on American civic life, finds that "evangelicalism is growing, but like all religion in a modern context, it is becoming less relevant as a legitimating force in public life."[6] He argues that "if conservative Protestantism must accommodate secular culture to survive in the long run, then the potential of resurgent evangelicalism—conservative southern religion—to reform the wider culture is limited."[7] In particular, Shibley finds that as evangelicalism outside the South "increasingly shape[s] itself to meet individual needs first and foremost . . . the restructuring of American religion and culture may, in the long run, be more public-to-private than liberal-to-conservative."[8]

Shibley makes his argument about a particular population that, while sharing some broad origins with those I study, is hardly identical to it. His specific focus is on how "new evangelicals" who share many of the characteristics of "conservative southern religion" manage to make this religion one which appeals to a much more transient and modern population outside the South. Among the many differences between those Shibley studies and those I study is the lesser reliance by the former on a literal interpretation of the Bible.

Yet the lessons he draws from the population he studies appear to have broad application, including to those I study. These insights stem from the focus both populations have on the individual needs of adherents, however differently this focus might be expressed. While the religion of local Baptists in the middle and uplands South appears unable to address itself to broad restructuring of local culture and society, Shibley's findings suggest this problem may be more widespread, with American religion increasingly focused on individual needs and growing more unable to address itself to the broad restructuring of national culture and society. The local Baptists I study lack a structure that might help them propagate their standards in broader settings, but Shibley's findings suggest it is not just the lack of such a structure that prevents their broader influence. It is also their appeal to individual needs and circumstances, coupled with a declining emphasis on religion in American civic life. Even if these churches had the ecclesiastical means to influence broader spheres, broader cultural and religious trends could prevent them from doing so.

Difficulties between, on the one hand, a founding spirit based on individual needs and adaptation and, on the other, changing modern circumstances adherents face are not limited to traditional southern religion or even religion in general, but are shared to some extent by all organizations seeking to remain true to their founding charisma. In addition to the charisma they claim from Jesus and "John the Baptizer," these Baptists share a common charisma grounded in hostility to established ecclesiastical authority that extols individual and local authority over bureaucratic and cosmopolitan authority. For charismatic authority to persist and not become a purely transitory phenomenon, Weber writes, it "cannot remain stable, but becomes either traditionalized or rationalized or a combination of both."[9] Weber identifies "the ideal and also the material interests of the followers in the continuation and the continual reactivation of the community" as underlying this transformation.[10]

The founding charisma of these Baptists persists, both in their traditionalism and in their persisting adaptability to secular circumstances. They do face a tension between an inflexible core of traditionalism and changing social and economic circumstances that continually affects the influences their religion has on their politics.

There is no clear line among them between what has become "traditionalized" and what remains open to adaptability, or what serves only traditional religious needs and what serves only modern secular needs. The localized authority of this religion, which might seem most open to adaptability, itself has become "traditionalized," or largely a goal in itself, rather than a pure agent to meet material success. It can still meet many material needs, just as emphasis on patriarchal authority can still serve some economic needs. There are indications that these Baptists' emphases on traditional roles for each sex can work to the advantage of their communities, or can be modified somewhat, as in the case of changing dress codes or greater acceptance for working women among these local Baptists in metropolitan areas, or can be too constricting to allow for needed civic adaptations, such as accepting the need for women in civic leadership. This religion can serve some material needs of adherents while keeping them from meeting others. These constraints can appear both for religious and still other material reasons.

LOCAL THEMES REVISITED

This tension between traditionalism and contemporary circumstance is apparent in the north Alabama preacher who turned down a promotion from industrial mechanic to foreman. He did not choose his religion to advance bourgeois material ambitions. He chose a religion which gives him a secured, honored place in an area that does not have many advantages. Perhaps more material and fewer ideal advantages of his religion would appear if he practiced it elsewhere. Perhaps if he and others like him were to leave their homes in rural hinterlands and be exposed to more cosmopolitan standards then we would see how this religion could be adapted to newer material circumstances. But to consider such hypothetical possibilities in his circumstances may be the secular equivalent of asking in these churches how many angels dance on the head of a pin. Such questions may attract those with the means to undertake "leisures" such as systematic theology or theoretical social science. They are less alluring in rural industrial areas such as where this preacher lives, and where the local community, like all communities, retains an interest in stability, and not in exporting every last stable worker.

The emphasis on local authority that is alluring in such hinterlands, stemming from the founding spirit in this religion, can help adherents with many of the daily challenges of their lives, but it cannot spur them into a broader world of moral, evangelistic, or economic conquest. Adherents can use their faith for individual and immediate community needs, but cannot use it to prop up ecclesiastical establishments representing broader religious or secular interests. Their reluctance to enforce universal ecclesiastical demands leads to a reluctance to enforce universal political demands. They can no more enforce universal political demands than they can enforce universal ecclesiastical demands on all their congregations or accept the enforcement of such universal demands by external authorities.

In emphasizing local authority for local use, this religion places limits on the exercise of broader authority for any use. These local Baptists can have local authority, and they can shape much of their religion to local circumstances. But this means acquiescing to a religion that does not permit what adherents will not bear: the exercise of external authority over others, particularly such authority that would enforce universal commands over others. This is true even for authority seeking to enforce commands in the religious or secular interests of these groups, since they would resent such authority coming from outside their local community.

The Magoffin County United Baptist preacher who emphasizes restrictions his association places on "lording it over God's heritage" illustrates the limits this religion places on the exercise of external authority by adherents. In exchange for local authority within his church, this preacher and his church avoid exerting worldly authority over others. The founding spirit of their religion is one which emphasizes local authority for local use, but is also one which thereby limits the exercise of religious authority.

There are also worldly reasons local Baptists in Magoffin may wish to avoid worldly conflict. County politics may be as unseemly to some in the county as it is to some outside it. Continuing emphasis on the autonomy of the local congregation, accompanying a professed lack of interest in using the church to propagate wider community standards, can help local Baptists there maintain the reputation of humility and subtlety they have in the broader community. Not being able to affect broader county politics may be a small price to pay for this reputation, and a price that appears reasonable not just by the accounting of traditionalism.

In addition to a solid reputation in the broader community, local Baptists in Magoffin gain the more material benefit of an institution that can promote community and family stability as few others can in such a distressed area. Material benefits accruing to other Baptists of this study include local religious authority they can use for some limited needs when confronting external economic, political, and religious authorities who are indifferent or hostile to local needs. In the Clairfield strike, the adaptability of this authority was least limited, enabling the miners to find greater support from their sects than from churches with vaunted establishments, including those that are supposed to exercise a preferential option for the poor.

There is tension for these sects when encroaching worldly conflicts, or confronting such conflicts, threaten the values that give them what little economic, political, and social security they possess. This tension emanates from the core of the particular tradition of these Baptists, which honors and recognizes individual needs and local authority, but in its logic limits the adaptability of religious authority for broader purposes.

Those in Clairfield resolved this tension with a modern accommodation: a wholehearted embrace of the labor movement. They had an advantage in confronting a problem that did not threaten immediately their social traditionalism, and for which they could identify a relatively fixed and definite solution. By embracing the labor movement wholeheartedly, they removed the problem posed by conflict with mine management to a completely secular arena, which they could approach from their religion as they saw fit.

The Magoffin sectarians had more difficulty confronting their problem of outside contact. The problems outside contact unveiled rested in venal local politics. Those strongest in such politics have been those best able to practice a politics focused on individual contact and needs. Such a style appeals to many local Baptists, but has not been conducive to the broader goals of "reform" government. The religious core local Baptists in Magoffin share continues to address in its patriarchal emphases many modern permutations of age-old spiritual and material problems, but it is not one that is flexible enough to address the most complex modern and cosmopolitan threats to the county.

To be sure, while local Baptist congregations in Magoffin would not become involved in the fight against the landfill, many individual adherents did. Opponents of the despised dump effectively invoked some religious resources in that particular, limited conflict. Yet as those most active against the landfill pursued more diffuse goals, or as they adapted political techniques that local Baptist tradition could not support, local Baptist influences dissipated. The peculiar circumstances of Magoffin work and education, for example, logically lead to female leadership in any complex or long-term secular grassroots struggle, but the complexities that lead to female leadership cannot be accommodated easily by these Baptists.

These sects can make limited concessions to accept the material benefits made possible by an increasing presence of women in the workforce. But they are not as adaptable in shifting their traditions from economic circumstances that keep women at home to social circumstances that lead to women's political authority. They can adapt when expanded roles for women grow slowly and steadily and bring material benefits to individual families, but they cannot adapt when the need for women's political leadership arises rapidly and contrasts so sharply with the traditional and material goals of their emphasis on patriarchal family authority. They cannot adapt as easily when confronting political circumstances that may be perceived as carrying an implicit radical challenge to their fundamental social assumptions.

We cannot calibrate the range of this religious adaptability by simply measuring traditional attitudes and cosmopolitan challenges to them. As illogical to modern circumstances as such traditionalism may seem in Magoffin politics today, it still has some secular uses and, hence, attractions. It regulates the labor market and can provide for family needs better than nearly any other social institution can in an impoverished area. Historically, the spirit that animates these Baptists' traditionalism developed in response to church establishments of colonial days and the first years of the American republic. This spirit continues among them today and can still be called upon to assist some material needs, even as limits to such adaptation become more apparent.

These Baptists continue to pursue both spiritual and, inadvertently or not, material interests through their religion. In persisting outside the mainstream of southern evangelical Protestantism, they maintain and follow a disestablishmentarian precedent. They call repeatedly upon this precedent for differing reasons and in varying forms. They continue to adhere to prohibitions of any form of religious establishments and nearly all forms of churchly accouterments. Their hostility to establishment and a corresponding emphasis on the "primitive" elements of faith ensure that a sectarian spirit, or a charisma of local authority and local religion, will always be present among them. This spirit enables any male, without regard to social or economic standing, to claim equality and authority with any other in these congregations. It animates what is the only institution, their religion, that these Baptists can invariably call upon, without interference from hostile, external bodies, in confronting local needs. At the same time, this spirit, by opposing the authority of ecclesiastical establishments, limits the establishment of ecclesiastical bodies by these groups, even those that conceivably might provide needed resources for other, more complex struggles.

Perhaps the relatively late settlement of many of the regions these sects occupy encouraged a continuing frontier spirit and independence in their religion.[11] Perhaps the loss of control over local economic production, common to those in areas dependent on industries such as coal mining, continually fosters a need for some type of local independence, religious or otherwise, and this religion remains a needed local institution that residents can seize at will. Perhaps workers in rural industrial hinterlands, increasingly dependent on distant corporations, similarly need a local institution that they can control and use for their own purposes. There are many reasons unique to these areas that give adherents a special predilection to religion emphasizing the sufficiency of local authority and based on the supposedly literal interpretation of a sacred text, but there are likely similar incentives for poor adherents elsewhere to turn to such a religion for social stability and locally controlled authority. Likewise, the social and economic circumstances of those I study may be in many ways unique. But there is no reason to suppose the process leading to the tension between adaptability and the traditional core is also unique.

Material and Traditional Goals

There are some traditional material concerns that continue to influence these Baptists, but they are not the bourgeois considerations similar religion has sometimes supported. The hostility of these Baptists toward many organized forms of "benevolence" has ensured that charity for the poor would stay among their own needy. This is a particularly touchy issue for these Baptists, given both the many poor in their home communities and the historical experience they have had in seeing how mission monies have been spent in ill-informed attempts to "convert" them. This hostility toward outside benevolence and ecclesiastical establishment, while tied to material interests, also has intangible community benefits, including local self-empowerment.

Traditional sex roles among these Baptists serve an economic role, but also provide intangible benefits to the community. Their enforcement enables these sectarians to foster family and community stability for themselves, material goals that can also provide a more tranquil setting for spiritual growth.

Despite its material advantages, there is a core of this religion that will not bend or, at the very least, increasingly will not change as fast as secular circumstances may. The more dire influences of this core are apparent in Magoffin County. There, the same traditions that enforce disciplined male behavior and that enable these churches to create stable, respected communities in impoverished circumstances are also those that prevent adaptation of more sophisticated politics, such as those needed to reform a venal county government, or to accept the reasons for female civic leadership, or more generally to adopt the politics needed to confront the threats facing the county, not all of which can be managed through local, individual action.

Even the most affluent among these Baptists have boundaries, such as those on women's roles or on acquisition of middle-class church accouterments, that they will not cross. The most affluent tend to align themselves with broader movements of cultural conservatism. This serves the purpose of reaffirming select elements of their sectarian roots that do not contradict their newfound affluence and that help develop other elements of their religion that may affirm it. But these new elements may be no more accepting of the need for more complex structures to accommodate more complex needs than is the religion of local Baptists in Magoffin. For many historical, political, and sociological reasons, including the precedents established among these groups and their rural roots, the sectarian spirit remains strong enough among them to require reaffirmation of some of the original elements of their faith. These elements, and their reaffirmation, prevent the religion from becoming merely a tool of bourgeois economic interests. A congregation that debates whether acquisition of a piano—much less mission support—is too great a concession to affluence will not foster institutions tying the interests of adherents to broader forms of cultural or economic conservatism, even if more affluent adherents seek such ties.

There are also limits to economic adaptability of this religion for those who would use it for more proletarian purposes. Some labor union members of these sects do not participate in militant union activities because of a desire to remain unspotted from the world. Others feel conflict with issues of cultural conservatism and, while supporting their particular union's activities, are leery about supporting culturally heterodox allies in liberal labor politics.[12] There is a group of enthusiastic supporters for broadly liberal labor politics among these sects. But this group is small, it is exceptional, it faces local circumstances allowing it to separate even more strictly the religious from the secular than the other sectarians do, and it is not clear that it can always adapt from the relatively specific goals of organized labor to more general goals.

The question of more "worldly" participation for these Baptists is not how "otherworldly" religion inhibits political participation, but what is the nature of the worldly challenges confronting them and how much their religion can accommodate to meet these challenges without upsetting both the traditional and material goals they have won and wish to maintain. We may wonder, for example, why these Baptists do not see that practicing some form of compulsion is sometimes needed to ensure the existence of a labor union, and thereby adjust their religious and political attitudes accordingly, but we may wonder this only because we have the leisure to do so. We may not have to worry, as they do, about more pressing community concerns or about losing all too easily an honored local reputation of humility and stability. The question for these Baptists is not necessarily one of worldliness confronting a desire to be unworldly. Rather, it is one of balancing worldly concerns with the challenges, or even threats, such concerns can pose to the core values of this religion, including values that provide both traditional and worldly benefits.

The material needs of these groups and how they use their churches to meet them are not always recognized by others, particularly when such needs conflict with those that might seem, at least to outsiders, to be more pressing. These Baptists have many reasons for seeking local community and authority and stability in their religion, even when these prevent them from confronting broader challenges. They do not always choose their religion because of what others might recognize as the most pressing material challenges confronting them. Rather, their religion typically attracts them because of the modest economic circumstances they face, because of the stability it offers, and because it may be the only institution in their communities that is always open and amenable to their local control and authority.

Implications for Broader Themes of Religion and Politics

The spirit of sectarian Protestantism that animates these groups also helps animate more widely recognized forms of biblically oriented Protestantism. The advantage of studying sectarian Protestantism in these groups is that two inherent tensions of this spirit affecting both the context and the extent of church-motivated political activity often overlooked in larger populations can be highlighted.

The first of these tensions is between ascetic origins and changing local circumstances. The ascetic spirit is both the greatest strength and weakness of such religion as a political and social secular resource. Its strength lies in allowing individuals to interpret sacred commands to local circumstances, free of disagreeable "experts" or establishments over which the individual adherent may have no control. It may even foster or justify some political behavior and attitudes appropriate to local needs. Its weakness lies in continuing to carry with it demands that adherents feel they must meet even after they appear to have become a hindrance in secular struggle. The ascetic spirit may inhibit development of more sophisticated political attitudes or behavior needed to confront diffuse problems. This religion can still benefit from emphasizing individual needs, but faces increasing circumstances in which its traditionalism causes its adaptability to falter.

Some labor union members among these sects feel a need, based on some of their traditional goals, to curtail union activities. Others try to live with a tension between their cultural concerns and an outside liberalism supportive of their unions but disdaining their cultural concerns. This tension immobilizes them politically. Still others devise a means by which they reinvigorate the spirit of the first Baptists and separate completely their politics from the demands of their religion. This enables political activism, but can neuter the political influence of their religion, particularly concerns grounded in their cultural traditionalism.

It appears that these sects' older members have accomplished an accommodation between this religion and liberal labor politics more easily than younger members. On the one hand, this raises questions about the long-term effectiveness of broadly liberal politics of labor unions among these groups, given increasingly wider knowledge of cultural standards and their partisan implications. On the other hand, the tension could conceivably become so great for younger members that they may adapt their religion even more than it has been adapted in the past. Circumstances could enable them to make their churches the true religious supporters in the cause of labor, as miners of all ages made the Clairfield churches. Some political entrepreneurs among these local Baptists may wish to foster a broader politics combining cultural conservatism with liberal labor politics giving these adherents a broader standard to follow in pursuing a similar faith of politics, economics, and religion. Perhaps if such a politics were to become more prominent, then broader political and social circumstances would make such adaptability easier for churches otherwise lacking any structure that could affect the culture to aid such a transition.[13]

Some of the most affluent among these Baptists tie themselves to broader cultural conservatism. Yet this does not help them escape the conflict between their sectarian traditions of highly localized authority and conservative Protestant establishments seeking to propagate universal standards. The goal of conservative Protestantism seeking public enforcement of religiously based standards is traceable to a Weberian notion of sectarian Protestantism, but it is far removed from the notion's original spirit. This particular goal is so far removed that this religion's adherents may find themselves subject to the same economic, political, and social forces that created the sects of this study, a religious revolt of the poor or the disinherited taking the form of a local seizure of religious authority.

The enduring possibility of revolt shows the second tension inherent to the religion of these local Baptists and similar religions. This religion faces an increasing threat that the newfound affluence of adherents can cause it to have the characteristics of church establishments, which in turn repels the "outcasts" attracted to the movement. Broader establishments of such religion, with their shunning of liberal, nontraditional theology, have avoided the pitfalls that ensnared other churches rising from sects, but the tension remains. It is unclear whether these establishments, by emphasizing traditional theology, have overcome permanently this inherent economic tension or simply suppressed it for a longer period than previously seen. Some of the local Baptists I study, and many more of similar religion, have reached levels of affluence unknown to their spiritual ancestors, and they will not feel this economic tension. To the extent that they congregate in their own denominations is the extent to which this economic issue will disappear for them, or even the extent to which they have transcended their origins. Most others among these local Baptists, and many others among similar religion, however, have not reached these levels of affluence. These may be subject to the ecclesiastical—and political—influences of a sectarian rebirth. They may not support indefinitely a religious traditionalism hostile to their economic interests.

The original and fundamental appeal of this religion lies in its emphasis on individual and local autonomy. The continuing appeal to the local Baptists in this study lies in an even stronger emphasis on individual autonomy, by which the most humble, poorest, and uneducated male receiving the "call" to preach can become a religious leader without any formal training and outside the standards set by external authorities. The extent to which such religion becomes led by a formally qualified clergy, trained to meet external rather than local standards, may mark the extent to which it becomes open to sectarian schism and regeneration.

The economic interests of the Clairfield miners and most others in this work, and maybe even most others of other, similar religions, are not those espoused by Jerry Falwell or Ralph Reed. In other circumstances where those similar to these sects become the voice of cultural tradition and economic populism, they may draw strength not only away from poorer adherents of more formal mainline churches, but also from more formal churches of conservative Protestantism, which may be perceived as too closely linked to more affluent forces. Cultural conservatism and economic populism may no longer form a sustainable platform in American electoral politics, but these viewpoints can sustain any church that does not require a majority of the population, or even a plurality of all religious adherents, for viability. The logic of "selling" American religion does not just mean that churches may find political aggregation difficult. It can also mean that religious bodies, in the midst of the other features they "sell" to potential adherents, may disregard what is needed for political influence and combine a sectarian message of economic populism and cultural traditionalism in its "product" regardless of how it might "sell" in another (e.g., political) marketplace.

The dual forces of ascetic Protestantism's cultural demands and the appeal of individual autonomy and ability to shape religion to local circumstances, within the boundaries of a concern for local authority placed on the exercise of external authority, make up the social and political heart of the religion of these local Baptists and other similar populations as well. It is a heart that often goes undetected under the muscle of recently burgeoning establishments of "Bible-based" Protestantism, but it is one that will beat as long as the religion lives. Both among the sects of this study and other, similar populations, these dual forces have moved adherents in their politics anywhere from populism to cultural conservatism to liberal labor politics to a shunning of broader politics to some combination of these or to some other point altogether.

The point of my analyses of the politics of cultural conservatism, populism, affluence, and secular organizations is not that these are the only forms of politics open to such populations. I do not analyze the sects of this study, who differ profoundly in many ways from more recognized forms of "Bible-based" Protestantism, to introduce and analyze a substantially different form of such religion. Rather, my analysis is meant to show a broader range of possibilities for political attitudes and participation among adherents of such religion, particularly as shaped by local community contexts that can give this religion of local authority its appeal. These are possibilities that social scientists should remind themselves of, even as other research presenting ever more specific definitions of religion and active political participation as measured by survey research instruments point to different contemporary directions in the politics of theologically conservative Protestants.

The politics of this population, like the politics of most Americans, cannot be analyzed strictly by analyses of voting, which for most is only an activity of sporadic interest, or by examining certain, limited forms of organizational activity. These Baptists, like most Americans, weigh many political issues and consequences in their lives that analyses with a broad geographic but narrow topical focus may sometimes miss. The fact that most of these Baptists may not vote in presidential elections or participate in civic organizations does not really mean, as they might say, that politics is of no personal concern to them. These Baptists are political, like most Americans are political, in ways we do not always recognize. Even their decision not to be "political" often is a political decision in that it is one they undertake in establishing the relationship they want with the body politic, and often one that helps them maintain an honored and respected place (however precarious) in the broader life of the community. The reader, like the author, may feel these Baptists sometimes avoid political decisions that would prove to be of greater utility. But this does not mean that these Baptists have ignored the issues that the combination of religion and politics pose in their lives. Likewise, if these Baptists among themselves disagree on political participation and its direction, it does not mean that the force of religion on politics works on some of them but not others, only that it works in various ways on the same, locally focused population in different circumstances.

There are nebulous borders to the possibilities of religion and politics I identify among these local Baptists. These borders do not always conform to economic determinism or cultural conservatism, the latter being increasingly featured in so much analysis of similar groups today. My point is not that these are the wrong categories for analysis, but that those relying on them for political analysis should always remember the full range of politics open to such groups as evident in history and even today in often overlooked places. We do well to remind ourselves of the full implications of the sectarian spirit for this religion, a spirit with both an immovable core and continuing potential for adaptability.

Those I have presented have drawn from their religion political skills needed for broader political participation, but the religion can also inhibit them from developing or exercising political skills, particularly when doing so would conflict with other goals of the religion, including differing material goals. Religion has instilled in these local Baptists a deep concern for cultural conservatism, but political action on this concern is often inhibited by conflicting (e.g., economic) interests arising from a common cause (e.g., a religion allowing adaptation to local spiritual and material needs).

Those ignoring the broader history and possibilities of "Bible-based" Protestantism and their operation in many local or regional bases of politics among varying populations risk being caught unaware of new, future political possibilities for such populations. These include changes in broader politics affecting the political alignments of these populations, changes in their religion affecting their political beliefs, and changes in local circumstances affecting what type of political participation can best be engaged without affecting other values the religion cherishes. Biblically oriented Protestantism can present an intriguing mix of traditional cultural concerns and evolving local adaptation. Neither acts alone in shaping the political influences of this religion on adherents. Both point to how other religions that likewise stress the sufficiency of local authority to interpret literally an ambiguous sacred text and its social implications often reflect local needs and concerns in confronting hostile outside authority, and how the traditions found in such religion can help meet many secular needs but fail to meet others. The secular, political, and social implications of such religion, like the faith itself, open to local and individual adaptation, remain open to change.

Appendix: Sources and Methodology

As noted in the text, all biblical citations are to the King James Version of the Bible, which is the biblical translation used by these Baptists. All pronoun references to the Christian God are also in the masculine in deference to the sensitivities of these Baptists.

In addition to interviews, correspondence, and newspaper accounts cited in the notes to this work, my research included primary source material from the associations (and one church) listed below, all of which (excepting Pleasant Hill Church) were counted in *CCMUS 1990*. As I explain in the text, not all associations listed were visited, but I did have contact for this work with either every association listed or one of its correspondents. All archival material remains in the possession of the author.

There are six groupings of associations that roughly, but not exactly, match the categories under which these associations were counted for *CCMUS 1990*. For a complete listing of associations by grouping in *CCMUS 1990*, see Appendix C of that work (pp. 445–49). Readers should consult the text and notes of this work to identify the reasons I made some minor changes to the *CCMUS 1990* classification.

The groupings for this work and their component associations were:
Central Baptist Association.
Duck River and Kindred, or the General Association of Baptist: Duck River, East Union, Mount Pleasant #1, Mount Pleasant #2, Mount Zion, New Liberty, and Union Associations; Pleasant Hill (Ky.) Church.

Old Missionary Baptist: Barren River, Enon, Siloam, and Wiseman Associations.

Old Regular Baptist: Bethel, Cumberland, Friendship, Old Friendship, Indian Bottom, Old Indian Bottom, Little Dove, Mountain (Feltner faction), Mountain (Gross faction), Original Mountain Liberty, Mud River, New Salem, Northern New Salem, Philadelphia, Sardis, Thornton Union, Union.

Eastern District Primitive Baptist Association.

United Baptist: Ancient Christian, Bethel, Bethlehem, Centerpoint, Cumberland River, Green River, Iron Hill, Jasper, Laurel River, Little Friendship, Mount Zion, Old Mount Zion, New Bethel, New Hope, Paint Union, Old Paint Union, Pleasant Valley, Second North Concord, South Concord, South Fork, Stockton Valley, Tri-State, Tri-State Zion, Union, West Union, Zion.

Notes

POLITICS AND THE BIBLE

1. For a more detailed discussion of the differences between "Fundamentalism" and more "popular" variations of the Baptist faith in the South, see Samuel S. Hill, *One Name but Several Faces: Variety in Popular Christian Denominations in Southern History* (Athens: Univ. of Georgia Press, 1996), 39–42. I am indebted to correspondence from Hill for the description of the particular Baptists I study as being neither "self-conscious rationalists nor rabid textualists."
2. See Martin Riesebrodt, *Pious Passion: The Emergence of Modern Fundamentalism in the United States and Iran,* trans. Don Reneau (Berkeley: Univ. of California Press, 1993), 176–208.
3. Nancy T. Ammerman, "Accounting for Christian Fundamentalisms: Social Dynamics and Rhetorical Strategies," in *Accounting for Fundamentalisms: The Dynamic Character of Movements,* ed. Martin E. Marty and R. Scott Appleby (Chicago: Univ. of Chicago Press, 1994), 151.
4. See William M. Clements, "The American Folk Church: A Characterization of American Folk Religion Based on Field Research Among White Protestants in a Community in the South Central United States" (Ph.D. diss., Indiana Univ., 1974), 85–88, 146–49.
5. H. Richard Niebuhr, *The Social Sources of Denominationalism* (1929; reprint, Cleveland: Meridian Books, 1965), 15.
6. See Glenn Tinder, *The Political Meaning of Christianity: An Interpretation* (Baton Rouge: Louisiana State Univ. Press, 1989), particularly 129–30.
7. Allan Gleason, *Encounters with the Bible: Use and Authority in the Churches* (Winfield, British Columbia: Wood Lake Books, 1991), 95–101.

8. James A. Davis and Tom W. Smith, *General Social Surveys* [machine-readable file], National Opinion Research Center, Chicago, 1994. I limit the ethnicity of my control group to non-Hispanic whites for two reasons. First, the Baptists that I study are overwhelmingly non-Hispanic white. The small population of African Americans among them number more than one hundred, but comprise well less than 1 percent of the aggregate church memberships of the groups I study. Second, while many African Americans and Latinos also claim belief in a literally true Bible and belong to fundamentalist churches, nearly all analyses of the politics of such Protestants focus on non-Hispanic whites. The fact that many African Americans of such faith, in particular, have far different politics than those prevalent among similar non-Hispanic whites in itself demonstrates the adaptive possibilities of the religion.
9. Sidney Verba, Kay Lehman Schlozman, and Henry E. Brady, *Voice and Equality: Civic Voluntarism in American Politics* (Cambridge, Mass.: Harvard Univ. Press, 1995), 245.
10. Ibid., 327–28.
11. Nancy T. Ammerman, *Bible Believers: Fundamentalists in the Modern World* (New Brunswick, N.J.: Rutgers Univ. Press, 1987), 201–3.
12. A 1998 *New York Times* account of South Carolina resistance to gay rights demonstrates this point. As Charles W. Dunn of Clemson University remarks, "People here perceive themselves on the defensive, defending their culture, their religion, their communities, against outside forces. They see these changes, such as homosexuality, and they want to rebel." In May 1996, for example the Greenville County Council joined the rebellion, adopting a "resolution declaring homosexuality incompatible with community standards." Still, a Baptist minister in Greenville warns that "what is about to happen to Greenville has already happened in places like San Francisco and New York City. We really believe this is the last bastion of moral decency left in America, and they're trying to push their agenda into this part of the county." Again, the point is that opposition to gay rights is largely based on a perception of threats from outside the community (although the *Times* article also documented gay life and activism within South Carolina). The same could likely be said for the opposition of these Protestants to abortion. Abortion rates in most of the South are lower than they are nationwide. For biblically oriented Protestants, opposition to abortion and gay rights may not be opposition to immediate community threats as much as opposition to broader cultural trends over which they have little control. On gay rights in South Carolina, see *New York Times*, 7 July 1998. On abortion rates by state, see *Statistical Abstract of the United States 1997*, table 116 (Washington, D.C.: Bureau of the Census, 1997).
13. Bruce B. Lawrence, *Defenders of God: The Fundamentalist Revolt Against the Modern Age* (San Francisco: Harper and Row, 1989), 27.

14. Kenneth D. Wald, Dennis E. Owen, and Samuel S. Hill Jr., "Churches as Political Communities," *American Political Science Review* 82 (1988): 531–48. For more on the particularly pronounced conservatism of "fundamentalists," see, among others, Lyman A. Kellstedt, "Religion, the Neglected Variable: An Agenda for Future Research," in *Rediscovering the Religious Factor in American Politics,* ed. David C. Leege, Lyman A. Kellstedt, et al. (Armonk, N.Y.: M. E. Sharpe, 1993), particularly 282; Kathleen Murphy Beatty and B. Oliver Walter, "Fundamentalists, Evangelicals, and Politics," *American Politics Quarterly* 16 (1988): 43–59; Ted G. Jelen, *The Political Mobilization of Religious Beliefs* (New York: Praeger Publishers, 1991); Clyde Wilcox, *God's Warriors: The Christian Right in Twentieth Century America* (Baltimore: Johns Hopkins Univ. Press, 1992).
15. At a press conference presenting findings from *Churches and Church Membership in the United States 1990* (hereafter referred to as *CCMUS 1990*), William McKinney classified the Baptist churches I counted, six of which make up the focus of this work, as "conservative Protestants." Personal correspondence from Lou McNeil, co-author of *CCMUS 1990* and former director of the Glenmary Research Center, publisher of *CCMUS 1990*, 5 July 1992. A copy of McKinney's complete classifications for churches counted in *CCMUS 1990* is available from the Church Growth Research Center at the Church of the Nazarene headquarters, Kansas City, Missouri.
16. Wade Clark Roof and William McKinney, *American Mainline Religion: Its Changing Shape and Future* (New Brunswick, N.J.: Rutgers Univ. Press, 1987), 90–91.
17. Lyman A. Kellstedt and John C. Green, "Knowing God's Many People: Denominational Difference and Political Behavior," in *Rediscovering the Religious Factor,* ed. Leege, Kellstedt, et al., 70–71.
18. Ibid., 58.
19. Peter L. Benson and Dorothy L. Williams, *Religion on Capitol Hill: Myths and Realities* (New York: Oxford Univ. Press, 1986), 111.
20. Ibid., 157–58.
21. Ibid., 155, 179.
22. Quoted in Ted G. Jelen, *The Political World of the Clergy* (Westport, Conn.: Praeger Publishers, 1993), 53. For more on the limits of linking "evangelical Protestantism" to broader politics, see ibid., 39–69.
23. Laurence R. Iannaccone, "The Economics of American Fundamentalists," in *Fundamentalisms and the State: Remaking Polities, Economies, and Militance,* ed. Martin E. Marty and R. Scott Appleby (Chicago: Univ. of Chicago Press, 1993), 360.
24. Stephen Hart, *What Does the Lord Require? How American Christians Think About Economic Justice* (New York: Oxford Univ. Press, 1992), 171–72.
25. The adjective "Bible-based" is one I use with some hesitation. All Christian

churches claim some basis in the Bible. My use of the term "Bible-based"—which, in deference to some readers of earlier drafts of my work, I try to use sparingly—is meant to draw attention to those most like the Baptists I study, whose only formal claim to religious authority is the local interpretation of the literal Bible. I use the term only to help generalize my findings to some others beyond the small number of Baptists I study.

26. See "The great environment divide," *The Economist* 339 (6 Apr. 1996): 23.
27. For more on "thick description," see Clifford Geertz, *The Interpretation of Cultures* (New York: Basic Books, 1973), 3–30.
28. Niebuhr, *The Social Sources of Denominationalism*, 15–17.
29. Unless otherwise cited, all quotations in this work are from interviews personally conducted by the author or other correspondence of the author with other parties. Notes, tapes, and other documentation remain in the possession of the author.
30. I recognize that not all Christian readers, much less all readers, exclusively use masculine pronouns in reference to the divine. Nevertheless, in deference to those I study, who invariably use masculine pronouns in reference to God, this work does also.
31. We might view the theological beliefs of these Baptists as located somewhere vaguely between free-will Arminianism and predestinarian Calvinism. For a discussion of Arminianism among southern churches, see Robert E. Cushman, "Arminianism," in *Encyclopedia of Religion in the South*, ed. Samuel S. Hill (Macon, Ga.: Mercer Univ. Press, 1984), 69–71. For a discussion of Calvinism in southern churches, see Shirley C. Guthrie Jr., "Calvinism," in ibid., 125–27.
32. Ernst Troeltsch, *The Social Teaching of the Christian Churches*, trans. Olive Wyon (1931; reprint, Chicago: Univ. of Chicago Press, 1981), 331.
33. Ibid.
34. Max Weber, *The Protestant Ethic and the Spirit of Capitalism*, trans. Talcott Parsons (1905; New York: Charles Scribner's Sons, 1958), 145–46.
35. Max Weber 1993 [1963, 1956, 1922], *The Sociology of Religion*, trans. Ephraim Fischoff (1922; Boston: Beacon Press, 1963), 230–31.
36. Ibid., 231.
37. Niebuhr, *The Social Sources of Denominationalism*, 17–18.
38. Ibid., 18.
39. Ibid.
40. Ibid., 21.
41. Werner Stark, *The Sociology of Religion: A Study of Christendom*, vol. 2, *Sectarian Religion* (New York: Fordham Univ. Press, 1967), 53.
42. Ibid., 54.
43. Roger Finke and Rodney Stark, *The Churching of America, 1776–1990*:

Winners and Losers in Our Religious Economy (New Brunswick, N.J.: Rutgers Univ. Press, 1992), 43.
44. See Bryan R. Wilson, "An Analysis of Sect Development," *American Sociological Review* 24 (1959): 3–15.
45. Ibid., 5–6.
46. Ibid., 6.
47. David A. Martin, "The Denomination," *British Journal of Sociology* 13 (1963): 5.
48. Ibid., 9.
49. Ibid., 11–12.
50. Ibid., 13.
51. Sidney E. Mead, *The Lively Experiment: The Shaping of Christianity in America* (New York: Harper and Row, 1963), 111–14.
52. Ibid., 111.
53. Ibid., 113–14.
54. Ibid., 115.
55. W. J. Cash, *The Mind of the South* (1941; reprint, Garden City, N.Y.: Doubleday, 1954), 292.
56. Robert Emil Botsch, *We Shall Not Overcome: Populism and Southern Blue-Collar Workers* (Chapel Hill: Univ. of North Carolina Press, 1980), 186–88.
57. J. Morgan Kousser, *The Shaping of Southern Politics: Suffrage Restriction and the Establishment of the One-Party South, 1880–1910* (New Haven, Conn.: Yale Univ. Press, 1974), 17, 247–49.
58. V. O. Key Jr., *Southern Politics in State and Nation* (Knoxville: Univ. of Tennessee Press, 1984), 283.
59. Corwin Smidt, "Born-Again Politics: The Political Behavior of Evangelical Christians in the South and the Non-South," in *Religion and Politics in the South: Mass and Elite Perspectives,* ed. Tod A. Baker, Robert P. Steed, and Laurence W. Moreland (New York: Praeger, 1983), 71.
60. Deborah Vansau McCauley, *Appalachian Mountain Religion: A History* (Urbana: Univ. of Illinois Press, 1995), 54.
61. Ibid., 7.
62. United States Department of Commerce, Bureau of the Census, *Census of Population and Housing 1990: Summary Tape File 3* [machine-readable file] (Washington, D.C., 1995).
63. Ibid. The national per capita income for 1989 reported in the last census was $14,420. In Kentucky ARC counties, it was approximately $8,400.
64. Jeff Todd Titon, *Powerhouse for God: Speech, Chant, and Song in an Appalachian Baptist Church* (Austin: Univ. of Texas Press, 1988), 79.
65. Samuel S. Hill, *Southern Churches in Crisis* (New York: Holt, Rinehart and Winston, 1967), 25.

66. J. Wayne Flynt makes a similar point that, however accurate Hill's typology may be, it does not follow that Southern religious thought must be static, and, indeed, it was not in confronting social problems of the early twentieth century. See J. Wayne Flynt, "Southern Protestantism and Reform," in *Varieties of Southern Religious Experience,* ed. Samuel S. Hill (Baton Rouge: Louisiana State Univ. Press, 1988), 146–47.
67. Clements, "The American Folk Church," 85–138.
68. Ibid., 20.
69. Åke Hultkrantz, *General Ethnological Concepts* (Copenhagen: Rosenkilde and Bagger, 1960), 228, as quoted in Clements, "The American Folk Church," 157.
70. Clements, "The American Folk Church," 157.
71. Ibid., 20–21.
72. For a general discussion on the problems of aggregating the preferences of religious groups for concerted political action, see Ted G. Jelen, Review of *The Churching of America: Winners and Losers in Our Religious Economy,* in Roger Finke and Rodney Stark, *Review of Religious Research* 36 (1995): 315–17. "Religious particularism" has been identified elsewhere as a characteristic of Protestants who base their faith on a literal interpretation of the Bible. See, for example, Jelen, *The Political World of the Clergy,* 59–63. Jelen remarks that such populations emphasize differences among themselves first before addressing differences between themselves and others. I encountered the same phenomenon in my field work. When I asked members of these sects what differentiates them from other churches, many told me first what differentiates them from other Baptists, and not what differentiates them within Christendom at large, much less from the world's non-Christian majority.
73. See, for example, Ammerman, *Bible Believers,* 103–19.
74. Davis and Smith, *General Social Surveys,* pooled data, 1989–93.
75. Ibid. Ammerman notes that many of the church-related organizations that attract fundamentalists have a secular purpose.
76. Davis and Smith *General Social Surveys,* 1994. Among non-Hispanic white fundamentalist Protestant households, 9 percent have a union member, compared with 17 percent of all households.
77. Garry Wills argues that Roger Williams, Thomas Jefferson, and James Madison sought separation of church and state at least as much to protect the church in its role as a civil guardian as to protect the state from religious influence. See Garry Wills, *Under God: Religion and American Politics* (New York: Simon and Schuster, 1990), 341–80.

1. National Themes in Local Settings

1. Lawrence W. Levine, *Defender of the Faith—William Jennings Bryan: The*

Last Decade, 1915–1925 (1965; Cambridge, Mass.: Harvard Univ. Press, 1987), 261.
2. David Edwin Harrell Jr., "The Evolution of Plain-Folk Religion in the South," in *Varieties of Southern Religious Experience,* ed. Hill, 42.
3. Troeltsch, *The Social Teaching of the Christian Churches,* 98.
4. Ibid.
5. George M. Marsden, 1980, *Fundamentalism and American Culture—The Shaping of Twentieth-Century Evangelicalism: 1870–1925* (New York: Oxford Univ. Press), 204–5.
6. See Riesebrodt, *Pious Passion,* 177, on urban fundamentalists in early-twentieth-century America.
7. Lyman A. Kellstedt and Mark A. Noll, "Religion, Voting for President, and Party Identification, 1948–1984," in *Religion and American Politics from the Colonial Period to the 1980s,* ed. Mark A. Noll (New York: Oxford Univ. Press, 1990), 248.
8. Kenneth D. Wald, *Religion and Politics in the United States* (New York: St. Martin's Press, 1987), 185.
9. Wilcox, *God's Warriors,* 78.
10. Wald, *Religion and Politics in the United States,* 185.
11. Michael Barone and Grant Ujifusa, *The Almanac of American Politics 1984* (Washington, D.C.: National Journal, 1983), 2.
12. Wills, *Under God,* 119–21.
13. Among others demonstrating this point are Robert E. Botsch, "A Microanalytic Return to the Mind of the South," in *Contemporary Southern Political Attitudes and Behavior,* ed. Laurence W. Moreland, Tod A. Baker, and Robert P. Steed (New York: Praeger, 1982), 24–47.
14. Hertzke develops this point throughout *Echoes of Discontent: Jesse Jackson, Pat Robertson, and the Resurgence of Populism* (Washington, D.C.: CQ Press, 1993), his analysis of the Jackson and Robertson campaigns. Hertzke adds an intriguing point about racial politics among these populations and their candidates, noting it was political operatives of the ideological middle, rather than those on the culturally traditional "extremes," that exploited race animosity in the campaign of 1988. See ibid., 209, 233.
15. Ann L. Page and Donald L. Clelland, "The Kanawha County Textbook Controversy: A Study of the Politics of Life Style Concern," *Social Forces* 57 (1978): 265.
16. Ibid., 276.
17. Scott Cummings, Richard Briggs, and James Mercy, "Preachers versus Teachers: Local-Cosmopolitan Conflict over Textbook Censorship in an Appalachian Community," *Rural Sociology* 42 (1977): 7–8.
18. For one analysis of conservative religion and conservative political activism, see Kenneth D. Wald, Lyman A. Kellstedt, and David C. Leege, "Church

Involvement and Political Behavior," in *Rediscovering the Religious Factor in American Politics,* ed. Leege, Kellstedt, et al., 121–38.
19. The minor exceptions made are typically for abortions in the cases of rape, incest, or for the health of the mother. A typical comment is that of a preacher who told me he would be satisfied with the laws "the way they used to be," i.e., pre-*Roe v. Wade.*
20. See Bertram Wyatt-Brown, "The Antimission Movement in the Jacksonian South: A Study in Regional Culture," *Journal of Southern History* 36 (1970): 501–29.
21. This preacher is paid about four thousand dollars annually, as published in the minutes for his association.
22. Ammerman, "Accounting for Christian Fundamentalisms," in *Accounting for Fundamentalisms,* ed. Marty and Appleby, 157.
23. The Baptists examined in this work all use the King James Version of the Bible, some doing so exclusively. In deference to their practice, all biblical citations and quotations in this work are from the King James translation.
24. Ammerman, "Accounting for Christian Fundamentalisms," in *Accounting for Fundamentalisms,* ed. Marty and Appleby, 157.
25. Bertram Wyatt-Brown, "The Antimission Movement," 502–3.
26. Ibid., 503.
27. Ibid., 510.
28. Ibid.
29. *Chicago Daily Tribune,* 28 May 1925, as quoted in Levine, *Defender of the Faith,* 274.
30. Ibid., 261.
31. See Wills, *Under God,* 101–7.
32. Lawrence Goodwyn, *The Populist Moment: A Short History of the Agrarian Revolt in America* (New York: Oxford Univ. Press, 1978), 263. By nominating Bryan and accepting his free silver platform, the People's Party abandoned its preference for a fiat currency, which, to Goodwyn, was the essence of late-nineteenth-century Populism.
33. A. James Reichley, *Religion in American Public Life* (Washington, D.C.: Brookings Institution, 1985), 206.
34. Ibid.
35. Harrell, "The Evolution of Plain-Folk Religion," in *Varieties of Southern Religious Experience,* ed. Hill, 42.
36. Flynt, "Southern Protestantism and Reform," in Hill, editor, *Varieties of Southern Religious Experience,* 145.
37. Ibid., 147.
38. Ibid.
39. Ibid., 147 ff.

40. Iannaccone, "The Economics of American Fundamentalists," in *Fundamentalisms and the State,* ed. Marty and Appleby, 355.
41. Martin E. Marty, "Fundamentalism as a Social Phenomenon," *Bulletin: The American Academy of Arts* 42 (Nov. 1988): 20, as quoted in Iannaccone, "The Economics of American Fundamentalists," in *Fundamentalisms and the State,* ed. Marty and Appleby, 360.
42. Iannaccone, "The Economics of American Fundamentalists," in *Fundamentalisms and the State,* ed. Marty and Appleby, 360–61.
43. Donald G. Mathews, "Antimission Movement," in *Encyclopedia of Religion in the South,* ed. Hill, 37.
44. Ibid.
45. Ibid.
46. Ibid.
47. John H. Spencer, as revised and corrected by Burrilla B. Spencer, *A History of Kentucky Baptists from 1769 to 1885* (Cincinnati: J. R. Baumes, 1885), 1: 488. I caution that much of Spencer's work reads as a polemic for the faith and practices of missionary Baptists, rather than a denominational history, which colors his interpretation.
48. Ibid., 676.
49. Ibid.
50. Ibid., 677. I Corinthians 12:24–25 states, "For our comely parts have no need: but God hath tempered the body together, having given more abundant honour to that part which lacked. That there would be no schism in the body; but that the members should have the same care for one another."
51. Ibid., 677.
52. Ibid., 678. Unlike Spencer, Deborah Vansau McCauley is sympathetic to such claims. Her history of Appalachian religion emphasizes that many of these groups did not depart from any movement so much as they saw their religion hijacked by those seeking to foster greater church establishments. See McCauley, *Appalachian Mountain Religion,* 126–42.
53. Spencer, *A History of Kentucky Baptists,* 1: 694.
54. This comment was from a preacher who supports many of Pat Robertson's causes. His concerns on Masonry reflect some of Robertson's, who believes Masonry leads to devil worship. See Hertzke, *Echoes of Discontent,* 92.
55. Loyal Jones, "Old-Time Baptists and Mainline Christianity," in *An Appalachian Symposium: Essays Written in Honor of Cratis D. Williams,* ed. J. W. Williamson (Boone, N.C.: Appalachian State Univ. Press, 1977), 127–28.
56. Ibid.
57. For an illuminating discussion of how affluence can foster religious institutions in certain nations, including the United States, and some general implications of this for "fundamentalism," see Robert Wuthnow and Matthew

P. Lawson, "Sources of Christian Fundamentalism in the United States," in *Accounting for Fundamentalisms*, ed. Marty and Appleby, 18–56.
58. Weber, *The Protestant Ethic and the Spirit of Capitalism*, 174.
59. Ibid., 174–75.
60. Weber, *The Sociology of Religion*, 101.
61. Ibid., 107.
62. Ibid.
63. Finke and Stark, *The Churching of America*, 173–75. The three characteristics of the SBC that Finke and Stark identify as having helped it avoid liberalization included the extremely autonomous and democratic nature of SBC congregations, which gave laity an extraordinary amount of control over the clergy; the difficulty of rooting out factions within the SBC, which prevented liberalization by default through expulsion and defection; and tighter control of denominational seminaries, which became more responsive to the conservative strains among the laity with more sectarian traditions. David Harrell notes that in the early twentieth century "most poor and rural Baptists still felt at home in the Southern Baptist Convention . . . heartened by periodic assurances of Baptist orthodoxy. . . ." See Harrell, "The Evolution of Plain-Folk Religion in the South," in *Varieties of Southern Religious Experience*, ed. Hill, 34.
64. Mark Shibley takes this discussion further in claiming that social strictness, in itself, is not what leads to church growth. He points out that many growing "evangelical" churches are growing because they can accommodate the desires of more mobile and affluent adherents, including, for example, golfing club and surfing group "ministries." See Mark A. Shibley, *Resurgent Evangelicalism in the United States: Mapping Cultural Change since 1970* (Columbia: Univ. of South Carolina Press, 1996), particularly 83–92. Shibley writes that the "new evangelicals" are theologically traditional, but it is a tradition that has apparently shed belief in a literal, though still inspired, Bible.
65. See, inter alia, Wald, *Religion and Politics in the United States*, 206–7.
66. Wald, *Religion and Politics in the United States*, 206–7; Nancy T. Ammerman, "North American Protestant Fundamentalism," in *Fundamentalisms Observed*, ed. Martin E. Marty and R. Scott Appleby (Chicago: Univ. of Chicago Press, 1991), 41. But see also Shibley, *Resurgent Evangelicalism in the United States*, 5, 6, and 136, on how "evangelical" religion, in order to survive, must adapt to individual adherents' needs first and foremost, and thus become less relevant in public life. I will return to this point in my concluding chapter.
67. Donald G. Mathews, *Religion in the Old South* (Chicago: Univ. of Chicago Press, 1977), 36.
68. Ibid., 128.
69. Ibid. Mathews mentions Primitive Baptists in particular as developing from

this conflict. I note again that McCauley emphasizes a different historical perspective, by which many of these groups, outside the quarrels Mathews analyzes, saw those supporting rising evangelical establishments as the ones who left the tradition, and not the opposite.
70. Ibid.
71. Services in this congregation are now similar to those in a "new evangelical" church that Mark Shibley said can be "more like a rock concert than a religious gathering." See Shibley, *Resurgent Evangelicalism in the United States,* 94–95.
72. Titon, *Powerhouse for God,* 223.
73. Howard Dorgan, *The Old Regular Baptists of Central Appalachia: Brothers and Sisters in Hope* (Knoxville: Univ. of Tennessee Press, 1989), 236.
74. Earl Black and Merle Black, *Politics and Society in the South* (Cambridge, Mass.: Harvard Univ. Press, 1987), 72.
75. Martin E. Marty, "Churches as winners, losers," *Christian Century* 110 (1993): 88–89.

2. Histories and Their Implications

1. Martin Bradley et al., *Churches and Church Membership in the United States 1990* (Atlanta: Glenmary Research Center, 1992).
2. I Chronicles 21:1–14.
3. Michael Barone and Grant Ujifusa, *The Almanac of American Politics 1992* (Washington, D.C.: National Journal, 1991), 4.
4. For a complete listing of associations by grouping, see the appendix of this work and Appendix C of *CCMUS 1990,* 445–49. I emphasize that while these bodies appear in some scattered references, most do not appear in any single standard reference book on religion (e.g., *Handbook of Denominations, Yearbook of American and Canadian Churches, Encyclopedia of American Religions*).
5. Central Baptists are also discussed in Frank S. Mead and Samuel S. Hill, *Handbook of Denominations in the United States,* 9th ed. (Nashville: Abingdon Press, 1990), 44–45.
6. For definitions of "churches," "members," and "adherents," see *CCMUS 1990,* xiv–xv, 439–43. As stated there, I believe the church membership study methodology underestimates the total number of "adherents" for these groups. The membership counts, however, are accurate for the associations that cooperated, and the underestimation of adherents likely does not affect much my analyses of the distribution of these Baptists.
7. Joshua 1:17.
8. Joshua 23:6.
9. John 13:1–17.

10. Richard Alan Humphrey, "Foot Washing," in *Encyclopedia of Religion in the South*, ed. Hill, 267.
11. For an extended treatment of the particulars of foot washing among many of these churches, see Howard Dorgan, *Giving Glory to God in Appalachia: Worship Practices of Six Baptist Subdenominations* (Knoxville: Univ. of Tennessee Press, 1987), 113–46.
12. Population counts are from the 100 percent counts of each Census. Social and economic data are from Summary Tape File 3 (STF3) statistics from the 1990 Census. See U.S. Bureau of the Census, *Census of Population and Housing: Summary Tape File 3* [machine-readable file] (Washington, D.C., 1992). Presidential election returns are from Richard M. Scammon, ed., biennial, *America Votes* (New York: Macmillan); in the interest of brevity, I present only the percentage of Democratic votes for president among those voting for major candidates in the past five elections. Again, all these data are for these areas as a whole, and not just for the Baptists I study within these areas. There are certainly many hazards in using ecological data to consider groups within them. Yet such data help focus attention on the central theme of this work, that is, how broader local conditions where these groups reside help shape the influence their religion has on their politics.
13. This study uses a slightly different definition of Duck River and Kindred Baptists than that used in *CCMUS 1990*. In addition to those associations listed in *CCMUS 1990*, Appendix C, this study includes Pleasant Hill Church, a Crittenden County, Kentucky, congregation with forty members and forty-nine estimated adherents. Pleasant Hill Church is not affiliated with any other association and has long corresponded with the General Association of Baptist. I was not able to obtain its statistics in time for publication in *CCMUS 1990*. Its inclusion completes an exhaustive count of all Duck River and Kindred Baptist congregations and members.
14. See the comments of S. F. Shelton, Duck River Association clerk, in *Religious Bodies: 1936*, ed. T. F. Murphy (Washington, D.C.: Bureau of the Census, 1941), 2: 210.
15. J. Gordon Melton, *The Encyclopedia of American Religions*, 5th ed. (Detroit: Gale Research, 1996), 461.
16. Mead and Hill, *Handbook of Denominations in the United States*, 46.
17. Duck River Baptists have grown by at least 23 percent in these core counties since 1936, while total population growth since 1950 has been 28 percent. There is no way to calculate exactly the rate of Duck River and Kindred Baptist growth in these counties from the Census Bureau report on *Religious Bodies: 1936* and *CCMUS 1990*, since the former did not report county-level statistics for Duck River and Kindred Baptists. The 1936 report did count 7,420 Duck River and Kindred Baptist members in all of Alabama and Tennessee. Comparing the *CCMUS 1990* Duck River and Kindred Bap-

tist membership count of the seventeen core rural counties with the 1936 figure for all of Alabama and Tennessee gives those in the core counties a growth rate of at least 23 percent in the past fifty years. I suspect the growth rate in the core counties was even higher.
18. Among those mentioning Missionary Baptists are Mead and Hill, *Handbook of Denominations in the United States*; Hill, ed., *Encyclopedia of Religion in the South*; McCauley, *Appalachian Mountain Religion*; Dorgan, *Giving Glory to God in Appalachia*; and Jones, "Old-Time Baptists and Mainline Christianity," in *An Appalachian Symposium*, ed. Williamson.
19. John R. Woodard, "North Carolina," in *Encyclopedia of Religion in the South*, ed. Hill, 533.
20. James E. Tull, "New Hampshire Confession of Faith," in *Encyclopedia of Religion in the South*, ed. Hill, 540.
21. My definition of Old Missionary Baptists here is slightly larger than that used in *CCMUS 1990*. A misunderstanding on correspondence patterns led me to list an Old Missionary Baptist association (Barren River) as a separate denomination in the church membership study. After fieldwork for the present work was completed, correspondence with Robert L. Vaughn of Mt. Enterprise, Texas, convinced me that I seriously underestimated the number of Old Missionary Baptists nationwide, particularly in their associations outside the South. Vaughn has documentation on several other associations similar to those that I study which, combined, have nearly three times the number of members. Despite the apparent inadequacies of my count, I decided to leave those I had interviewed in this study, because, even considering the evidence Vaughn has shared with me, they still formed a coherent and cohesive cluster and because they helped highlight many of the issues, particularly of bridging traditional concerns and modern environs, confronting similar Baptists.
22. Maps 4 and 5 do not show Denver County, Colorado, which is home to 0.1 percent of the Old Missionary Baptists I study.
23. Dorgan, *The Old Regular Baptists of Central Appalachia*, 8–9. There are two small Old Regular Baptist associations that do not trace their ancestry to New Salem, but these are the only exceptions. Both are in correspondence with those that do trace their origins to New Salem.
24. Spencer, *A History of Kentucky Baptists from 1769 to 1885*, 2: 394.
25. Ibid. See also Chester R. Young, "Old Regular Baptists," in *Encyclopedia of Religion in the South*, ed. Hill, 569. Burning Spring is now a Primitive Baptist association, indicating how some of these sects not only may find the SBC but even some of the more traditional of these sects to be too liberal.
26. Unfortunately, the most complete contemporary account of this period is Spencer's *A History of Kentucky Baptists*. As McCauley notes in *Appalachian Mountain Religion*, Spencer is not an objective source, since he had more

concern for increasing Baptist ranks through missions than he did in respecting the tradition and theology of groups like New Salem. To complicate matters further, McCauley, who is more concerned with documenting what she argues is a unique Appalachian regional religious heritage than with documenting individual group histories, does not present all historical particulars on those I study. For example, as Spencer notes and McCauley does not, there were nonreligious organizations involved in the controversy, such as political organizations and "secret societies," like Masonic orders.

27. See Young, "Old Regular Baptists," in *Encyclopedia of Religion in the South*, ed. Hill, 569; Spencer, *A History of Kentucky Baptists*, 2: 394; and Dorgan, *The Old Regular Baptists of Central Appalachia*, 37. Dorgan finds the "Old Regular" title was not in formal use until 1891.
28. Spencer, *A History of Kentucky Baptists*, 2: 395.
29. Harrell, "The Evolution of Plain-Folk Religion in the South," in *Varieties of Southern Religious Experience*, ed. Hill, 32.
30. Spencer, *A History of Kentucky Baptists*, 2: 395.
31. Ibid.
32. Dorgan, *The Old Regular Baptists of Central Appalachia*, 37.
33. Ibid.
34. Ibid.
35. Melton, *The Encyclopedia of American Religions*, 461.
36. Ibid.
37. On additional doctrinal differences that split Kyova and other Old Regular Baptists, see Dorgan, *The Old Regular Baptists of Central Appalachia*, 12.
38. A *New York Times* story of 19 April 1998, citing evidence for and against the authenticity of the Shroud of Turin as Christ's burial cloth, notes that "some scholars argue that Jesus would not have had long hair, which was typical of the Nazarite Jews who had taken special ascetic vows and could not touch cadavers or drink wine," unlike Jesus, who did both.
39. See photos of Old Regular Baptist males in Rufus Perrigan, *History of Regular Baptist and Their Ancestors and Accessors* (Haysi, Va.: The Author, 1961).
40. Not shown in map 6 are one Arizona county, five Florida counties, and two Washington counties that are home to a combined 1.8 percent of all Old Regular Baptists.
41. See Dorgan, *The Old Regular Baptists of Central Appalachia*, 189–94, and Ron Short, "We Believed in the Family and the Old Regular Baptist Church," *Southern Exposure* 4 (3) (1976): 65.
42. Michael J. Bradshaw, *The Appalachian Regional Commission: Twenty-five Years of Government Policy* (Lexington: Univ. Press of Kentucky, 1992), 20.
43. The decision to lump all Primitive Baptists together was an administrative one made in light of the fact that I was not able to get anywhere near an exhaustive count of most of the five different Primitive Baptist groups. For a

succinct discussion of the differences between the four most recognized groups of Primitive Baptists, see Chester R. Young, "Primitive Baptists," in *Encyclopedia of Religion in the South,* ed. Hill, 612–13.
44. Allan Gleason, in correspondence with the author, says there may be a distinct "antiresurrectionist" group in Carroll County, Virginia. For more on a Primitive Baptist group with unique beliefs in the afterlife, see Howard Dorgan, *In the Hands of a Happy God: The "No-Hellers" of Central Appalachia* (Knoxville: Univ. of Tennessee Press, 1997).
45. Dorgan, *Giving Glory to God in Appalachia,* 8.
46. See statement of C. H. Cayce, a Primitive Baptist elder, in *Religious Bodies: 1936,* ed. Murphy, 2: 224. Descriptive material below on Primitive Baptist doctrine and nineteenth-century history is primarily from this same source.
47. Ibid.
48. Ibid.
49. Ibid.
50. See James L. Peacock and Tim Pettyjohn, "Fundamentalisms Narrated: Muslim, Christian, and Mystical," in *Fundamentalisms Comprehended,* ed. Martin E. Marty and R. Scott Appleby (Chicago: Univ. of Chicago Press, 1995), particularly 120–23.
51. Map 9 does not show one Arizona county, two Florida counties, one Idaho county, and one Wisconsin county, which are home to a combined 0.13 percent of all United Baptists. The definition of United Baptists in this work is different from that used in *CCMUS 1990*. The chief difference is the addition of two north Georgia associations that I had classified as a separate denomination but whose history and doctrine, I later learned, places them within the United Baptist tradition.
52. See the statement of J. P. Adams in Murphy, ed., *Religious Bodies: 1936,* vol. 2: 206. Many United Baptist associations today correspond with those outside the tradition who are greatly similar in faith and practice.
53. There is an irony, of course, in the fact that, in these churches emphasizing the sufficiency of local authority, there is little discussion as to why there should be an "Authorized" Bible.
54. See Kathleen C. Boone, *The Bible Tells Them So: The Discourse of Protestant Fundamentalism* (Albany: State Univ. of New York Press, 1989), particularly 31–32.
55. See Gleason, *Encounters with the Bible,* 107–20.
56. McCauley, *Appalachian Mountain Religion,* 77.
57. For one version of this history, see Short, "We Believed in the Family," 77.
58. Hill, *One Name but Several Faces,* 29.
59. Harrell, "The Evolution of Plain-Folk Religion in the South," in *Varieties of Southern Religious Experience,* ed. Hill, 34.
60. Hill, *One Name but Several Faces,* 29–30.

61. Ibid., 30.
62. John 21:15–17.
63. Matthew 16:18–19.
64. Charles Thomas Davis III and Richard Alan Humphrey, "Appalachian Religion: A Diversity of Consciousness," *Appalachian Journal* 5 (1978): 393–94.
65. Titon, *Powerhouse for God,* 209.
66. See, for example, Dorgan, *Giving Glory to God in Appalachia,* particularly 9–11, 24–25, and Dorgan, *The Old Regular Baptists of Central Appalachia,* 37, 64.
67. See Dorgan, *Giving Glory to God in Appalachia,* 9, and Mathews, *Religion in the Old South,* 10, 126–35.
68. Dorgan, *The Old Regular Baptists of Central Appalachia,* 37.
69. See, for example, Mathews, *Religion in the Old South,* 59–61.
70. Finke and Stark, *The Churching of America,* 45.
71. McCauley, *Appalachian Mountain Religion,* 78.
72. Mathews, *Religion in the Old South,* 127. Mathews traces Primitive Baptists to this schism, but I again note McCauley emphasizes that many of these groups did not depart from any movement so much as they saw their religion hijacked by those seeking to foster greater church establishments. See McCauley, *Appalachian Mountain Religion,* 126–42.
73. Jones, "Old-Time Baptists and Mainline Christianity," in *An Appalachian Symposium,* ed. Williamson, 121. See also John C. Campbell, *The Southern Highlander and His Homeland* (New York: Russell Sage Foundation, 1921), 302.
74. Mark 16:15; see also Matthew 28:19.
75. Not all similar churches in these Baptists' rural stronghold oppose Sunday schools. The opposition is limited to those that, like those I study, have Calvinist traditions. Free Will Baptist and Holiness churches in the highlands have Sunday schools, but they rely on local interpretations of the Bible, rather than Sunday school materials published elsewhere. See McCauley, *Appalachian Mountain Religion,* 76.
76. For a concise review of many of these sects' preaching styles and their variations, see Dorgan, *Giving Glory to God in Appalachia,* 55–85. A "lined" hymn is one where a leader will speak, shout, or chant out the line of the hymn that the congregation will then sing. The practice appears to have originated with English Baptists in the seventeenth century. For more on lined singing, see, among others, ibid., 6–7; McCauley, *Appalachian Mountain Religion,* 82, 428–29; and William Tallmadge, "Baptist Monophonic and Heterophonic Hymnody in Southern Appalachia," *Yearbook for Inter-American Musical Research* 11 (1975): 106–36.
77. Mathews, *Religion in the Old South,* 42.

78. For a more general discussion of how these preachers adapt their sermons to specific local needs, see Dorgan, *Giving Glory to God in Appalachia,* 86–112.
79. McCauley, *Appalachian Mountain Religion,* 82.
80. On Saul, see I Samuel 16:14–18.
81. See Titon, *Powerhouse for God,* 374. For more on women's shouting in Old Regular Baptist churches, see Dorgan, *The Old Regular Baptists of Central Appalachia,* 68–69, 109–11.
82. Clements, "The American Folk Church," 133–34. The emphasis on the "priesthood of all believers," Clements writes, comes from I Peter 2:5, which reads, "Ye also, as lively stones, are built up a spiritual house, an holy priesthood, to offer up spiritual sacrifices, acceptable to God by Jesus Christ."
83. Some churches located elsewhere but founded by migrants from an association stronghold may still "letter," or correspond with, the association.
84. McCauley, *Appalachian Mountain Religion,* 68.
85. Stark, *The Sociology of Religion,* 2: 60.
86. Stark recognizes American exceptionalism to sectarian processes. See ibid., 61, 333–45.
87. On the roles of women in Old Regular Baptist governance, see Dorgan, *The Old Regular Baptists of Central Appalachia,* 118–19. On more general social roles for Old Regular Baptist women, see ibid., 238–40. While Old Regular Baptists are generally the most conservative on sex roles and mores, the most traditional association I have encountered on these matters was a United Baptist association, concentrated in Pike County, Kentucky, that had dropped correspondence with all others because of their allegedly lax enforcement of these rules.
88. Mathews, *Religion in the Old South,* 107–8.
89. Finke and Stark, *The Churching of America,* 35. The same disciplining effect of religion can be seen in areas to which many from the uplands South have migrated. See, for example, William E. Powles, "The Southern Appalachian Migrant: Country Boy Turned Blue-Collarite," in *Blue-Collar World: Studies of the American Worker,* ed. Arthur B. Shostak and William Gomberg (Englewood Cliffs, N.J.: Prentice-Hall, 1964), 270–81.
90. Titon, *Powerhouse for God,* 425.
91. Ammerman, "Accounting for Christian Fundamentalism," in *Accounting for Fundamentalisms,* ed. Marty and Appleby, 159.
92. Titon, *Powerhouse for God,* 75.
93. Clements, "The American Folk Church," 135.
94. For a discussion of growth among Duck River and Kindred Baptists, see text and notes above. For a discussion of growth among Old Regular Baptists, see Dorgan, *The Old Regular Baptists of Central Appalachia,* 222–29.

3. The Strengths of Adaptation for Labor

1. E. P. Thompson, *The Making of the English Working Class* (New York: Vintage Books, 1966), 391.
2. Ibid.
3. Ibid., 43–44.
4. Ibid., 673.
5. Hugh Kelly, *The Stone Cut Out of the Mountain* (Newcastle, England; no publisher given, 1821), 13, and Hugh Kelly, *An Impartial History of Independent Methodism* (Newcastle, England; no publisher given, 1824), as quoted in Thompson, *The Making of the English Working Class*, 393.
6. Thompson, *The Making of the English Working Class*, 397. We should not overlook the ambiguity that is available to Methodists in their General Rules. While these have been the chief factor influencing many Methodists' attitudes and activities, they are not specific legal rules, but general principles which are ambiguous in detail. For a nineteenth-century example, see Edward G. Andrews, ed., *The Doctrines and Discipline of the Methodist Episcopal Church* (New York: Eaton & Mains, 1896), particularly 26–34.
7. Levine, *Defender of the Faith*, 200–201.
8. Ibid.
9. Riesebrodt, *Pious Passion*, 69.
10. Ibid., 68.
11. Ibid., 68–69.
12. J. Wayne Flynt, "Alabama White Protestantism and Labor, 1900–1914," *Alabama Review* 25 (1972): 198.
13. J. Wayne Flynt, *Dixie's Forgotten People: The South's Poor Whites* (Bloomington: Indiana Univ. Press, 1979), 99.
14. Liston Pope, *Millhands and Preachers: A Study of Gastonia* (New Haven, Conn.: Yale Univ. Press, 1942), 160.
15. Ibid.
16. Ibid., 165.
17. Ibid., 164.
18. Ibid.
19. Friedrich Engels, "The Peasant War in Germany," in Karl Marx and Friedrich Engels, *On Religion* (1850; New York: Schocken Books, 1982), 108–9.
20. On tithing by sectarian congregation members, see Pope, *Millhands and Preachers*, 101–2.
21. Ibid., 165.
22. Ibid.
23. F. Ray Marshall, *Labor in the South* (Cambridge, Mass.: Harvard Univ. Press, 1967), 341.
24. Ibid., 343. The biblical command is from II Corinthians 6:14, which encour-

ages believers to follow the ways of God and forsake then prevailing pagan practices.
25. Others have considered the role of religion in southern labor strife, but their perspective differs from that of Pope, whose concerns are closest to those of this work. Generally, such works consider religion as one of several variables affecting workers, rather than by itself, as this work does. They often focus on company-sponsored churches, on churches that are more "established" (even if occasionally siding with workers) than those I consider, or on how workers sustain their own religion outside church during labor strife, or on the adaptation of Marxist themes to religion. See, among others, David L. Carlton, *Mill and Town in South Carolina, 1880–1920* (Baton Rouge: Louisiana State Univ. Press, 1982); David A. Corbin, *Life, Work, and Rebellion in the Coal Fields: The Southern West Virginia Miners, 1880–1922* (Urbana: Univ. of Illinois Press, 1981); Ronald D Eller, *Miners, Millhands, and Mountaineers: Industrialization of the Appalachian South, 1880–1930* (Knoxville: Univ. of Tennessee Press, 1982); John Gaventa, *Power and Powerlessness: Quiescence and Rebellion in an Appalachian Valley* (Urbana: Univ. of Illinois Press, 1980); and William J. B. Livingston, "Coal Miners and Religion: A Study of Logan" (Th.D. thesis, Union Theological Seminary, 1951). Livingston's work is helpful for understanding how and why coal miners adhere to indigenous religion, which supported their aims, over mainline and company-sponsored churches (see particularly 224–41). Corbin also demonstrates how family interests led to union support (particularly among black miners). He writes: "Not only did married men make the best miners, they later made good union men. Single miners often left struck coal fields for more peaceful areas where thy could make more money. The married miner viewed the coal fields as more of a permanent home. They found it more difficult to move and recognized that they had a vested interest in improving their working conditions. Consequently, it was the married miner who stuck out the strikes and fought the hardest for the union, and their families helped sustain them" (Corbin, *Life, Work and Rebellion in the Coal Fields,* 266).
26. Correspondence with Michael Szpak, 14 May 1991. Szpak, a religious bodies liaison for the AFL-CIO, uncovered this phenomenon in researching the Church of God headquartered in Cleveland, Tennessee.
27. Livingston, "Coal Miners and Religion," 233.
28. Melton, *Encyclopedia of American Religions,* 462–63.
29. Dorgan, *The Old Regular Baptists of Central Appalachia,* 12, 250.
30. Michael Walzer, for example, in his *Exodus and Revolution* (New York: Basic Books, 1985), documents the use of the Exodus story to justify a wide variety of leftist politics, including the goals of the labor movement.
31. In fact, this preacher's home county voted for George Bush in 1992 and Bob Dole in 1996. Nevertheless, it is certainly conceivable that many white Bap-

tists in this rural, nearly all-white community voted for Clinton, who received about 40 percent of the vote there in his two presidential elections. Furthermore, some Virginia counties close to this preacher's home, which are nearly all white, traditional mining areas and in the Old Regular Baptist geographic core, cast roughly two-thirds of their ballots for Clinton in both 1992 and 1996.
32. Jones, "Old-Time Baptists and Mainline Christianity," in *An Appalachian Symposium,* ed. Williamson, 128.
33. Ibid.
34. The following account is based in part on information in a file compiled by the Commission on Religion in Appalachia (CORA) in Knoxville, Tennessee. The CORA file includes correspondence from public, union, and church officials and local newspaper accounts. Fieldwork interviews among religious and union leaders supplement the information I present from the CORA file.
35. *LaFollette Press,* 8 Aug. 1991.
36. Ibid.
37. Ibid.
38. For full details on the relationship between the owners of the mines, see, among others, *Morgantown Dominion Post,* 29 Sept. 1991.
39. See, among others, *Coal Outlook,* 3 Dec. 1990.
40. See, for example, *UMWA Journal,* Oct. 1991; correspondence from attorney John L. Quinn to Freddie Wright of the UMW, 19 July 1993, in CORA file.
41. See, among others, correspondence from Jim Sessions of CORA to Bernard Schmitt, Catholic Bishop of Wheeling-Charleston, 15 Jan. 1991, in CORA file.
42. *Clinch Valley Chronicle,* 21 Aug. 1991.
43. See correspondence from Jim Cooper, Jim Sasser, and Al Gore to Marvin Runyon of the TVA, 13 Aug. 1991, a copy of which is in the CORA file. The TVA declined to terminate its contract at the time of the request of Cooper, Gore, and Sasser (see correspondence from Runyon, 4 Sept. 1991), but three years later it would cite Kopper-Glo's failure to supply coal in terminating the contract.
44. The 1989 per capita income in Claiborne, at $8,371, ranked eighty-first among the ninety-five counties in Tennessee. The 1989 per capita income in Campbell, at $8,098, ranked eighty-eighth. The per capita income for Tennessee in 1989 was $12,255; that for the nation was $14,420.
45. See, for examples, *Clinch Valley Chronicle,* 21 Aug. 1991; *LaFollettee Press,* 22 Aug. 1991; *Knoxville News-Sentinel,* 1 Sept. 1991.
46. *Knoxville Journal,* 11 Nov. 1991.
47. McCauley, *Appalachian Mountain Religion,* 456.
48. The ad appeared in the *Knoxville News-Sentinel* on 24 Oct. 1991. Circula-

tion data are from Mark S. Hoffman, ed., *The World Almanac and Book of Facts 1992* (New York: Pharos Books, 1991), 299–300.
49. A Jewish rabbi also signed.
50. See, among others, correspondence from Bernard Schmitt, Catholic Bishop of Wheeling-Charleston, to Darlene F. Flaim of the UMWA, 11 Feb. 1992, in CORA file.
51. See correspondence from Jim Sessions to Bernard Schmitt, 13 Feb. 1992, in CORA file.
52. See correspondence from Jim Sessions to Bernard Schmitt, 3 Aug. 1992, in CORA file.
53. The Morgantown ad, too, had a Jewish signatory.
54. *Knoxville News-Sentinel,* 21 Feb. 1992.
55. See *Clinch Valley Chronicle,* 7 Aug. 1991; *UMWA Journal,* Oct. 1991.
56. On conservative Protestant establishment support of North, and Trumka's support for Robb, particularly in southwestern Virginia mining areas, see, among others, *Washington Post,* 7 Nov. 1994, and *Norfolk Virginian-Pilot,* 7 Nov. 1994.
57. On conservative Protestant establishment support of Forgy and Trumka's support of Patton, see, for examples, *Louisville Courier-Journal,* 6 and 10 Nov. 1995, and *Washington Times,* 26 Nov. 1995.
58. *Lexington Herald-Leader,* 28 May 1998.

4. THE LIMITS OF ADAPTATION FOR REFORM

1. See Mancur Olson, *The Logic of Collective Action* (Cambridge, Mass.: Harvard Univ. Press, 1971), 66–97.
2. For more on Olson's discussion of intermediate groups, latent groups, and their goals, see ibid., 49–52.
3. Joseph Nathan Kane, *The American Counties: Origins of County Names, Dates of Creation and Organization, Area, Population, Historical Data, and Published Sources,* 4th ed. (Metuchen, N.J.: Scarecrow Press, 1983), 201.
4. *Salyersville Independent,* 4 Mar. 1993.
5. See, for example, *Cincinnati Enquirer,* 19 Jan. 1997; *Lexington Herald-Leader,* 12 Jan. 1997; and *Louisville Courier-Journal,* 11 Jan. 1997.
6. A concerted effort to improve the accuracy of the church membership study by including counts of more sectarian bodies "raised" the county church membership rate from 7 percent in *CCMUS 1980* to 34 percent in *CCMUS 1990,* and the number of churches counted from 7 to 42. Most county observers whom I asked said there were likely at least 80 churches in the county, which I think may be a conservative estimate. *CCMUS 1990,* like its predecessors in 1952, 1971, and 1980, primarily relies on data from self-reporting churches belonging to denominations listed in the *Yearbook of*

American and Canadian Churches. While this policy is certainly defensible given the level of funding available to the study, the fact remains that the survey misses many small, independent congregations in many places that are not affiliated with a larger body. In Magoffin, I believe such churches are likely all small, "Bible-based" Protestant churches. Church membership rates look much lower than what the reality probably is in places like Magoffin and others where such congregations are concentrated.

7. United Press International Regional News, 12 July 1982.
8. United Press International Regional News, 31 July 1987, 5 Aug. 1987.
9. *Louisville Courier-Journal*, 11–14 Oct., 1987.
10. A *Lexington Herald-Leader* article on 14 May 1992 reported that there were 9,643 registered voters in the county, and a *Herald-Leader* article of 21 Feb. 1997 indicated there were approximately 10,000 registered voters in the county for the 1996 election. The total Magoffin population eighteen years and over in the 1990 Census was 9,025.
11. *Lexington Herald-Leader*, 9 Oct. 1991.
12. *Salyersville Independent*, 19 Sept. 1991; *Lexington Herald-Leader*, 25 Sept. 1991.
13. *Louisville Courier-Journal*, 28 Dec. 1991.
14. *Lexington Herald-Leader*, 7 Nov. 1991.
15. *Lexington Herald-Leader*, 2 Oct. 1991.
16. *Lexington Herald-Leader*, 15 Oct. 1991.
17. *Lexington Herald-Leader*, 14 Oct. 1991.
18. *Louisville Courier-Journal*, 18 Mar. 1992.
19. Ibid.
20. *Lexington Herald-Leader*, 20 June 1992, 28 June 1992; *Louisville Courier-Journal*, 27 June 1992.
21. *Lexington Herald-Leader*, 7 Nov. 1991.
22. *Lexington Herald-Leader*, 25 Feb. 1995.
23. *Lexington Herald-Leader*, 21 Dec. 1991.
24. *Salyersville Independent*, 26 Dec. 1991.
25. *Lexington Herald-Leader*, 21 Dec. 1991.
26. *Louisville Courier-Journal*, 28 Dec. 1991.
27. *Lexington Herald-Leader*, 28 Dec. 1991.
28. *Louisville Courier-Journal*, 28 Dec. 1991.
29. *Philadelphia Inquirer*, 17 Feb. 1994.
30. *Lexington Herald-Leader*, 26 Sept. 1991.
31. *Philadelphia Inquirer*, 17 Feb. 1994.
32. Ibid.
33. Ibid.
34. *Louisville Courier-Journal*, 28 Dec. 1991.

35. *Louisville Courier-Journal,* 3 Mar. 1992; *Lexington Herald-Leader,* 3 Mar. 1992.
36. *Lexington Herald-Leader,* 14 Mar. 1992.
37. *Lexington Herald-Leader,* 14 May 1992.
38. *Lexington Herald-Leader,* 21 May 1992.
39. *Lexington Herald-Leader,* 9 Jan. 1993.
40. *Lexington Herald-Leader,* 8 Oct. 1992; *Louisville Courier-Journal,* 16 Oct. 1992.
41. *Louisville Courier-Journal,* 18 Oct. 1992.
42. *Louisville Courier-Journal,* 20 Oct. 1992; *Lexington Herald-Leader,* 20 Oct. 1992.
43. *Lexington Herald-Leader,* 28 Oct. 1992.
44. Ibid.
45. *Lexington Herald-Leader,* 17 Nov. 1992.
46. *Lexington Herald-Leader,* 30 May 1992.
47. *Louisville Courier-Journal,* 23 May 1993.
48. I use the term "old guard" loosely to describe those politicians and officials who were more traditional than MCBE supporters and held or shared power before the landfill controversy. There are, to be sure, many divisions within this "old guard," including over the landfill, which is one reason this or no other singular term in the county is used to describe those whom, in the brevity needed for this work, I must consider as one group.
49. *Lexington Herald-Leader,* 13 May 1993.
50. *Lexington Herald-Leader,* 26 May 1993.
51. *Louisville Courier-Journal,* 23 May 1993.
52. *Lexington Herald-Leader,* 16 July 1992, 11 Aug. 1993.
53. Many listed as "miners" in table 7 are not coal miners but workers in county oil fields. Magoffin shares, with neighboring Johnson County, a community called Oil Springs. For a map of county oil fields, see Karl B. Raitz, Richard Ulack, and Thomas R. Leinback, *Appalachia—A Regional Geography: Land, People, and Development* (Boulder, Colo.: Westview Press, 1984), 78.
54. Data on education by sex in the civilian labor force are from U.S. Department of Commerce, Bureau of the Census, 1992, *1990 Census of Population and Housing: Equal Employment Opportunity File* [machine-readable data] (Washington). A similar but weaker pattern exists in educational data by sex for all workers nationwide. Among all males in the civilian labor force, 80 percent have graduated from high school, 51 percent have some education beyond high school, and 24 percent have a bachelor's degree or higher. Among females, 84 percent have graduated from high school, 53 percent have some education beyond high school, and 21 percent hold a bachelor's degree or higher.

55. The county was experiencing a heavy rainstorm during our interview which would cause the Licking River to overflow its banks for the third time within three months.
56. I emphasize that this minister's response was to a question I asked about the involvement of his church and association in secular affairs. Although his response appears to emphasize the autonomy of the church in all matters, Howard Dorgan, in personal correspondence, notes that his fieldwork among some of the churches we both study finds that some associations recently have enforced stringently rules on "twice-married," i.e., divorced and remarried, ministers. This trend appears to have no implication for secular politics among these Baptists, but it may signal a trend for which future students of these groups may wish to account.
57. The Methodist minister was born in another eastern Kentucky county and had a Bardstown, Kentucky, pastorate before being assigned to Salyersville. In 1998, after ten years in Magoffin, he resigned his pastorate to assume duties at another eastern Kentucky congregation.
58. *Lexington Herald-Leader,* 18 May 1993.
59. *Lexington Herald-Leader,* 8 July 1993.
60. *Lexington Herald-Leader,* 25 Sept. 1993.
61. *Lexington Herald-Leader,* 13 Oct. 1993.
62. Ibid.
63. *Lexington Herald-Leader,* 10 Nov. 1994.
64. Ibid.
65. *Lexington Herald-Leader,* 28 July 1995.
66. *Lexington Herald-Leader,* 21 Jan. 1998.
67. Ibid.
68. *Lexington Herald-Leader,* 27 May 1998, 28 May 1998.
69. *Louisville Courier-Journal,* 22 Feb. 1998.
70. *Lexington Herald-Leader,* 4 Dec. 1996, 9 Dec. 1996.
71. *Louisville Courier-Journal,* 22 Feb. 1998.
72. *Louisville Courier-Journal,* 13 May 1993, 20 May 1993.
73. *Lexington Herald-Leader,* 9 Nov. 1993.
74. Ibid.
75. Ibid.
76. *Louisville Courier-Journal,* 3 Mar. 1992.
77. *Lexington Herald-Leader,* 22 Nov. 1996.
78. The case, filed in the sixth circuit, was *Eastern Kentucky Resources, et al., v. The Fiscal Court of Magoffin County, Kentucky, et al.,* No. 95-6360.
79. *Salyersville Independent,* 30 Apr. 1998.
80. *Lexington Herald-Leader,* 25 Jan. 1997, 1 May 1997; *Salyersville Independent* 26 June 1997, 25 Sept. 1997.
81. *Lexington Herald-Leader,* 7 June 1996.

82. *Salyersville Independent,* 7 May 1998.
83. *Salyersville Independent,* 13 Mar. 1997.
84. *Salyersville Independent,* 27 Mar. 1997.
85. Ibid.
86. Ibid.
87. Ibid.
88. For the story of Hardin's apology, see *Salyersville Independent,* 17 Apr. 1997.
89. *Salyersville Independent,* 30 Apr. 1998.
90. Even zoning supporters said existing land use would be "grandfathered."
91. *Salyersville Independent,* 21 May 1998.
92. *Lexington Herald-Leader,* 26 Sept. 1997.
93. Robert H. Wiebe, *The Search for Order 1877–1920* (New York: Hill and Wang, 1967), 74.
94. Richard Hofstadter, *The Age of Reform: From Bryan to F.D.R.* (New York: Alfred A. Knopf, 1955), 131–34.

5. A Theme and Its Variations

1. Max Weber, *Economy and Society: An Outline of Interpretive Sociology,* ed. Guenther Roth and Claus Wittich (New York: Bedminster Press, 1968), 1204.
2. Ibid.
3. Ibid., 1208.
4. Hill, *Southern Churches in Crisis,* 183–84.
5. Ted G. Jelen, "Research in Religion and Mass Political Behavior in the United States: Looking Both Ways After Two Decades of Scholarship," *American Politics Quarterly* 26 (1998): 124–25.
6. Shibley, *Resurgent Evangelicalism in the United States,* 136.
7. Ibid., 6.
8. Ibid., 6–7.
9. Weber, *Economy and Society,* 246.
10. Ibid.
11. For a graphic presentation of the relative recession of the frontier in some areas where these Baptists flourish, see Raitz, Ulack, and Leinbach, *Appalachia—A Regional Geography,* 99.
12. Culturally liberal activists are likewise leery about backing culturally conservative supporters of liberal labor politics. A recent example of this is the 1998 gubernatorial campaign in Illinois. Glenn Poshard, a long-time supporter of liberal labor politics in the U.S. House, won the Democratic nomination with staunch early support from the state chapter of the AFL-CIO. Nevertheless, Poshard, a culturally conservative Baptist from southern Illinois—a region that borders and greatly reflects the South—continually had

problems with culturally liberal activists who were wary of Poshard's anti-abortion politics and his skepticism about some gay rights measures. Some culturally liberal activists intimated their neutrality in the gubernatorial contest, or even supported Poshard's Republican opponent, George Ryan, despite Ryan's own anti-abortion politics and his key role as a state legislator in thwarting passage of the Equal Rights Amendment in the general assembly. See, for example, *New York Times,* 28 July and 1 Aug. 1998; *Chicago Tribune,* 7 and 11 Aug. 1998.

13. Although current political alignments and broader electoral concerns may prevent an outside political entrepreneur from adopting this strategy, there have been noteworthy, electorally successful practitioners of cultural conservatism and economic liberalism in relatively recent politics. Former House Speaker and New Dealer Sam Rayburn, for example, was a Primitive Baptist. For more on Rayburn's religion, see D. B. Hardeman and Donald C. Bacon, *Rayburn: A Biography* (Austin: Texas Monthly Press, 1987), 412–13. Hardeman and Bacon note that the religion does not appear to have shaped much of Rayburn's politics, though it was one he was proud to claim. Several Primitive Baptists I met and interviewed for this and other works proudly, and without prompting, mentioned that Rayburn was of their faith. Any church, even one as small as the Primitive Baptist church, that can claim both Guy Hunt and Sam Rayburn can accommodate many political viewpoints. A more vivid and recent example of combining liberalism on economic issues with modern cultural conservatism is in the politics of the late Carl D. Perkins, who represented eastern Kentucky, including large areas of United Baptist and Old Regular Baptist concentration, in Congress for nearly four decades. While Perkins, as chairman of the Education and Labor Committee, was well known for championing the causes of organized labor, his last significant legislative victory was an "equal access" bill, pushed by much of the Religious Right, allowing religious student groups to use public school facilities after hours. See Michael Barone and Grant Ujifusa, *The Almanac of American Politics 1986* (Washington, D.C.: National Journal, 1985), 541. Even as the politics of cultural conservatism and the Religious Right were reaching new heights in the mid-1980s, a most skillful politician was still uniting, successfully, the themes of cultural conservatism and liberal economic policy. The difficulties of the Poshard campaign, noted above, however, raise questions about how soon such politics can become viable on more than a local level.

Bibliography

Ammerman, Nancy T. 1987. *Bible Believers: Fundamentalists in the Modern World*. New Brunswick, N.J.: Rutgers Univ. Press.
Andrews, Edward G., editor. 1896. *The Doctrines and Discipline of the Methodist Episcopal Church*. New York: Eaton & Mains.
Baker, Tod A., Robert P. Steed, and Laurence W. Moreland, editors. 1983. *Religion and Politics in the South: Mass and Elite Perspectives*. New York: Praeger Publishers.
Barone, Michael, and Grant Ujifusa. Biennial. *The Almanac of American Politics*. Washington, D.C.: National Journal.
Beatty, Kathleen Murphy, and B. Oliver Walter. 1988. "Fundamentalists, Evangelicals, and Politics." *American Politics Quarterly* 16: 43–59.
Benson, Peter L., and Dorothy L. Williams. 1986. *Religion on Capitol Hill: Myths and Realities*. New York: Oxford Univ. Press.
Black, Earl, and Merle Black. 1987. *Politics and Society in the South*. Cambridge, Mass.: Harvard Univ. Press.
Botsch, Robert Emil. 1980. *We Shall Not Overcome: Populism and Southern Blue-Collar Workers*. Chapel Hill: Univ. of North Carolina Press.
Boone, Kathleen C. 1989. *The Bible Tells Them So: The Discourse of Protestant Fundamentalism*. Albany: State Univ. of New York Press.
Bradley, Martin B., Norman M. Green Jr., Dale E. Jones, Mac Lynn, and Lou McNeil. 1992. *Churches and Church Membership in the United States 1990*. Atlanta: Glenmary Research Center.
Campbell, John C. 1921. *The Southern Highlander and His Homeland*. New York: Russell Sage Foundation.

Carlton, David L. 1982. *Mill and Town in South Carolina, 1880–1920*. Baton Rouge: Louisiana State Univ. Press.

Cash, W. J. 1954 [1941]. *The Mind of the South*. Garden City, N.Y.: Doubleday & Company, Inc.

Clements, William M. 1974. "The American Folk Church: A Characterization of American Folk Religion Based on Field Research Among White Protestants in a Community in the South Central United States." Ph.D. diss. Indiana Univ., Bloomington.

Corbin, David A. 1981. *Life, Work, and Rebellion in the Coal Fields: The Southern West Virginia Miners, 1880–1922*. Urbana: Univ. of Illinois Press.

Cummings, Scott, Richard Briggs, and James Mercy. 1977. "Preachers versus Teachers: Local-Cosmopolitan Conflict over Textbook Censorship in an Appalachian Community." *Rural Sociology* 42: 7–21.

Davis, Charles Thomas III, and Richard Alan Humphrey. 1978. "Appalachian Religion: A Diversity of Consciousness." *Appalachian Journal* 5: 390–99.

Davis, James A., and Tom W. Smith. 1989–1994. *General Social Surveys* [machine-readable file]. Chicago: National Opinion Research Center.

Dorgan, Howard. 1987. *Giving Glory to God in Appalachia: Worship Practices of Six Baptist Subdenominations*. Knoxville: Univ. of Tennessee Press.

———. 1989. *The Old Regular Baptists of Central Appalachia: Brothers and Sisters in Hope*. Knoxville: Univ. of Tennessee Press.

———. 1997. *In the Hands of a Happy God: The "No-Hellers" of Central Appalachia*. Knoxville: Univ. of Tennessee Press.

Eller, Ronald D. 1982. *Miners, Millhands, and Mountaineers: Industrialization of the Appalachian South*. Knoxville: Univ. of Tennessee Press.

Finke, Roger, and Rodney Stark. 1992. *The Churching of America, 1776–1990: Winners and Losers in Our Religious Economy*. New Brunswick, N.J.: Rutgers Univ. Press.

Flynt, J. Wayne. 1972. "Alabama White Protestantism and Labor, 1900–1914." *Alabama Review* 25: 192–217.

———. 1979. *Dixie's Forgotten People: The South's Poor Whites*. Bloomington: Indiana Univ. Press.

Gaventa, John. 1980. *Power and Powerlessness: Quiescence and Rebellion in an Appalachian Valley*. Urbana: Univ. of Illinois Press.

Geertz, Clifford. 1973. *The Interpretation of Cultures*. New York: Basic Books.

Gleason, Allan. 1991. *Encounters with the Bible: Use and Authority in the Churches*. Winfield, British Columbia: Wood Lake Books.

Goodwyn, Lawrence. 1978. *The Populist Moment: A Short History of the Agrarian Revolt in America*. New York: Oxford Univ. Press.

Hardeman, D. B., and Donald C. Bacon. 1987. *Rayburn: A Biography*. Austin: Texas Monthly Press.

Hertzke, Allen D. 1993. *Echoes of Discontent: Jesse Jackson, Pat Robertson, and the Resurgence of Populism.* Washington, D.C.: CQ Press.

Hill, Samuel S. 1967. *Southern Churches in Crisis.* New York: Holt, Rinehart and Winston.

———. 1996. *One Name but Several Faces: Variety in Popular Christian Denominations in Southern History.* Athens: Univ. of Georgia Press.

———, editor. 1984. *Encyclopedia of Religion in the South.* Macon, Ga.: Mercer Univ. Press.

———, editor. 1988. *Varieties of Southern Religious Experience.* Baton Rouge: Louisiana State Univ. Press.

Hofstadter, Richard. 1955. *The Age of Reform: From Bryan to F.D.R.* New York: Alfred A. Knopf.

Jelen, Ted G. 1991. *The Political Mobilization of Religious Beliefs.* New York: Praeger Publishers.

———. 1993. *The Political World of the Clergy.* Westport, Conn.: Praeger Publishers.

———. 1995. Review of *The Churching of America: Winners and Losers in Our Religious Economy,* by Roger Finke and Rodney Stark. *Review of Religious Research* 36: 315–17.

———. 1998. "Research in Religion and Mass Political Behavior in the United States: Looking Both Ways After Two Decades of Scholarship." *American Politics Quarterly* 26: 110–34.

Kane, Joseph Nathan. 1983. *The American Counties: Origins of County Names, Dates of Creation and Organization, Area, Population, Historical Data, and Published Sources.* 4th ed. Metuchen, N.J.: Scarecrow Press.

Key, V. O., Jr. 1984 [1949]. *Southern Politics in State and Nation.* Knoxville: Univ. of Tennessee Press.

Kousser, J. Morgan. 1974. *The Shaping of Southern Politics: Suffrage Restriction and the Establishment of the One-Party South, 1880–1910.* New Haven, Conn.: Yale Univ. Press.

Lawrence, Bruce B. 1989. *Defenders of God: The Fundamentalist Revolt Against the Modern Age.* San Francisco: Harper and Row.

Leege, David C., Lyman A. Kellstedt, et al. 1993. *Rediscovering the Religious Factor in American Politics.* Armonk, N.Y.: M. E. Sharpe.

Levine, Lawrence W. 1987 [1965]. *Defender of the Faith—William Jennings Bryan: The Last Decade, 1915–1925.* Cambridge, Mass.: Harvard Univ. Press.

Livingston, William J. B. 1951. "Coal Miners and Religion: A Study of Logan," Th.D. thesis. Union Theological Seminary, Richmond, Va.

Martin, David A. 1963. "The Denomination." *British Journal of Sociology* 13: 1–14.

Marty, Martin E. 1993. "Churches as winners, losers." *Christian Century* 110: 88–89.

Marty, Martin E., and R. Scott Appleby, editors. 1991. *Fundamentalisms Observed.* Chicago: Univ. of Chicago Press.
———. 1993. *Fundamentalisms and the State: Remaking Polities, Economies, and Militance.* Chicago: Univ. of Chicago Press.
———. 1994. *Accounting for Fundamentalisms: The Dynamic Character of Movements.* Chicago: Univ. of Chicago Press.
———. 1995. *Fundamentalisms Comprehended.* Chicago: Univ. of Chicago Press.
Marsden, George M. 1980. *Fundamentalism and American Culture—The Shaping of Twentieth-Century Evangelicalism: 1870–1925.* New York: Oxford Univ. Press.
Marshall, F. Ray. 1967. *Labor in the South.* Cambridge, Mass.: Harvard Univ. Press.
Marx, Karl, and Friedrich Engels. 1982. *On Religion.* New York: Schocken Books.
Mathews, Donald G. 1977. *Religion in the Old South.* Chicago: Univ. of Chicago Press.
McCauley, Deborah Vansau. 1995. *Appalachian Mountain Religion: A History.* Urbana: Univ. of Illinois Press.
Mead, Frank S., and Samuel S. Hill. 1990. *Handbook of Denominations in the United States.* 9th ed. Nashville: Abingdon Press.
Mead, Sidney E. 1963. *The Lively Experiment: The Shaping of Christianity in America.* New York: Harper & Row.
Melton, J. Gordon. 1996. *The Encyclopedia of American Religions.* 5th ed. Detroit: Gale Research.
Moreland, Laurence W., Tod A. Baker, and Robert P. Steed, editors. 1982. *Contemporary Southern Political Attitudes and Behavior.* New York: Praeger Publishers.
Murphy, T. F., editor. 1941. *Religious Bodies: 1936.* 2 vols. Washington, D.C.: Bureau of the Census.
National Council of the Churches of Christ in the U.S.A. Annual. *Yearbook of American and Canadian Churches.* Nashville: Abingdon Press.
Niebuhr, H. Richard. 1965 [1929]. *The Social Sources of Denominationalism.* Cleveland: Meridian Books.
Noll, Mark A., editor. 1990. *Religion and American Politics from the Colonial Period to the 1980s.* New York: Oxford Univ. Press.
Olson, Mancur. 1971. *The Logic of Collective Action.* Cambridge, Mass.: Harvard Univ. Press.
Page, Ann L., and Donald L. Clelland. 1978. "The Kanawha County Textbook Controversy: A Study of the Politics of Life Style Concern." *Social Forces* 57: 265–81.
Perrigan, Rufus. 1961. *History of Regular Baptist and Their Ancestors and Accessors.* Haysi, Va.: The Author.

Pope, Liston. 1942. *Millhands and Preachers: A Study of Gastonia.* New Haven, Conn.: Yale Univ. Press.
Raitz, Karl B., Richard Ulack, and Thomas R. Leinbach. 1984. *Appalachia—A Regional Geography: Land, People, and Development.* Boulder, Colo.: Westview Press.
Reichley, A. James. 1985. *Religion in American Public Life.* Washington, D.C.: Brookings Institution.
Riesebrodt, Martin. 1993. *Pious Passion: The Emergence of Modern Fundamentalism in the United States and Iran.* Trans. Don Reneau. Berkeley: Univ. of California Press.
Roof, Wade Clark, and William McKinney. 1987. *American Mainline Religion: Its Changing Shape and Future.* New Brunswick, N.J.: Rutgers Univ. Press.
Scammon, Richard M., editor. Biennial. *America Votes.* New York: Macmillan.
Shibley, Mark A. 1996. *Resurgent Evangelicalism in the United States: Mapping Cultural Change since 1970.* Columbia: Univ. of South Carolina Press.
Short, Ron. 1976. "We Believed in the Family and the Old Regular Baptist Church." *Southern Exposure* 4 (3): 60–65.
Shostak, Arthur B., and William Gomberg, editors. 1964. *Blue-Collar World: Studies of the American Worker.* Englewood Cliffs, N.J.: Prentice-Hall, Inc.
Spencer, John H., as revised and corrected by Burrilla B. Spencer. 1885. *A History of Kentucky Baptists from 1769 to 1885.* 2 vols. Cincinnati: J. R. Baumes.
Stark, Werner. 1967. *The Sociology of Religion: A Study of Christendom.* Vol. 2, *Sectarian Religion.* New York: Fordham Univ. Press.
Tallmadge, William. 1975. "Baptist Monophonic and Heterophonic Hymnody in Southern Appalachia." *Yearbook for Inter-American Musical Research* 11: 106–36.
Thompson, E. P. 1966. *The Making of the English Working Class.* New York: Vintage Books.
Tinder, Glenn. 1989. *The Political Meaning of Christianity: An Interpretation.* Baton Rouge: Louisiana State Univ. Press.
Titon, Jeff Todd. 1988. *Powerhouse for God: Speech, Chant, and Song in an Appalachian Baptist Church.* Austin: Univ. of Texas Press.
Troeltsch, Ernst. 1981 [1931]. *The Social Teaching of the Christian Churches.* Trans. Olive Wyon. Chicago: Univ. of Chicago Press.
United States Dept. of Commerce, Bureau of the Census. 1992. *Census of Population and Housing 1990: Summary Tape File 1* [machine-readable file]. Washington, D.C.: Bureau of the Census.
———. 1992. *Census of Population and Housing 1990: Summary Tape File 3* [machine-readable file]. Washington, D.C.: Bureau of the Census.
———. 1992. *Equal Employment Opportunity File* [machine-readable file]. Washington, D.C.: Bureau of the Census.

———. 1997. *Statistical Abstract of the United States, 1997.* Washington, D.C.: Bureau of the Census.

Verba, Sidney, Kay Lehman Schlozman, and Henry E. Brady. 1995. *Voice and Equality: Civic Voluntarism in American Politics.* Cambridge, Mass.: Harvard Univ. Press.

Wald, Kenneth D. 1987. *Religion and Politics in the United States.* New York: St. Martin's Press.

Wald, Kenneth D., Dennis E. Owen, and Samuel S. Hill Jr. 1988. "Churches as Political Communities." *American Political Science Review* 82: 531–48.

Walzer, Michael. 1985. *Exodus and Revolution.* New York: Basic Books.

Weber, Max. 1958 [1930]. *The Protestant Ethic and the Spirit of Capitalism.* Trans. Talcott Parsons. New York: Charles Scribner's Sons.

———. 1968. *Economy and Society: An Outline of Interpretive Sociology.* Ed. Guenther Roth and Claus Wittich. New York: Bedminster Press.

———. 1993 [1963]. *The Sociology of Religion.* Trans. Ephraim Fischoff. Boston: Beacon Press.

Wiebe, Robert H. 1967. *The Search for Order 1877–1920.* New York: Hill and Wang.

Wilcox, Clyde. 1992. *God's Warriors: The Christian Right in Twentieth Century America.* Baltimore: Johns Hopkins Univ. Press.

Williamson, J. W., editor. 1977. *An Appalachian Symposium: Essays Written in Honor of Cratis D. Williams.* Boone, N.C.: Appalachian State Univ. Press.

Wills, Garry. 1990. *Under God: Religion and American Politics.* New York: Simon and Schuster.

Wilson, Bryan R. 1959. "An Analysis of Sect Development." *American Sociological Review* 24: 3–15.

Wyatt-Brown, Bertram. 1970. "The Antimission Movement in the Jacksonian South: A Study in Regional Folk Culture." *Journal of Southern History* 36: 501–29.

Index

Abortion politics, 35, 54, 125, 135, 163, 208n12, 214n19
Affluence, 45–53, 98, 115; and cultural traditionalism, 47–48, 201; and ecclesiastical authority and structures, 45–49, 50–51, 198, 201, 215n57, 216n54; and politics, 11, 22, 36, 52; see also Cosmopolitan authority and influences
Age of accountability, 99
Agentic religion, 7
Agriculture, 72, 85, 93, 109, 110
Ammerman, Nancy T., 2, 5–6, 38, 109
Antimission movement, 32, 39–40, 42–43, 77, 83, 111
Appalachian region, 11, 18–19, 79, 88, 90, 101–2
Arminianism, 210n31
Arnett, William Grover, 178–80
Asceticism, 46, 200
Associations, 58–59, 76

Bakker, Jim and Tammy, 46
Bardstown, Kentucky, 230n57
Behavior codes, 21, 32–33, 49–50, 103, 106–9, 183, 197–98; in Baptist associations, 62, 69, 84, 90, 223n87; and political participation, 139, 155–58, 167; and religious adaptation, 111–12, 193, 196

Benevolence, 43–44, 77, 83, 84, 197
Benson, Peter L., 7
Biblical ambiguity, 3, 12, 27, 95, 100, 120
Brady, Henry E., 5
British Commonwealth, 16
Brookside strike, 126
Bryan, William Jennings, 28, 30, 40–41, 42, 44, 114, 214n32
Buchannan County, Virginia, 134
Bureaucratic authority, 24
Burning Spring Association of Primitive Baptist, 76, 219n25
Bush, George, 35, 225n31

Calvinism, 66, 71, 83, 88, 98, 209n15; see also Predestination
Campbell County, Tennessee, 128, 226n44
Carroll County, Virginia, 163
Carter, Jimmy, 30
Cash, Wilbur, 17–18
Catholicism, 96, 97–98, 130–32
Central Baptists, 50–51, 60–65, 83–84, 104–5
Charisma, 192
Christian Broadcasting Network, 10, 36
Christian Coalition, 32, 134
Church-sect typology, 13, 14, 16, 29,

Church-sect typology, *cont.*
  37, 46, 53, 55, 201–2, 216n63; *see also* Sectarianism
Churches and Church Membership in the United States 1990 (CCMUS 1990), 56, 57, 60, 65, 140, 142, 160, 205, 209n15, 217n4, 217n6, 218n13, 218n17, 219n21, 227n6
Claiborne County, Tennessee, 128, 226n44
Clairfield, Tennessee, 127, 195, 200, 202
Class conflict, 39–40, 42–44, 47–48, 53–54, 77, 96, 99, 100, 105, 111, 114–17, 131, 162
Clements, William, 20–21, 103, 110, 223n82
Clergy qualifications, 72, 84, 90, 99–100
Clinton, Bill, 10, 11, 33, 34, 36, 124, 125, 164, 226n31
Coffee County, Tennessee, 65
Collective goods, 31–32, 112, 137–38, 195
Collins, Martha Layne, 33
Colquest Energy, Inc., 127–33, 137–39, 190
Combs, Ollie, 45
Communion, 58, 95–96
Consumerism, 11–12, 22, 28, 31, 46, 63
Conversion narratives, 107
"Conversionist" sects, 16
Cooper, Jim, 226n43
Corbin, David, 225n25
Correspondence (of Baptists), 58
Cosmopolitan authority and influences, 4, 11, 19, 31–32, 48, 52–53, 99, 109–10, 193; and Baptist associations, 51, 63, 65, 71, 76, 79, 85, 88, 101; and behavior codes, 106, 109; and cultural traditionalism, 195, 197
Cultural traditionalism, 28–39; and culturally conservative politics, 11, 47, 52–55, 135–36, 198, 200, 202, 213n18, 231n12; and Magoffin County, Kentucky, 139, 154, 177, 183–86; and organized labor, 23–25, 126; and religious adaptability, 22, 27, 189–90, 192–93, 195, 196, 204

Decker, Montana, 128
Denominationalism, 9, 16, 25, 56–57, 104–5
Dickenson County, Virginia, 134
Divorce, 62, 78
Dole, Bob, 35, 225n31
Dorgan, Howard, 230n56
Dress codes, 8, 49–50, 108, 122, 193, 220n38; and Baptist associations, 62–63, 69, 78–79, 84, 90
Duck River and Kindred Baptists, 65–71, 88, 98, 106, 120–21, 190–91, 218n13, 218n17
Dukakis, Michael, 35
Dunn, Charles, 208n12

Eastern District Association of Primitive Baptists, 50–51, 60, 62, 83–88, 98
Eastern Kentucky Resources (EKR), 148–52, 168–69, 173–74, 176, 181
Ecclesiastical authorities and structures, 24, 35, 36, 42–43, 48, 98, 104–6, 114, 116, 137, 192, 193–94, 197; and affluence, 45–49, 50–51, 100, 201, 215n57, 216n64; and antimission movement, 39, 111; and Baptist associations, 62, 66, 77, 83–84, 159–60, 162, 194; and Magoffin County, Kentucky, 159–66, 168; and sectarianism, 187–88, 196–97
Elk River Association, 66
Engels, Friedrich, 116

Falwell, Jerry, 34, 36, 37, 42, 52, 134, 202
Finke, Roger, 47, 216n63
Flynt, J. Wayne, 41, 115, 212n66
Flynt, Larry, 140
Folk religion, 2, 20, 21, 103, 110
Footwashing, 63, 102
Ford, Gerald, 30
Forgy, Larry, 134–35
Four Leaf Coal Company, 127, 130, 131
Fraternal organizations, 44, 77–78, 84, 118–19
Free will doctrine, 71, 77–78, 88, 98; *see also* Arminianism
Free Will Baptists, 159, 161–62
Freemasonry, 44, 77, 118–19, 215n34, 220n26
Fundamentalism, 1, 2, 27, 32; and Baptist associations, 83, 100; and behavior codes, 109; and economic

issues, 8, 11, 41, 42, 114–15, 215n57; and King James Bible, 94–95; and politics, 6, 28–30, 35, 38, 40, 209n14

Gastonia, North Carolina, 115–17
Gay rights, 6, 33, 35, 124, 208n12
General Association of the Baptist, 65–66, 106; *see also* Duck River and Kindred Baptist
Gibson, Dan, 45
Gingrich, Newt, 93
Gleason, Allan, 3, 65, 69, 84, 94, 163, 221n44
Goldwater, Barry, 30
Goodwyn, Lawrence, 214n32
Gore, Albert, 34, 226n43
Great Commission, 101; *see also* Missions
Green, John, 7
Greenville County, South Carolina, 208n12

"Hard-Shell" Baptists, 39
Hardin, Charles, 151–53, 162, 167, 169–70, 173–74, 178–80
Harrell, David, 77, 216n63
Hertzke, Allen, 31, 213n14
Hill, Samuel S., 20, 96, 189, 207n1, 212n66
Hillsville, Virginia, 163
Hofstadter, Richard, 180
Hunt, Guy, 57, 232n13
Husbandry, 109; *see also* Behavior codes

Illinois gubernatorial politics, 231n12
International Brotherhood of Electrical Workers, 124
Interstate and Foreign Landmark Missionary Baptist Association, 57
"Introversionist" sects, 16

Jackson, Andrew, 32, 40, 42
Jackson, Jesse, 31, 213n14
Jefferson, Thomas, 212n77
Jelen, Ted, 189, 190, 212n72
Jones, Brereton, 151, 152, 153, 170

Kellstedt, Lyman, 7
Kennedy, John F., 30

Kentuckians for the Commonwealth, 167
Kentucky, environmental law, 148, 151; electoral politics, 134–36, 145, 153; history of Baptists in, 43; supreme court, 174, 177
Kentucky Education Reform Act (KERA), 170–71
Key, V. O. Jr., 18
King, Otis, 45
King James (i.e., Authorized) Bible, 94–95, 109, 165, 205, 214n23, 221n53
Knoxville News-Sentinel, 130
Kopper-Glo Fuel, Inc., 127, 128, 130, 131, 132, 226n43
Kousser, J. Morgan, 18
Kyova Association of (Old) Regular Baptist, 44, 78, 118

Labor unions, *see* Organized labor
"Lamb's Book of Life," 56
Landmark movement, 95–96
Lawrence, Bruce, 6
Lawrence County, Kentucky, 174
Lee County, Virginia, 85
Lewis, Ron, 93
Liberation theology, 19
Licking River, 148, 150–51, 230n55
Line singing, 103; *see also* Music
Livingston, William J. B., 225n25
Local authority, 4 (seizure of in external conflict); 9 (sufficiency of for biblical interpretation), 23 (seizure of in external conflict)
Luther, Martin, 116

Madison, James, 212n77
Magoffin, Beriah, 140
Magoffin Countians for a Better Environment, 149–58, 164, 169–78
Magoffin County, Kentucky, 24, 138–86; and Kentucky, 140, 146–47; cosmopolitan influences, 146, 182; Democratic party, 152, 162, 172, 174; demographics, 142, 156; electoral politics, 144–45, 152–54, 158, 163, 173, 175–76, 179–80; environmental problems, 148, 150–51, 161; fiscal court, 144, 148–52, 154, 158, 162–63, 174–75, 181;

Magoffin County, Kentucky, *cont.*
  Free Will Baptists, 159, 161–62; landfill controversy, 138–39, 144, 147–64, 166–69, 173–74; Pentecostals, 159–60, 162–63; personal and familial ties, 145–46, 178–79, 182–85; political participation, 144–45, 147, 158–66, 182–83, 198; political reform, 138–39, 153, 154, 169–71, 180–86, 195; political violence, 144, 149, 152, 158, 159, 166, 181; prohibition, 157–58, 164, 166, 183; public schools, 144, 155, 169–71, 181, 182; religious ethos, 140, 142, 145, 153, 158, 168, 183; United Baptists' prominence, 140, 142, 154–55, 184, 194; United Methodists, 159–61, 167; vote fraud, 140, 144, 149–50, 172–73, 181, 227n10; zoning, 174–78
Marsden, George, 29
Martin, David, 16
Mathews, Donald G., 216n69, 222n72
Matriarchal authority, 107; *see also* Behavior codes
McCauley, Deborah Vansau, 18–20, 95, 100, 102–4, 129, 215n52, 217n69, 219n26, 222n72
McKinney, William 6, 209n15
Mead, Sidney E., 16–17
Methodism, 114, 224n6
Methodology, 56–60
Migration, 65, 79, 85, 88, 93, 110–11
Missions, 77, 100–102; opposition to, 90, 99, 159, 162, 197; support of, 51, 62, 66, 72, 84
Moderators, 58, 59
Morgantown, West Virginia, 131–32
Mountain Parkway, 146, 148
Mulberry Gap Baptist Association, 84
Music, 49, 69, 78, 84, 90, 103

Natcher, William, 93
National Labor Relations Board (NLRB), 127, 131, 132
National Opinion Research Center—General Social Survey (NORC-GSS), 4, 23, 208n8
"New evangelicals," 191, 216n64
New Hampshire Confession of Faith, 71

New Salem Association of Old Regular Baptist, 44, 76–77, 219n23, 220n26; *see also* Old Regular Baptists
Niebuhr, H. Richard, 3, 9, 112, 187; on churches and sects, 13–14, 53, 99
Norris, J. Frank, 114–15
North, Oliver, 134

"Old" Missionary Baptists, 33, 71–76, 99, 219n21
Old Regular Baptists, 45, 76–82, 88, 96–97, 118, 142, 147, 219n23, 220n40, 223n87; and benevolence, 44, 77; and ecclesiastical establishments, 51, 77; and politics in core areas, 134–35; and salvation doctrine, 98, 99
Olson, Mancur, 138–39, 182, 183
Ordinances (religious), 63, 69, 78, 84, 88, 90, 102
Organized labor, 113–36; and collective goods, 137–38, 195; and cultural traditionalism, 122–26, 133, 200, 225n25, 231n12; militancy, 35, 117, 120, 121; politics, 23–24, 90, 113–16, 122, 123, 124; religious adaptability for, 120, 122, 125, 126, 133–34, 198–99; religious doctrine on, 10, 78, 84, 114, 119, 120, 121, 124, 126; secular justification of, 120, 121, 123, 124, 129; support of, 117–18, 132, 133
Otherworldliness, and organized labor, 116, 122, 133; and politics, 33, 37, 135–36, 160, 199; and sectarianism, 13, 15, 17–19, 187

Page County, Virginia, 19, 97, 107
Palmer, Paul, 71
Patriarchal authority, 1, 2, 17, 22, 27, 46, 49–50, 55, 106–7, 109, 184, 195, 197
Patton, Paul, 78, 134–36, 153, 162, 168–69, 180
Pentecostals, 159–60, 162–63
Perkins, Carl, 232n12
Pike County, Kentucky, 78, 223n87
Political aggregation, 25, 190, 202, 212n72
Political mobilization, 24

Political participtiion, 5–6, 8, 32, 36, 52, 55, 139, 165, 203, 216n66; and behavior codes, 155–58, 167; and ecclesiastical structures, 165–66, 192–94; and fundamentalism, 37, 38, 209n14; Magoffin County, Kentucky, 144–45, 147, 149, 155–67, 182–83, 195; and organized labor, 114, 119–20, 122–24; and sectarianism, 33, 135–36, 159, 167, 188, 199–200
Political parties and churches, 34–36, 125, 147, 162, 164–67
Political pragmatism, 33–34, 37, 119
Pope, Liston, 115–17, 225n25
Populism, 28, 30–31, 39–45, 54–55, 180, 182, 202, 214n32
Poshard, Glenn, 231n12
Postmillenialism, 6
Predestination, 62, 66, 77–78, 83, 98; see also Calvinism
Premillenialism, 6
Primitive Baptists, 56–57, 83, 142, 216n69, 219n25, 220n43, 222n72; see also Eastern District Association of Primitive Baptists
Progressivism, 180, 182
Prohibition, 37, 157–58, 162
Promise Keepers, 46
"Prooftexts," 3

Racial politics, 18, 30
Rayburn, Sam, 232n13
Redistributionist politics, 28
Reed, Ralph, 32, 37, 202
Regular Baptists, 88
Religious adaptability, 1, 4–5, 17, 23, 27, 44, 95, 98, 101–2, 111–12; and affluence, 47, 50–51; and Baptist associations, 62–63, 77–78, 84–85, 93–94; and behavior codes, 29–30, 50, 107–9; limits of, 21, 154, 185–86, 189–93, 196–99, 204; and organized labor, 114, 116–20, 122, 125–26, 133–34; and politics, 35, 38–39, 204, 216n66; and preaching, 100, 102–3; and sectarianism, 12, 16, 47, 53, 97, 118–19, 133–34, 197–99
Religious right, 10, 30, 32, 37, 135, 190–91

Republican Party, 47
Riesebrodt, Martin, 2
Robertson, Pat, 10, 31, 34, 36–37, 52, 134, 213n14, 215n54
Robb, Chuck, 134
Roof, Wade Clark, 6
Ryan, George, 232n12

Salvation doctrine, 99, 101; see also Calvinism, free will, predestination
Salyer, Paul Hudson, 153–54, 162, 173–74, 178–80
Salyersville, Kentucky, 146, 148, 162, 163, 173, 176, 230n57; see also Magoffin County, Kentucky
Schlozman, Kay Lehman, 5
School textbook controversies, 31
Scopes trial, 40
Scott County, Virginia, 60, 63, 65
Secret societies, 44, 77–78, 118–19, 219n26
Sectarianism, 7, 13, 14, 18–19, 22, 48–49, 77, 97, 99, 106; ahistorical, 17, 27, 32; and ecclesiastical structures, 187–88, 196–97; and organized labor, 116–19, 132–34; and politics, 15, 25, 28, 38, 135–36, 138, 159, 167, 188, 204; and religious adaptability, 12, 118–19, 185
Separate Baptists, 88
Sermon preparation, 102–3
Shibley, Mark, 189, 190, 191, 192, 216n64, 216n66, 217n71
Social Darwinism, 28, 40
Social vices, 6, 32, 33, 41
Southern Baptist Convention (SBC), 7, 35, 105, 117, 142; and Baptist associations, 71–72, 84, 88, 219n25; and church-sect typology, 16, 47, 216n63
Southern evangelicalism, 48 (origins)
Southern Labor Union, 130
Southern religion, 17–18, 20, 24, 27, 189, 191
"Southern white evangelicals," 18
Spencer, John H., 215n47, 215n52, 219n26
Sunday schools, 101–2, 222n75
Stark, Rodney, 47, 216n63
Stark, Werner, 14–15, 105, 185

"Status politics," 31
Strategic lawsuits against public participation (SLAPP), 150
Syncretism, 20–21

Taylor, John, 40
Tennessee Valley Authority, 128, 226n43
Thompson, Edward P., 114
Tithing, 52
Titon, Jeff Todd, 19, 97, 107, 109
Tri-Cities area (Tennessee), 50, 51, 60, 63, 85
Troeltsch, Ernst, 13, 29, 187
Tropology, 97
Trumka, Rich, 134–35

United Auto Workers, 123
United Baptists, 76, 88, 90–93, 221n51, 223n87; and Magoffin County, Kentucky, 140, 142, 147, 154–55, 157, 159, 162, 164, 166–67, 184, 194; and organized labor, 121–22, 129–30, 133
United Methodists, 159–61, 167; see also Methodism

United Mine Workers of America (UMW), 11, 24, 78, 127–34, 137–38
United States Supreme Court, 174

Vaughn, Robert L., 219n21
Verba, Sidney, 5
Virginia U.S. Senate politics, 132
Voluntaryism, 17

Wales, 95
Wallace, George, 30
Walzer, Michael, 225n30
Weber, Max, on charisma, 189, 192; on Protestant ethic, 46; on sectarianism, 13, 15, 187–88
"White evangelical Protestantism," 7
"White Protestant conservatives," 6–7
"Widow Combs" bill, 45
Wiebe, Robert, 180
Williams, Dorothy L, 7
Williams, Roger, 212n77
Wills, Garry, 40, 212n77
Wilson, Bryan R., 16
Worship styles, 102–3; see also Foot washing, Music, Ordinances
Wyatt-Brown, Bertram, 39–40

www.ingramcontent.com/pod-product-compliance
Lightning Source LLC
Chambersburg PA
CBHW030512080526
44586CB00011B/161